VIY

Building Brands & Believers

How to Connect with Consumers

using Archetypes

Building Brands & Believers

How to Connect with Consumers

using Archetypes

KENT WERTIME

John Wiley & Sons (Asia) Pte Ltd

To Nok, Toby and Nong Boo, who fill my days with happiness.

Contents

Acknowledgments ix

Introduction xi

Section I — **The Image Market**

Chapter 1: The Image Economy 3

Chapter 2: The Growth Engine 11

Chapter 3: Hitting the Image Wall 29

Chapter 4: The Persuasion Process 43

Section II — **The Mythic Connection**

Chapter 5: Archetypes: The Source Code 59

Chapter 6: Making Modern Mythology 71

Section III — **Mythic Profiles**

Chapter 7: Mythic Profile: The Ultimate Strength 87

Chapter 8: Mythic Profile: The Siren 97

Chapter 9: Mythic Profile: The Hero 107

Chapter 10: Mythic Profile: The Anti-Hero 117

Chapter 11: Mythic Profile: The Creator 125

Chapter 12: Mythic Profile: The Change Master 135

Chapter 13: Mythic Profile: The Powerbroker 145

Chapter 14: Mythic Profile: The Wise Old Man 153

Chapter 15: Mythic Profile: The Loyalist   163

Chapter 16: Mythic Profile: The Mother of Goodness   173

Chapter 17: Mythic Profile: The Little Trickster   183

Chapter 18: Mythic Profile: The Enigma   191

Chapter 19: Mythic Figures in Combination
        and in Local Cultures   201

Section IV — **Harnessing Archetypes**

Chapter 20: Managing the Intangible   211

Chapter 21: Improving Consumer Connections   223

Endnotes   241

References   255

Index   259

Acknowledgments

I owe a debt of gratitude to several people who have helped shape my thinking or assisted me as I put together *Building Brands and Believers*. First, I'd like to thank my father, Dr. Richard Wertime, who gave me invaluable guidance and encouragement in the early stages of the book. Next, I'd like to thank Dr. John Ricketts for some intense and fascinating conversations that opened new channels in my thinking at critical points. Thanks, too, to Yuranan Somsak, who provided research and secretarial support for the book. Also, a word of thanks to the people at John Wiley & Sons and to John Owen for their exceptional professionalism. Lastly, I'd like to express my appreciation to Professor Joanne Hutchinson for her wisdom and encouragement many years ago when, unbeknownst to me, I set out on the path that eventually led to this book.

Introduction

A WORLD OF CONNECTIONS

My job is to sell things. Frankly, it doesn't much matter what I'm selling. Soap, cars, insurance, milk powder, dishes or computers: you name it, I can help my clients sell it. My experience developing advertising for a lot of different products over the years has shown me that each type of product has its own unique qualities and demands. Selling a bar of chocolate, for example, requires a different focus than selling a new laptop computer. What has struck me most though is not the difference in the products but, rather, the consistency of the process of successful selling. Regardless of whether you want to convince a grandmother in New York to buy a new set of dishes or a businessman in Hong Kong to buy a new Mercedes-Benz, the process of persuasion is fundamentally the same: it is all about making a connection with people.

The insights I've gained into human connections, and the thinking I've done about how to create them, have led to this book. It is, in fact, the essence of this book's subject matter. The intention, however, is not to cover traditional selling techniques, since plenty of other books have already covered this topic, and it is not what is most intriguing or critical to understand. Rather, the focus is on the deeper level of how this process actually works. What enables a watch or a car or a pair of shoes to establish a meaningful connection with a person? This is the key type of question this book has set out to answer. And bear in mind, products and their related "brand values" do indeed connect with consumers.

Brands have an influence that extends well beyond the purely functional role they play in people's lives: they genuinely affect the way people feel. Increasingly, brands influence the way consumers define themselves, their standing in society and their sense of accomplishment. Many Mercedes-Benz owners, for example, feel great sitting behind the wheel of their car because it is a sign of having "made it". The benefits are more than just a great ride. The advertising that is done to create this type of brand connection ultimately affects the basic decisions people make about most things in their daily lives: what they eat, how they dress, where they spend their money and what they do with their leisure time. Moreover, advertising not only persuades them which products to choose, it also convinces them to try new types of products they might never have used before. It should be no wonder then that people form emotional bonds with products and brands.

This magical connection that consumers feel is certainly not limited to products alone. The various personalities and stars who populate entertainment, sports and the news worldwide also have a substantial impact on the public psyche. These connections are also easy to see in daily life. People are intrigued, and sometimes obsessed, by celebrities. They follow stories about them in newspapers, magazines and TV shows. Who is Leonardo Di Caprio dating now? What is David Beckham like at home? The tabloids and gossip columns thrive because the public craves the latest news about their personal lives. Teenagers proudly don T-shirts of their favorite rock groups and singers as a badge of personal honor. People weep at the death of public icons whom they have never met, because they feel a personal connection to them.[1] People of all ages, in fact, make genuine and meaningful connections with the public personalities that fill their lives.

Unfortunately, there can also be a downside to the connection that stars and advertising make with consumers. Studies have shown, for example, that if a teenager's favorite film star smokes in his or her films, there's a higher likelihood that the teenager will smoke too.[2] This motivational power of images should be no surprise. The fact that many countries ban some forms of cigarette and liquor advertising is a tacit acknowledgment that advertising does indeed drive personal habits and the demand for products.[3] But it doesn't stop there. Some images are attributed with causing serious damage, not just bad habits. There are people who argue that violence on TV and in the movies triggers increased violence in society at large. The potential for video games to motivate violence has come under special scrutiny, particularly in the wake of a chain of shootings in America's public schools over the past few years.[4] Ironically, all of this provides further evidence that people do realize the motivational power of contemporary images and the connection they make with individuals.

Adding to the power of commercial images is the fact that they are more intertwined with both the sales and entertainment processes. This makes it hard to tell today exactly where the entertaining ends and the selling begins. Take, for example, Mickey Mouse. He was originally created to entertain people. But he is now a global merchandising icon. Mickey's face can be found on shirts, dishes, baby bibs and key rings around the world. The same could be said of the M&M's characters, which were originally created as a mascot for a product, but have become popular figures, with a variety of merchandise following. Sports, too, are now part of this great fusion of commerce and entertainment. The pre-game show and pyrotechnics of any NFL Super Bowl should easily convince you that professional sports have learned some valuable tricks from theater. The failed attempt in the U.S. to launch the XFL — a blend of American football and professional wrestling — just blurred the lines further.

This cohabitation of marketing and entertainment through sponsorships, tie-ins and merchandising has become the business norm. And it works because both marketing and entertainment are designed to marry form and function by creating material and characters which interest, amuse and capture your imagination while they also motivate you for a specific purpose — to part you from your money. Enabling the linkage of brands, personalities and entertainment is ultimately one common power source, which is the strength of images. So while this book is broadly about human connections, it aims more specifically to be a study in the DNA of images and how this power source actually functions in many different forms.

This is an important issue to examine, because powerful images are increasingly central to a number of business-building tasks today. Images help propel products, build brand loyalty for local and global brands, and guide corporate reputations both inside and outside of companies. While the process of connection happens at an individual level, with each person having his or her own unique tastes and interests, effective images also tap into something that is universal. The power source of images is indeed common to us all and can cut across cultures. This is the reason power brands have managed to become global in their reach. Plus, as the U.S. entertainment industry has proven, *The Terminator* and *Forrest Gump* can generate as much interest in Kuala Lumpur as they do in Kansas.[5] So companies or individuals who hope to manage their images successfully must know how to tap into this universal pool of feelings to harness its global potential.

Failing the Challenge

However, it's stunning how often companies don't fully understand the process of connection. Many can't define the deeper meaning of their own brands or company images, let alone the key reasons consumers are really attracted to them. This should set off alarm bells, because the key to every successful brand or personality is to have a clearly defined and meaningful image. The feelings and aspirations that consumers associate with a brand or public personality are critical to creating an emotional bond, which is the essence of what's commonly called "brand equity". This equity can be a durable asset for a company. In many cases, brands are *the* key asset for companies, with some even putting their brands on their corporate balance sheets. Can you imagine how stockholders would react if they realized that the management of many companies today don't fully understand how to tend to their most valued assets?

It's not that these companies are uninterested — far from it. The problem is that companies often focus on managing the superficial parts of their brands without ever really attaining a profound understanding of what makes them tick with consumers. Of course, if they can't fully articulate what their brand represents to people, it then becomes difficult for them to control and exploit that image. That is why so many companies make changes they shouldn't, or they fail to make changes they should. Sometimes companies stumble into rash decisions about their brands or their company image. Sales aren't good, so some corporate wizard decides it's time for a change. They then set out on a new path to re-launch their image — to change everything, until poor marketplace results show them their error. But it's too late. The mistakes have already been made, and consumers are now either confused or turned off by the changes. This is much more than an advertising or PR problem, because it can cause long-term damage to one of their key assets — their image. This can be truly disastrous for companies. And believe me, it happens to even the biggest and brightest of them. Remember New Coke?

So there is a genuine need today for companies to get better at managing images as intangible but valuable assets. However, companies are often not adequately equipped to guide the deeper essence of what they do. Even the advertising business is full of people who develop work based more on instinct than genuine insights. Perhaps the reason some companies aren't able to define the essence of their image is that the contemporary business environment tends to focus more and more on the present and near future. Quarterly earnings and annual sales tend to be the key drivers — it's all about delivering *now*. Consequently, there is very little time to delve into the deeper psychological strata of how consumers make connections with their brands. "Who cares?", some would argue, as long as their image is working and sales are strong.

But many aren't making it work. Sure, we can all name some famous brands and companies: Coke, Gillette, Nokia and others come readily to mind. However, these power brands are the exception rather than the rule. For every brand that is recognized and effective, there are thousands that wither and die without our notice every year. And for every successful superstar out there, the Michael Jacksons, Julia Robertses, Ronaldos or Tom Cruises of the world, there are countless thousands of struggling wannabes looking for a way to make it big. So, creating and managing effective images that truly connect is indeed a difficult process. And it's not something that happens by accident — it takes conscious decisions to develop and guide an image successfully.

More companies today are realizing that the quality of the images they create has become the great determiner of their success. So they hire a battery of consultants who then turn to various testing methodologies to shape and tune their clients' messages. In the process, billions of dollars are spent annually to build better communications mousetraps. But success can prove to be elusive. A big wallet does not guarantee success. Companies can't simply spend their way into cut-through commercial images and communication. What is required is a deep insight into the dynamics of images and how to exploit them.

Consequently, companies have a clear need to find a way to tap into the source code for more effective imagery to reach consumers. This is essential, since images aren't all on the surface. They have underlying currents and psychological dynamics that consumers react to on sub-conscious levels. In fact, every image you see is based on a common set of subconscious mechanisms that create fascination, persuasion and consumer beliefs. So while companies in the early 20th century derived increased success by organizing the means of production — tangible assets — companies at the start of the 21st century must find better ways to manage the intangible assets of their brands and corporate reputations. More and more, these types of amorphous assets are vital to business success.

The following pages are intended to examine and demystify the most inner workings of the image business, to help unlock the secrets to consumer connections. *Building Brands and Believers* will examine the psychological underpinnings of the Image Economy — an increasingly significant part of the general economy that is formed by a number of image-centric industries, such as advertising, marketing and entertainment. It will explain how the personalities and products that surround us form contemporary culture and a modern mythology that has as powerful an effect on people today as mythologies of the past had in ancient times. The premise is simple: you can create better communications if you understand the subconscious mechanisms of communication and how they create modern mythology.

Building Brands and Believers will walk you through the process of how various archetypes, the building blocks of images, create and drive consumer motivation. Specifically, 12 mythic figures — the popular personifications of various archetypes — will be profiled using contemporary examples from advertising and entertainment. These examples will be used to illustrate the traits that are unique to each mythic figure and to demonstrate how others are using their power today to sell products or to entertain you. Lastly, the closing chapters of this book will offer you some best practices so that you are armed with theoretical and practical insights to then harness the power of archetypes.

In total, the promise is to provide you with a new way of looking at the issue of effectively building brands, shaping images and identifying universally appealing ways to communicate. The goal is to put the keys to persuasive images, and the critical connections they create, into your hands.

Section I

The Image Market

The
Image
Economy

When Michael Jordan stepped back into professional basketball, after a three-and-a-half year retirement, it heralded more than the return of a great athlete: it also marked the re-booting of one of this century's most potent images. According to *Fortune* magazine, Jordan had added an estimated US$10 billion to the U.S. economy during his career prior to his retirement.[1] To put it in perspective, US$10 billion is more than the market capitalization of some of America's best-known companies. It's even more than the total annual exports of many small countries. Anyway you cut it, it's a lot of wealth for one individual to create with little more than a ball, a hoop and a pair of sneakers.

Granted, Michael Jordan is probably the greatest player to ever step onto the court. Perhaps no future basketball player will ever quite match his skills or competitive intensity, both of which are keys to his phenomenal success. Plus, Jordan delivered winning results: he led the league in scoring 10 times, he captained the Chicago Bulls to six NBA championships and he was a leader of the United States' star-studded team that took the gold in two successive Olympics. But this US$10-billion "Jordan effect"[2] points to more than athletic prowess. It is a reflection of both the financial drawing power and extensive reach of stardom today. While Jordan has dazzled spectators on the court, he has also been a potent commercial force off the court because he has a winning image.

The drawing power of stars and personalities is certainly not new. Many decades ago, people flocked to Yankee Stadium to see the likes of

Babe Ruth. Pele, too, packed sports stadiums in his native Brazil and around the world as he led Brazil to World Cup fame. Screaming, fainting fans awaited the Beatles at each stop on their tours, as did Elvis fans a generation earlier. In Hong Kong, Bruce Lee became a revered star and still today is considered one of its favorite sons. The list goes on and on. Clearly, for generations, stars in a variety of fields have been magnets of public attention.

What has changed though, particularly in the past two decades, is the sophistication of the industries that build and milk fame. The business of image management has become increasingly complex, as are the support structures that foster stardom. Today's stars, irrespective of what field they come from, can count on a battery of agents and handlers who focus on spinning them into as many lucrative areas as possible, some of which are quite removed from the star's actual skills. Endorsements, TV appearances, infomercials and public appearances ensure, too, that the public see a celebrity's face as frequently as they do some of the most heavily advertised products. Stardom rarely happens by luck anymore.

In the case of Michael Jordan, his ascent to commercial success began with one of the most effective sports-marketing deals ever struck. As Jordan began his basketball career, the U.S. sports-shoe company Nike hitched itself to the young talent, putting him in commercials which featured awe-inspiring footage of Jordan soaring gracefully, legs spread wide, through the air. This image of Jordan came to define an era in sports, and it motivated an entire generation of young basketball players. Who didn't want to be Jordan? Not surprisingly, his 1989 sports video *Come Fly With Me*, which followed, is still among the best-selling sports videos of all time.[3] But the Nike deal went further than simply associating the star with the brand through commercials. Nike was bold enough to incorporate Jordan's name in the product itself, bringing the Air Jordan to the market. This represented the leading edge of sports marketing at the time, and it paid off handsomely, as Nike enjoyed strong sales growth during his early playing years.

The fact that Jordan was an effective icon for Nike didn't preclude him from being an equally effective endorser for others. Interestingly, this is often the case. Even when a star is heavily aligned as an endorser with a particular brand or product, he or she is often able to endorse others effectively as well. Jordan eventually signed on as a pitchman to represent a variety of products that included Gatorade, McDonald's, Oakley, Rayovac and WorldCom. As his fame grew on court, his commercial potency gained too. Gatorade, for example, more than doubled its sales during Jordan's tenure as an endorser.[4] And despite a brief, unsuccessful interlude to try his hand at baseball, Jordan's image was truly bankable. This even included a Warner Bros. film, *Space Jam*, in which he starred with Bugs Bunny. Not surprisingly, it was a commercial (if not an artistic) success, pulling in US$250 million in global box-office sales.

The most substantial impact of the "Jordan effect", however, was felt in the basketball business itself. Fundamentally, great sports heroes sell tickets and build an interest in their sport. This was clearly the case with Jordan and the NBA. He was literally the one-man driving force for the entire league, despite the fact that there were many other highly paid and talented players. According to *BusinessWeek*, Jordan pumped US$1 billion into the NBA by bolstering attendance, merchandise sales and the value of broadcast rights.[5] Game tickets sold out not only on his home court but also in visiting cities. Wherever he went, people would turn out specifically to see him play. Even in far-off countries such as China, Jordan, or *Qiao Dan* as he is known there, was the key to building the appeal of the NBA from a largely American sport into a worldwide sports brand name. It's all pretty amazing for a man who failed to make his varsity team as a high school sophomore.

Jordan is just one example. The contemporary business landscape is full of commercial endorsements, movie rights and merchandising deals for both superstars and even flash-in-the-pan personalities of the day. As a result, the financial value of stardom has continued to climb, with singers, athletes and movie stars earning tens or even hundreds of millions of dollars. Not surprisingly, in just the few years that Jordan was in retirement, the sporting world saw commercial deals that eclipsed Jordan's prolific haul. Tiger Woods, at an early point in his career, is arguably already as dominant in the golf world as Jordan was in the basketball world. Woods has effectively taken over the mantle of sports "power brand" from Michael Jordan. Tiger entered the ranks of professional sports at a time when the mechanisms of stardom pushed images even farther and faster than they did when Jordan started. Nike placed an intelligent corporate bet on Tiger too by signing him to a lucrative, multi-year sponsorship, just as they did with Michael Jordan.[6] However, in Tiger's case, they did it before he had ever won a PGA golf tournament. Not surprisingly, Tiger Woods has a host of commercial deals that could well make him the first athlete in history to earn US$1 billion in his career.[7]

Even in this world of hype and marketing overdrive, superstars like Jordan and Woods are exceptional. However, a web of commercial activity, spun around the core of a star, is basically a standard practice today in the leveraging of most stars' commercial potential. The image ecosystem that grew around Jordan, for example, contained many elements that could be considered typical components in the image business today. Indeed, any agent or publicist who fails to consider all of these angles for their client would be considered negligent.

And this is not just the case with America's high-paid athletes. Even Pokemon, the cute little cartoon characters from Japan, became popular as worldwide icons through an integrated and well-tended strategy. Since Pokemons were first introduced in Japan in 1996, Pikachu and buddies have starred in their own TV show, appeared in a line of trading cards — which have sold millions — and graced a diverse range of merchandise available in shops from Seoul to Seattle. Nintendo has also sold millions of Pokemon Game Boy cartridges, making it one of the fastest-selling products in the company's history.[8]

Of course, all of these personalities wouldn't be hired if product companies didn't see a benefit from their end as well. Companies create the other side of the equation, funding the activities and benefiting from the endorsements. Today, many companies' success depends heavily upon their marketing activities that use the power of endorsers and other image associations. So they must play the image game as astutely as the stars. This involves determining which celebrities or partner-companies embody the right image to associate with their brands. Companies must also cut commercially savvy deals for sponsorships and options for future material such as merchandise, movie rights and possible product placements in shows. Some companies diversify their risks by engaging a number of stars or by signing multiple sponsorship and merchandising deals. Just as Michael Jordan can effectively endorse a number of products, a company such as Pepsi can benefit from a number of different endorsers, provided that each celebrity contributes effectively to their image. In fact, they must be effective, or companies would not continue to pay ever-higher prices for the association.

The Growing Importance of the Image Economy

What the examples of Jordan, Woods, Pepsi and even Pokemon all reflect are two key points. First, an increasingly complex image puzzle must fit together to work effectively. Each piece must contribute to improving the whole picture. Second, a huge business impact is being made by a diverse, yet interrelated set of industries that create, nurture and disseminate material that has an image at its center. In aggregate, these industries constitute an Image Economy that is a key component of the world economy today and that is poised to have an increasing business impact for years to come.

The New Economy may have garnered the press hype over the past few years, but the Image Economy is a more significant force in business. It is certainly more durable. The Image Economy isn't a fad or even a recent phenomenon. The businesses that constitute it have been growing steadily for several decades. And as the sum total of all the image-centric components of the overall economy, the Image Economy is a proven force in driving economic activity and consumer interest. So while many people now are starting to debunk various aspects of the New Economy[9] — or the notion all together — most companies are investing increasing sums in their image.

Big money is at stake in the industries that are directly responsible for creating and disseminating commercial images as well as in industries that rely upon an image to create consumer demand. These industries can be categorized into a few, key groupings:

• **Image-creation and image-management businesses:** A number of businesses derive revenue from creating the material and providing the communication that is seen in the Image Economy. Advertising, which is one of the largest of these businesses, is now a US$450-billion business worldwide.[10] Many other communications businesses, each worth billions, are included as well in this group: PR, corporate design, merchandising, Interactive design, and promotions businesses. By 1997, even corporate sponsorship, which creates a connection of products with events and stars, was projected to have reached US$15.3 billion.[11]

• **Entertainment businesses:** Entertainment constitutes a sizeable business segment. Included amongst this group are films, video games, music, publishing, plays, sports and theme parks. Across the board, these industries have seen tremendous growth over the past few decades. Video and computer games sales, for example, total nearly $8.5 billion in the U.S. On a worldwide basis, the industry generates US$20 billion in sales.[12] Included in this group too are the many individuals and companies that serve as agents, coaches and publicists to celebrities and sports personalities — again, billion-dollar businesses.

•   **Media businesses:** The media — which provides the Image Economy with the means to reach people — constitutes a global growth story with substantial financial impact. Media moguls such as Rupert Murdoch, Ted Turner and John Malone have built empires over the past couple of decades by satisfying an expanding worldwide appetite for more information and entertainment. Satellite and cable TV, home shopping and other new media — the Internet being the most celebrated — account in aggregate for hundreds of billions of dollars around the world. As we'll see later, it has also spawned celebrated brand names such as CNN. Not surprisingly, some of the biggest media players are also entertainment companies.

•   **Branded consumer products:** Arguably, virtually all consumer products, accounting for trillions of dollars, should be counted as part of this Image Economy as well, since almost all types of products today rely on a brand image, not just functional benefits, in order to connect with consumers.

The impact of the Image Economy, however, is more than just financial. Brands and personalities are fixtures and talking points in societies all over the world. Human fascination with images ensures that the content of the Image Economy influences contemporary societies. This influence begins with the ubiquity of commercial images today. The Image Economy touches people from the second they wake up until the time they go to sleep. Billboards and shop signs expose them to brand names and sales pitches. Packaging for products communicates values and personalities of the products. The media blasts out star-powered entertainment and advertising. According to some studies, people are bombarded with over 2,000 messages in this manner every day. As we'll explore in the following chapters, this ubiquity of images translates into persuasion and meaning for consumers.

Added to this is an overwhelming mound of data. The world is full of information, with bits and bytes floating around tracking virtually all forms of human activity. Giant databases carry phone numbers, addresses, bank balances, credit ratings and the like that coarse through computers every second of every day. Complex data-mining programs allow marketers to use data to analyze purchase patterns in detail. But there is an important distinction to draw here between *data* and *images* in creating consumer demand. Information ultimately has to come in a form that allows it to connect with people. Factual data alone rarely motivates people the way a great story does. Therefore, information must be turned into something digestible and persuasive for humans, not just machines. Images are what make both products and entertainment compelling. TV stations, magazines and websites rely on image-driven content that amuses, entertains and informs people. Manufacturers communicate brand images and product personalities to attract consumers. The image of sports and TV heroes provides the public with icons of the day. Images have, in effect, become the major currency of the Information Age.

The stakes have never been bigger in the Image Economy. The winners can win big. The losers, on the other hand, disappear quickly. So the great challenge for communicators is to find ways to stand out in the Image Economy while making relevant consumer connections. To achieve this, communicators must first understand the deeper nature of the images that power the Image Economy. The irony is that despite the huge size of the Image Economy, people are often blind to its true economic and social impact. That's because images are such a standard part of our daily lives that we are sometimes oblivious to the degree to which they surround and persuade us each day. Also, much of their persuasive power works on consumers on a subconscious level. The Image Economy is like a gigantic iceberg that is imposing on its surface but even larger below the water line. This requires companies to look deeper to understand its full contours, since much of its weight lies in the darkened depths of consumers' psyches.

If companies fail to understand this, or fail to contend with the growing complexity of the Image Economy, all of their efforts to create better, more cost-efficient and fault-free products will be in vain, since they will stumble at the critical step of connecting persuasively with consumers. This ultimately places image creation in a central role for most companies' survival. Our focus, however, is on more than just survival. So we will be diving deep into the mind to understand the mechanics of persuasion at the most rudimentary level. The aim is to help you win in this demanding, yet exciting, environment.

The Growth Engine

2

Given the ubiquity, financial significance and growing influence of the Image Economy, there are some critical questions that people should be asking. Where, for example, is the Image Economy heading, and what forces will continue to shape and guide it? What will be its key features and challenges? Most critically, what will be the secrets to succeeding and winning with images?

The answers to these questions are not easy to pinpoint, since the business world frequently generates surprises. Anyone involved in the Image Economy must therefore be prepared to adapt and change with it in the future. But there are also major factors that are subject to slower, more consistent change — evolution rather than revolution. So the vital answers to the future don't all lie in prophetic guesses. Rather, by observing discernible patterns from today, we can make some broad extrapolations about the likely shape and nature of the Image Economy in the future.

The important place to start, then, is by understanding the present forces at work, identifying the key trends most likely to influence and guide the Image Economy in the future. The following are six of the most critical trends. All of them point to continued growth and a front-and-center role for the Image Economy for the foreseeable future.

• Growth Trend I: Brands are multiplying as key corporate assets in the Image Economy.

The history of brands: Set in a historical perspective, the concept of branding is a relatively recent phenomenon. Commodities such as tea, spices and timber have been shipped to and from distant lands for centuries. But until the Industrial Revolution, the vast majority of goods and services were provided locally by the corner butcher, baker or cobbler, all of whom usually knew their clientele.

Eventually, however, the efficiency of shipping and manufacturing improved, allowing products to be sold at great distances from where they were actually created. Brands then grew as a way to build and retain trust for products when the manufacturer/consumer relationship was no longer a personal one. This brought about a shift from commodities and custom wares to branded goods. Paralleling this shift was the growth of the image-creation business. While Henry Ford and others were perfecting assembly-line production, nascent industries were also growing to create and disseminate mass messages to support these products. Brands and the image-creation business are therefore interlinked as by-products of the modern consumer society.

This history is the source of a very important distinction: there is a difference between a product and a brand. A product is most often tangible, with a form and a function (the notable exception being service industries). A brand, on the other hand, is intangible and exists largely in consumers' minds. Broadly defined, a brand is a promise that has significance and distinction for its consumers. Its underlying power stems from an idea and a consistent set of values. There are, of course, physical manifestations of a brand — the name, the logo and its corporate colors. But, in and of themselves, these are not the totality of the brand.

While the brand is linked to the product, it is often more than the product itself. For this reason, a brand can live on long after the products associated with it have changed or become obsolete. The IBM brand, for example, was once associated with one of its more important products at that time — great typewriters. Of course, IBM made the transition to the computer age and now most people under the age of 40 would not think of associating IBM with a typewriter. Yet, the brand has continued as a symbol of high-quality, reliable products, just as it was in the heyday of typewriters. Thus brands enable companies to constantly rejuvenate themselves through new types of products under the brand name.

Traditional fast-moving consumer-goods companies have long been seen as the main builders of brands. These companies have had a clear need to build personalities and values for the otherwise fairly mundane staples that fill most people's homes. Many of these companies, such as P&G, Unilever and S.C. Johnson, have a stable of brands, numbering in the hundreds, or even thousands, across a variety of categories, which they must manage. Companies of all types, however, must now be equally skilled in managing their brands as intangible assets.

Brand proliferation: The potential longevity and extendibility of brands are key reasons why more people are trying to build brands. One sign of this is the fact that the number of brands registered as trademarks — now nine million — has doubled since 1974, according to the World Intellectual Property Organization.[1] As just mentioned, a brand is not just a trademark alone. But this growth in trademarks is a signal that more and more companies are attempting to secure the proprietary property of a name as an initial step towards building brands.

There are not only more brands, there are more types of brands than ever before, since brands reflect what's on offer in the economy. So, as global business has diversified to include more services, media and digital products, the scope of brands has expanded too. MTV and CNN are examples of powerhouse media brands that have been built in the past couple of decades. They represent a consistent promise of a certain style and quality of news and entertainment. American Express is a world-famous example of a brand built on quality financial services. The New Economy has spawned a variety of e-brands from companies that provide information, buying clubs and digital services. A diverse range of industries today is attempting to create and manage brands.

Enduring value: The common link amongst these different types of brands is the desire to create enduring value, which stems from the customer loyalty that brands engender. The financial rewards for those who are successful can be amazing. One *Harvard Business Review* study noted that even for a category as simple as pizzas, loyalty over a consumer's lifetime could result in up to US$8,000 in residual sales.[2] Loyalty provides brands such as Coke, Marlboro and Gillette with recognition and devotion worldwide, adds billions to their balance sheets and helps them sustain sales year after year, even through economic downturns. No wonder so many companies want to build brands and customer loyalty.

A prerequisite to building loyalty is to create preference. A specific example from Pepsi and Coke illustrates the impact of brands in driving preference. As most people who have been involved in marketing these products know, there is a huge difference between what consumers say in blind taste tests and what they say in branded taste tests. The difference in these two testing methodologies is simple. Blind taste tests force consumers to determine which soda they prefer, based on taste alone, without seeing the brand. In branded taste testing, consumers sample the product with the brand logo in front of them.

The difference in the testing methodologies may be simple, but the implications can be profound. While most blind taste tests come out roughly even for Pepsi and Coke, the branded taste tests can be heavily skewed to either brand, depending upon which one has the dominant market share in the market in which the test is being conducted. This provides vivid evidence that brands are actually potent enough to affect the way products "taste" in people's minds. This nebulous thing called "brand values" distinguishes brands from the competition and drives preference across countless product categories.

Increasingly, then, there is recognition that a company's value resides not merely in the bricks and mortar of its plants and other physical assets but also in the intangible assets of its brands and reputation. As a result, brand building has become one of the business obsessions of the day, with companies looking for new, better ways to build brands quickly and more efficiently. Some turn to stars and endorsers, such as Michael Jordan. Others have turned from mass marketing to more customized, one-to-one options. These approaches, in combination with new technology that delivers greater efficiency, are driving a marketing trend to get closer to the consumer. However, the hype that surrounds some of today's hot business practices, such as CRM (customer relationship management) and customization software, should not blind brand builders to the fundamental lessons learned from the days of the village barber or butcher: know your customers, familiarize yourself with their needs, cater to their desires and build a human connection with them that is likely to bring them back through your door.

Future prognosis: *For the foreseeable future, the building of brand distinction and values will be a key activity in the Image Economy. Companies* *will have to place an even greater focus on managing these intangible assets. The closing chapters of* Building Brands and Believers *will address how this can be done better.*

•   Growth Trend 2: Personalities are increasingly ubiquitous in the Image Economy, making them a more pervasive part of people's lives.

The modern fame game: The growth of brand building is paralleled by the growth of the personality business. Put in historical perspective, the immediacy of fame and stardom, like brand building, is a relatively recent phenomenon. In the early part of the past century, there was a distance between the public and public figures. The stars of yesteryear were the gods and goddesses of the silent screen. They appeared in choreographed still shots in the newspaper or were simply heard over the radio. The public had only a rarefied view of celebrities and public figures, ensuring that Franklin Roosevelt, for example, was virtually never seen in the press using crutches or a wheelchair. People were interested in details of celebrities' lives, but, with a few exceptions, there wasn't the 24-hour-a-day, no-holds-barred fame game that exists today.

Perhaps the late Andy Warhol was right with his droll observation that "in the future everyone will be world famous for 15 minutes"[3], because today it seems that more and more people are using the mechanisms of the Image Economy to gain public exposure, if not enduring fame. Public personalities come from a variety of professions: CEOs are celebrities, TV broadcasters are celebrities, fashion models are celebrities, MTV VJs are celebrities, and even Wall Street analysts and other financial types are celebrities.

Some popular figures enjoy enduring fame. But most disappear from view after a few years or even just months, only to be replaced by new personalities of the moment who quickly fill the void. There are a lot of people out there itching to be famous.

Personalities as brands: As a result, personalities are managed in very much the same way as brands. Press agents tend carefully to their clients' every public move. The goal is the same as it is with any brand: extend their value and "shelf life" as long as possible so their fame can create enduring financial value. The mega-brands of the personality business are those rare individuals who reach icon status — who become lasting public emblems of a lifestyle, an attitude or a cause. Examples come readily to mind: Mick Jagger, Madonna or Richard Branson immediately evoke specific images and associations in the same way Pepsi, Volvo or McDonald's do. They are positioned in the public's mind, just like any product. Plus, great stars tap into a common human denominator that reaches a swath of people, just like mass brands appeal to millions of eager consumers.

The pervasiveness of stardom, like the ubiquity of brands, is being driven by the sophistication of the media mechanisms that enable it. Today's world is populated with well-known figures because the media helps make it so. It provides more and more outlets for stars to be seen by the public. But it also provides an outlet for fame itself to become the subject matter, like a two-headed monster that turns upon itself. Larry King and Oprah Winfrey's personal lives are of as much interest to people as the lives of the stars they interview. Switch on the TV, and programs such as *Lifestyles of the Rich and Famous* show you how the stars live. Talk shows from morning to late evening let stars and personalities talk about their feelings, their ambitions, their private lives and how they are coping with their fame. There is no shortage of print coverage too. Glossy magazines to checkout-aisle gossip-rags make stars, and stardom, their key focus. And these things sell. *People* magazine is one of America's most successful magazines ever.

The price of fame: All of this exposure comes at a price, however. The fame game is not just pervasive; it is also becoming increasingly invasive. Today's public figures are subjected to every in-your-face attempt imaginable to uncover the private details about their lives. Nothing seems too embarrassing or too personal to leave off-limits. This is partly the result of a hyper-aggressive paparazzi press corps. But it is also a reflection of the fact that the public wants the dirt. The immediacy of personalities breeds an almost unquenchable fascination with stars. The press would not be out there digging if the public weren't prepared to consume it.

But let's not get sentimental about stars. Invasiveness is a two-way street. Some stars today use their public platform to vent their personal problems and childhood traumas, such as abusive parents. It has become a veritable cottage industry for children of celebrities to write books about how lousy their famous parents really were. Meanwhile, some celebrities desperately try to manipulate the media in order to hold the public's interest, clawing to stay in the limelight and milk their fame.

New media channels, particularly the Internet, are creating more extensive ways for celebrities to work their way into fans' lives. Most stars today have websites and fan clubs on-line. Evolving technologies promise to extend the pervasiveness of images even further. At some future point, it might even be possible to have Bugs Bunny or your favorite soap-opera star provide you with the news. Wannabe stars are also benefiting from new ways to reach the public. Young bands and writers today are putting their material on the Net for free, hoping to build a following. Virtually anyone can create content and possibly become well known via the Internet. We can all reach the masses, if the masses want to listen. Maybe Warhol's vision wasn't so whimsical after all.

Future prognosis: Fame, notoriety and public recognition will continue to be cornerstones of the Image Economy. Personality builders will be as savvy as corporations about managing the image ecosystem and will seek increasingly invasive ways to stay in the public eye.

• Growth Trend 3: Fame is leveraged as an asset to the greatest extent possible in the Image Economy.

The familiarity of celebrities: This leads to the next reason why the Image Economy will continue to grow in both its scope and impact. The by-product of the frequency of exposure to celebrities, and the more engrossing nature of stardom, is a heightened sense of familiarity with celebrities. People often feel like they "know" their favorite stars or sports heroes. Who can blame people for feeling this way? After all, people can hear and read so much about stars, in addition to watching them perform. For example, people who regularly watch the *Tonight Show* with Jay Leno might well spend more hours per week watching Jay than they spend with most of their friends, even their close ones. And some consumers seem to enjoy it more, too. According to a recent Gallup poll, American viewers consider watching TV the most popular way to spend an evening — three-times more so than seeing their friends.[4]

This sense of familiarity with celebrities is an illusion, of course. There are plenty of seemingly friendly, affable personalities who throw backstage temper tantrums, rave at PAs and have nasty habits that stay hidden from view (until an investigative journalist exposes them). Yet the illusion of familiarity does breed a sense of trust and has a potent effect on the public all the same. The consistent role that celebrities play in some people's lives enhances and extends their commercial potency because it makes them credible. It seems only logical, in fact, that people should believe somebody they watch on the TV every day. This is one of the reasons that star endorsements can be so effective.

The image is the asset: Even if people don't have this sense of personal familiarity with a celebrity, they usually do have some expectations about the celebrity's personality and character. This too is a by-product of exposure and the familiarity it breeds. The great actors are expected to have consistent qualities. This is true of many different types of celebrities. You even expect Mickey Mouse to be, well, Mickey Mouse — friendly and light-hearted. Of course, real people are erratic and hard to control, unlike cartoon characters. But whether they're real-life stars or cartoon characters, a star's image must be managed consistently.

In today's image-savvy world, the image is the asset. It is the bankable commodity that handlers so carefully nurture and spin. For this reason, the image takes on a life of its own that often is quite separate from the star as an individual. This is true in the brand world as well, where most consumers have no idea or concern which company actually owns or makes a certain brand they like. In fact, some of the world's best-known branded products have traded corporate owners without the public ever noticing. What people buy is the story, not the reality.

Stretching the image: The critical question most image handlers must ask today is how far the influence of the image can be stretched. Should a celebrity be the host of the Miss World Contest? Will he or she be credible in a children's cereal commercial? Will anyone really buy a celebrity's watercolors for millions because it has his or her name on it? At what point does an image cease to have an impact on selling another product?

In the Image Economy, both stars and their handlers are prepared to stretch the limits of stardom for financial gain. Gone are the days when people like Jane Fonda or John Lennon used their public platform primarily for social commentary. Now, supermodels open theme restaurants and personalities put their images on coffee mugs to maximize their return on stardom. Personalities today are trading on their fame in inventive new ways. The Planet Hollywood restaurant chain, which was founded by a group of stars including Bruce Willis and Arnold Schwarzenegger, is one of the most obvious examples of stars merchandizing their fame. In this case, it wasn't just their names they banked on, but the Hollywood appeal in general. Although the restaurant chain eventually had financial difficulties, its early success demonstrates the power of leveraging star images. Oprah Winfrey provides another example. She has created an entire media empire around her name, including a magazine and an inspirational-lecture tour. Indeed, stardom today creates brand power for personalities, which must be managed and maximized.

Future Prognosis: Personalities will continue to command the public's attention. As long as this is the case, image handlers will continue to leverage "star power" into as many commercial spin-offs as possible in order to maximize the image as an asset.

• **Growth Trend 4: Branded products create a sense of meaning in the Image Economy.**

Products as markers of meaning: The Image Economy affects more than simply what we buy; it helps guide the way we feel and a lot of the things we do. Plenty of folks would decry this as a sign that modern societies are losing their way and abandoning the critical cultural markers that should define them. Some would argue that good character, talent and caring should help people define themselves, not bags, shoes and haircuts. It is tempting to make value judgments about this fact. However, the mission here is to analyze the forces shaping the Image Economy, not pass social judgments.

Brands as markers of individuality: The fact is, a lot of consumers do derive some degree of *meaning* from what they own and acquire. As we'll examine in greater depth in later chapters, the frequent exposure to images plays a role in creating the bond that helps sustain a sense of worth. Products can also be the fulfillment of an individual's dreams. So brands serve as relevant markers of progress in people's judgment about themselves. Additionally, brands become a key component of how people portray themselves to the outside world. Consumers often configure products in recognizable, somewhat predictable combinations because they want to convey a certain style or image with which they have an affinity. How they look and what they have is part of their self-definition. And that certainly has meaning for people.

Brands and social interaction: Brands work on a collective level as well. People not only choose brands because they like them but also, subconsciously or overtly, because they want others to enjoy or admire what they have. What's the thrill of having a shiny new car, for example, if your friends don't have a little envy and want you to take them for a spin and smell the fresh, new leather?

Brand images create meaning because they are relevant social markers. This is true in all types of societies. In the most economically advanced, status-conscious societies, Montblanc pens and Zegna suits might be the status symbols, while in a developing country, the first person in the village to have a TV might have bragging rights. It's still the same basic mechanism at work in both cases: people generally define material progress relative to their peers. For this to work, though, there has to be common exposure to images so that others recognize these social markers.

All one has to do is watch a group of school children, of almost any age in almost any country, to witness the role that brands play in the socializing of that group. Whether they are comparing Hello Kitty bags or their new tennis shoes, kids clearly place brands as meaningful symbols of belonging and mutuality in their circle of friends. The same is clearly true of entertainment figures too, since groups of friends often form around the worship of their favorite rock band or movie stars. The toys get bigger and more expensive over time, but the dynamic is consistent through adulthood as well.

Future prognosis: Branded items, driven by images, will continue as vital social markers. These markers will, no doubt, be subject to change. However, they will continue to provide value and meaning to contemporary generations.

• Growth Trend 5: The media and marketing channels that drive the Image Economy are continuing to multiply.

Image creators require avenues through which they can reach and persuade people. Today, there are more of those avenues than ever before, as options proliferate around world. A number of factors are contributing to this increase. Foremost amongst them, though, are competition, consumer demand and non-advertising alternatives.

Media competition: First, deregulation of media environments, coupled with new technology, is providing the opportunity for new players to enter and change the media businesses. Both the number and breadth of options are expanding in many countries around the world. This is ultimately a benefit to consumers since competition hotly follows the opening of new markets, bringing about innovation. A chance to feed the entertainment-hungry masses is a major business drawing card, so more companies are seeking a cut of the action. Even in state-controlled economies such as China, the programming choices have multiplied as a result of competition from regional and provincial stations.

The impact of competition is evident even when we examine so-called traditional media, such as television. Watching TV is probably the single most popular thing that human beings do around the world for entertainment and information. The Internet may have garnered a lot of attention over the past few years, but it still does not reach the kind of numbers that the TV does. In Asia, where much of the teeming populations of countries such as India or China (which together account for one-third of the world's population) live at or below the poverty level, television is virtually ubiquitous. It reaches 472 million households in the region.[5] Even in poor rural villages there is often a communal TV that everyone gathers around to watch sports or the popular soap operas.

TV is a mainstay, but this mainstay is also undergoing a revolution. Traditional "free to air" network TV is challenged in many markets by a variety of cable and satellite TV options. More of those villages today not only have a TV, they have one attached to a cable or satellite dish. The multi-channel future is quickly evolving on hundreds of millions of TV screens around the world. A case in point is India, where the introduction of cable and satellite TV has made a substantial impact on the viewing habits of millions of Indians.

Consumer demand for media options: This has led to the second driver of media proliferation — consumer demand. Consumers are expecting and demanding more choice wherever they go. For example, it used to be that the only entertainment on airplanes was the book you brought and the second-run movies they showed. Today, however, the quality of the in-flight entertainment is one of the battleground features amongst the airlines, with more of them offering dozens of channels of video entertainment and a similar number of radio channels too. Their purpose isn't to take your mind off the food. Rather, they know that consumers are expecting more variety of entertainment that caters to their specific needs and lifestyles. Other in-flight media options, such as Internet connections, are following today. In-flight shopping, too, is a growing segment. Even in the air, consumers today expect an outlet to the commercial images they prefer to consume.

A sort of chicken-and-egg relationship has therefore evolved between media availability and consumption. It's hard to tell whether there are more media choices today because people want more entertainment and information or if people are consuming more of it simply because there's more media around. Irrespective of which is ultimately the prime mover, a key by-product is that many consumers feel a need to be connected to all types of information. CNN and other 24-hour news services have both fostered and profited from this growing consumer need. Telecommunications, an evolving medium for non-voice data and images, is a part of this info-connection as well. More consumers are "constantly connected" via their hand-phones and frequent checks of the Internet and e-mail. For an increasing number of people, this isn't even a choice — there is an expectation from their peers or co-workers that they will be connected, so they feel anxiety about not doing so. This is not just the habit of business junkies, eager to stay up on the news and stock prices. It is indeed the reflection of a very basic trend of the way people consume media today. The generation of kids currently growing up is a multimedia generation. For many of them, it's natural to surf the Net or chat on the phone with friends, their pagers at the ready, with a TV and possibly a radio on in the background at the same time. They are perfectly comfortable with this multi-channel world.

The cacophony of media will only get louder over time as more advertisers turn to the growing number of alternative "new media". Some advertisers are abandoning traditional media because of the cost and the high clutter of messages. Instead, they are utilizing new media options. Ironically, these new media are often the ones making the clutter worse. Like mushrooms growing in a warm, moist environment, new forms of media are reaching into most crevices in our lives. They enable messages to be plastered on just about every imaginable place where people congregate or where there's a sufficient amount of passing traffic to justify charging an advertiser. Commercial messages can be found in subway stations, on the trains, turnstiles and platforms, in hospital and doctors' waiting rooms with medical television channels, in sports stadiums on revolving sign boards, and even on the back of public toilet doors or over urinals. One company even offers sticker space on fruit people buy in stores. Essentially, wherever entrepreneurs can negotiate to secure the space, there's a chance to turn it into a medium for images.

Non-advertising alternatives: The third major driver of media and marketing channel proliferation is the move beyond paid media to inventive ways to reach consumers with images.

Sponsorship is one of these growing channels. The benefits of sponsorship are twofold, since sponsorship provides exposure of the brand outside of expected channels while there is the image rub-off of the event being sponsored. Take Formula One racing as an example. A variety of companies are willing to pay millions to have their brand name and logo on a sports car. Why? Because TV coverage of Formula One races provides multiple exposures of the sponsor's brand, which is easily seen on the car during the races, without the interference of other TV commercials. Simultaneously, there's the benefit of having the brand associated with Formula One, which has its own "brand values" and personality. The hope is that some of the excitement and sex appeal of Formula One will rub off on the companies that sponsor a car. Given sponsorship's popularity, price tags continue to escalate for all types of deals. Nike, for example, paid an estimated US$160 million for a 10-year sponsorship of the Brazilian national soccer team.[6]

Merchandising, too, has boomed in the past decade because of companies seeking to associate their products with other potent images. As a result, companies are paying ever-bigger merchandising price tags as well. In what some considered an excessive attempt to bank on the *Star Wars* image, the launch of *The Phantom Menace*, the first in the new installment of *Star Wars* episodes, was surrounded by some of the most choreographed marketing ever. PepsiCo reportedly paid US$2 billion for rights to sponsor the trilogy. According to press reports, George Lucas, the creator of *Star Wars*, inked additional merchandising and toy deals in excess of US$500 million.[7] Interestingly, what sponsorship and merchandising deals of this magnitude generally entail is not just money paid for the sponsorship, but also a commitment of marketing dollars to support the property through other activities. This creates a symbiotic relationship. While *Star Wars* cups are likely to draw kids to purchasing PepsiCo products, the flood of this same merchandise will ensure further awareness of the movie, driving kids to the theaters too. At least, that's the theory.

Future prognosis: As long as the marketing dollars are flowing, new mechanisms will evolve to soak up the spending. Consumer demand will ensure that more options cater to their individual needs. In the future, a multiplicity of media and marketing mechanisms will be available to drive images, both locally and globally.

• Growth Trend 6: The Image Economy, a global force, is leading to greater commonality of lifestyles.

The global reach of images and products: The last of the key growth trends is globalization. More and more, product and entertainment images are propelled around the world, creating common icons and more-similar lifestyles as a result. This makes McDonald's and Arnold Schwarzenegger as recognizable in Beijing as they are in Boston. This fact is perhaps the most hotly debated topic related to the Image Economy. Each side has staunch advocates who argue their side of the debate about global trade and its social impact. Regardless of your point of view on this topic, though, one point is undeniable: images are the power behind increased globalization. This last growth trend, therefore, is perhaps the most important one for image creators. The requirement is increasingly to understand how to create images that will effectively cross virtually any border.

The impact of globalization starts with the goods that people choose to put on their dinner tables or park in their driveways every night. Many urban homes around the world contain a smorgasbord of international products. This is the result of the global marketplace for goods and services. French people buy Japanese electronics equipment, Japanese people buy Italian coffee, Italians buy Thai food, and Thais buy Swedish cars. Global trade in all directions provides the basic material for a more common lifestyle. This cross-border flow of goods, which has been growing over decades, is set to increase further according to global trade figures. In 1999, the dollar value of world merchandise exports was US$5.47 trillion.[8] Brands, and brand images, play a central role in this global trade.

Developing markets: The trend towards globalization is not just a function of wealthy economies. The worldwide movement of products is changing lifestyles in a number of developing economies as well. Global-product companies play a role in fulfilling people's basic needs for products such as soap and cooking oil. In fact, some of the best-known products in the developing world come from the multinational conglomerates. In addition, the wants of emerging-market consumers often migrate from basic household items to white goods and electronics and then later into entertainment and other pleasures. This pattern is repeated in market after developing market around the world. Multinational products play a role throughout, soaking up newly found discretionary spending as consumers attain higher levels of income. Not surprisingly, some of the fastest-growing markets for U.S.-style "junk food" are these developing countries. Cheeseburgers and video games have become familiar treats around the world.

Brand preference is at work affecting consumers at all levels of income, driving their purchasing decisions. In China, for example, while there are cheaper Korean electronic goods available, consumers know and want Japanese electronic products because of their brand cachet. Young Vietnamese dream of owning a Honda "Dream" motorcycle. Young Brazilians want Nike shoes. Brands play an aspirational role in people's improving lives. The Image Economy ensures that people everywhere are not just choosing products based upon functionality but also based upon image.

This is not to say that we all can or do consume exactly the same products. There are still huge differences in people's preferences and tastes around the world. Also, it's important to recognize that there is far-from-equal access to decent living standards. The sad fact, according to the World Bank, is that 1.2 billion of the world's six billion people live on less than US$1 a day.[9] Still, even amongst the world's poor, brand competition over even simple items such as soap powder can be intense. So while globalization doesn't necessarily imply that we all use the same thing, the growth of global trade does create a demand for product distinction wherever even basic products are sold.

The globalization of marketing practices: As a result, the process of creating and promoting products is becoming more common across markets. Globally, brand management is a relatively consistent practice. Although there are scores of local market and consumer nuances that must be considered by any marketer where they do business, the *process* has a lot of commonality worldwide. Consequently, the integrated marketing tactics that made Michael Jordan or Pokemon famous are replicated almost anywhere you go. Local Canto-pop singers, for example, endorse everything from fizzy drinks to furniture stores.[10] Indian cricket stars help hawk tea and skillets. Dragon boat races in Hong Kong and beach volleyball tournaments in Rio attract corporate sponsors and a raft of merchandise that follows. The local media pumps out a stream of commercial messages in fairly similar formats around the world. The marketing mechanisms tend to be the same.

Ultimately, this makes the impact of globalization social as well as economic. While the subject matter varies from market to market, it's common for consumers around the world to be surrounded by a marketing culture. Sponsorship, product promotions, advertising and entertainers are common fixtures in their lives.

Future prognosis: The Image Economy will continue to generate globally recognized symbols. Around the world, marketers will compete fiercely, using many of the same marketing tactics. This will lead to more commonality and the continued possibility for image makers to touch a global audience. However, as we will examine, this still requires local relevancy in order to persuade consumers.

The Image Economy as a Growth Engine

These six growth trends of the Image Economy add up to a powerful cocktail of opportunity: people around the world spending more time, more resources and more interest focused on brands, celebrities and entertainment — the outputs of the Image Economy. Customer affinity ensures that certain brands get selected over others, brand loyalty provides customer bonds that generate repeat sales, and the public's infatuation with stars ensures a constant flow of eager audiences. The financial rewards are spectacular for those who play the image-management game right — just ask George Lucas.

What this all highlights is a clear and pressing need for companies and individuals to master the mechanisms for building effective images. Consumers are clearly willing to devote a significant amount of their time to consuming what the Image Economy produces, provided that it's effective at connecting with them. In fact, with the Image Economy surrounding them daily, consumers appear to be open, willing targets for a multiplicity of commercial sales pitches and invitations to be entertained. What could possibly stand in the way?

Hitting the Image Wall

3

What stands in the way of most companies' success with images is the sheer mass of information that confronts consumers each day. Everyone faces this challenge. Huge corporations and small start-ups alike must figure out how to get past it with meaningful, refreshing images that connect with consumers. This can be a daunting task. Like a blind man feeling his way along the Great Wall in search of an opening, product marketers spend their days seeking some form of avenue to consumers. But this opening doesn't come easily.

The star business isn't any easier. One casting call by a company in Thailand resulted in over 5,000 applications. It seems that everyone wants to be a star. Even for those who do make it, stardom can be a precarious perch. In Hollywood, the land of big stars, there's fierce competition for good scripts, and careers can quickly wither like delicate roses in a sudden frost. There is also no guarantee that even the best-financed entertainment products will be successful. Many movies from Hollywood to Bombay's Bollywood fail to make a profit. The Image Economy can be both exacting and harsh.

So despite all the growth and impact of the Image Economy, there are powerful counter-forces at work. Ironically, a lot of this stems from the success of the Image Economy. The fact that some companies and individuals have enjoyed phenomenal success has led many others to try. This, in turn, has made the Image Economy a hyper-competitive space, leading to consumer overload and burnout.

Therefore, the six growth trends outlined earlier mean more than opportunity. They also signal the growing competition that lies ahead. Also, for each of the arguments that can be made supporting the future promise of the Image Economy, there are equally compelling counter-arguments about the challenges facing communicators. In fact, the challenges that must be surmounted are both increasingly immense and complex. This makes it critical to examine the challenges as well. In some way, they are perhaps even more important to understand than the growth forces just outlined, because they represent the pressing issues companies must contend with in their attempts to create a successful image. Once we get to the explanation of archetypes, you'll see that these challenges are not insurmountable. But the following six trends are, and will be, critical challenges to image-creation efforts.

• **_Challenge 1: As the Image Economy continues to expand, clutter, image overload, public confusion and cynicism are worsening._**

Clutter: It is getting harder to dent the public psyche, and the reason is clutter. Just like dirty clothes that pile up quickly in the corner of a kid's room, the overload of images is piling up in consumers' brains. According to estimates, American children have viewed 360,000 TV commercials before they graduate from high school.[1] The U.S., of course, has the highest marketing spending in the world. But this massive intake of images is approximated today in plenty of other markets around the world as well. And, simple marketing math virtually guarantees that there will be more clutter in emerging markets in the future.

Developing economies, most notably in Asia and Latin America, have young, growing populations and relatively low per-capita spending on advertising relative to the developed markets. Corporations are eyeing these markets for long-term future growth. Indeed, wherever there is opportunity, marketers will rush in with investment. As previously noted, this increased spending generally translates into both a larger volume of messages and more diversity in where those messages appear.

These images are added on top of an already substantial mound of basic data that the average consumer must deal with. If you need some medical information on-line, for example, you can choose from thousands of sites offering medical advice. Would you like to read a book? There are more than 50,000 books published every year in America alone. Meanwhile, the number of journals published globally is estimated at 400,000.[2] There's simply more for consumers to take in, to process and to comprehend. The information mound seems to grow every day, making us richer in data yet stressed with the overload.

Messaging contradiction: It's not just the volume of messaging that is tiring the public; it's also the contradictory nature of a lot of messages we see. One day a scientific study tells you it's good to drink wine; the next day one tells you it's bad for you. One soap powder says it's the strongest, but another one claims the same thing too. Who is telling the truth here? It's often not actual lying that causes these discrepancies. Rather, as most people in marketing know, there are many ways to cut a set of numbers. Multiple interpretations can be gleaned from the same research figures, depending upon your bias. Marketers often leverage factual information, skewed conveniently to substantiate their claims, to create greater persuasion for their product. But the credibility of these messages can, and does, erode over time because of all the contradictions.

Sponsorship overload: Adding further to the clutter are many other forms of corporate messaging besides advertising. As noted in the previous chapter, corporate names adorn all types of sports events, festivals and civic activities as companies attempt to extend their reach beyond media to become a part of communities. But as corporate sponsorship has become more popular, overload has rocketed too. Even the world's largest sporting events, the Olympic Games and the World Cup, now suffer from sponsorship clutter.

It's clear from the statistics why companies want to be involved with the World Cup. The event offers some truly awesome numbers to any corporation. The World Cup is broadcast in more than 200 countries, reaching an estimated three billion people, who watch at least one match. No wonder some of the world's biggest consumer-products companies are willing to pay the price tag of about US$40 million per main corporate sponsorship.[3] In 2002, there are 15 "official partners" that are sponsors for the event. In addition to this, there are 80 licensees in Japan that can sell a range of World Cup products.[4] After dishing out tens of millions of dollars just for the sponsorship, companies often spend tens of millions of dollars more to publicize their sponsorship in order to recoup their investment.

The resulting blur of sponsors trying to muscle their way through the pack leaves consumers feeling hit by a ton of marketing bricks for the weeks immediately before and during the matches. Adding further injury to this are clever "guerilla marketers". They often sabotage the real sponsors' efforts by intentionally confusing consumers. They achieve this by running sports-themed advertising and other activities, often involving star athletes, during the same time period as the event. Unsuspecting consumers often have no clue who the real sponsors are.[5]

The fed-up and cynical consumer: As a result, people are sick and tired of the media circus and all the hype that comes with it. Who can blame the public? Few athletes, it would seem, are in it for the real love of the game anymore. Instead, it all comes down to agents, lucrative contracts and marketing spin. Everything, and everyone, is for sale. Any star will be available for a TV commercial in Japan if you pay them enough. Space shots are suddenly prime space for brand sponsorships. Product placement — the practice of buying space in shows or movies to highlight a product — means that the soda machine or telephone you see in the background is there for a reason: money. Products are being sold to you even when you're trying to relax and just watch a movie. Nowhere, it seems, is safe.

Future prognosis: Public cynicism is likely to continue in the future, adding another layer of complexity to the challenge of breaking through with consumers.

• Challenge 2: As more companies seek to build brands as assets, brand distinction is difficult to create or maintain.

Product proliferation: Just as images must struggle through the overload, products themselves have become more numerous and must struggle for distinction. Our familiarity with power brands should not lull us into complacency about the complexity of this task. Since brands such as Coke, Nike and Nokia are common fixtures, people might consider them average. In truth though, these power brands are the very tip of the iceberg. They are the crème de la crème of marketing — the Michael Jordans of the brand and product world.

The brutal fact is that most brands never make it onto consumers' radar screens to begin with. They never even get a fair hearing. How can they? There are up to 40,000 products stocked in a typical supermarket.[6]

The mammoth hypermarkets that are cropping up all over the world carry more products still. Even on a very big shopping outing, at best only a hundred products will wind up in a consumer's shopping cart. And when consumers shop, they may spend only a few seconds in front of the product shelf before making their brand selection in a given category. Consumers give you an instant — that's it. That's how long you have to make contact with them and begin to break into their consideration set.

Waves of new products: The proliferation of existing products doesn't deter companies from continuing to introduce a plethora of new products each year. In 2000 alone, consumer-product makers in the U.S. introduced more than 31,000 new products. These weren't all from new companies, mind you. Many new products came from existing companies offering new types of products or variants of existing products.[7] This results in category after category becoming clogged with stock-keeping units (SKUs) of different sizes and variations. Consumers seeking staples such as shampoo can select from conditioning shampoo, 2-in-1 shampoo, shampoo for dry hair, shampoo for oily hair — and the list goes on. There's a dizzying array of choice.

An example from Taiwan illustrates how clogged categories are with brand competition. Up until 1987, Taiwan Beer had a monopoly in the market. It was the beer that Taiwanese consumers drank because they basically had no choice. But when the market was deregulated in 1990, competition quickly followed. Since Taiwan represented an attractive new market, beer brands from Japan, Europe, Mexico, America and many other places rushed in to capitalize on the opportunity. In the process, advertising spending shot up exponentially. Within a decade, there were 120 beer brands available on Taiwanese shelves.[8]

Just think what this meant for consumers. You could say that they should be grateful for the choice. After all, having the right to choose is what the Image Economy is all about. But what realistically follows when so many choices are introduced so rapidly is the large degree of consumer confusion already mentioned. It's not easy for consumers to tell the difference between 20 beer brands, let alone 120 different products. There is also an exponential effect, since the same thing is happening simultaneously in other product categories too. The result of this intense level of competition is that the cost of customer acquisition is rising. Companies have to spend more money to break through to reach and convert customers.

The lack of product distinction: Therefore, creating and maintaining product distinction is one of the biggest challenges today in the Image Economy. This challenge affects virtually all facets of products, starting with the basics of the way products are made. The truth is that products simply *are* more similar today. With multiple brands likely to be elbowing for a spot in any given category, the differences that separate them are often minute. So, from the day they are put on the shelves, many products are largely the same in consumers' eyes. Even when new features are developed, competitive matching through reverse engineering ensures that these benefits disappear after weeks or months. Competitors are obsessed with each other, so no move goes unnoticed. If one beer introduces a light variant, others follow. If a drink-maker decides to put in strawberry flavor, the others consider it too. This happens in virtually every type of business today. The days when unique features or benefits could give products a truly long-term advantage are dying.

The similarity of products is putting more pressure on marketing to create the relevant distinction for the brand. The brand image must step in to provide a difference, even if the product performance attributes are quickly matched. A well-positioned product will indeed stick out in consumers' mind. Volvo's "safety" positioning is an often-quoted example of a clear, effective positioning. But creating a distinctive image takes guts — more guts, in fact, than most marketers have. That's because a "category mentality" creeps in. Given the intense competition between brands, and the focus they tend to have on each other, marketers can easily find themselves in a closeted little world within their business category. So how they go about marketing and promoting the product is often influenced by what others in the category are doing.

The similarity of marketing approaches: This problem is most pronounced in their marketing and communications — the material they should be creating to tell the world about the uniqueness of their product. Many ads today in virtually any category will simply look the same. What shampoo-maker would dream of advertising its product without the shot of a lady swooshing her hair? What car-maker would dare to spend all those funds and then fail to show that automobile being put through its paces? Trying something completely out of the norm seems too risky, because so much is at stake. Marketers are afraid to make a big blunder, from which their image — and sales — can take a long time to recover. In the process, marketers themselves are wasting the opportunity they have to create distinction. They actually make it harder for consumers to tell them apart. Their biggest mistake turns out to be their failure to take a risk.

Future prognosis: Distinction will continue to be elusive for most players in the Image Economy of the future. Images will come under increased pressure to deliver the differentiation that is lacking in many products. This will ultimately require companies to look deeper at how archetypes can be used to create distinction — a topic that we will be looking at in detail.

• **Challenge 3: Business power shifts are putting structural pressure on brands.**

The formidable challenges that face brand-creators extend beyond the proliferation of products on store shelves. Basic structural changes in business are also making it more difficult for companies to get those products on the shelves in the first place. Price competition and generic products then threaten to erode the value of brands. Lastly, the investment community demands quicker payback from companies, hastening the brand-building process. These three factors pose a row of significant hurdles to brand-builders in the Image Economy.

Structural changes challenging brands: The first of these issues relates back to the balance of power between retailers and brand marketers. Today's retailers exert more control over manufacturers than ever before. This is a direct result of the way many retailers grow and manage their business. So-called category killers — mammoth shops that offer a huge range of products in any given category — have gobbled up more of the retailing pie in the past few decades. A notable example is the food hypermarkets such as Lotus and French operator Carrefour. As these types of retailers control a larger percentage of the trade distribution, they have been able to exert more control over the manufacturers' brands in their shops. This happens primarily through category management, the system by which shelf space is carefully and scientifically managed to maximize retailers' sales yields and profits. Products that sell well receive space. Those that do not are promptly de-listed from the store. Given all the products vying for consumers' attention, retailers are assured that other brands will be lined up, waiting for their crack at some shelf space.

The growth of retailers' power has been brought about by a related shift, which is the growing influence of retailers' brands. The goal of many retailers is to "own" the primary consumer relationship. They want consumers' main attachment to be with their shopping environment and selection, rather than manufacturers' brands sold in their shops. Therefore, retailers have aggressively promoted their own brand values. As a result, Walmart, K-Mart, Target and Makro are as well recognized as brand names as most of the products found in their stores.

Price competition and generics: Some retailers have extended this further by creating their own line of products. These "house labels" have become an effective way for retailers to extend their value to consumers and further lock-in their loyalty. No-name generic products have also grown dramatically as a facet of the retailing scene. These generics are based purely on low price. This erodes the power of brands, because they often cannot compete on price alone. Most brands count on consumers paying a price premium because of the attraction of the brand. Therefore, brands end up having to fight on three fronts: they must compete against other brands in the category, they sometimes have retailers' house brands to contend with, *and* they have generics nipping at their heels through rock-bottom pricing.

This pressure has caused many marketers to lose their focus on image building. Instead, promotions and giveaways have become the order of the day. The simplest evidence of this is the dramatic shift in the ratio of spending for image building vis-á-vis promotions. Spending patterns clearly show a move away from thematic advertising — generating a consumer image on television and other types of media — to more spending on promotionally oriented activities. Two decades ago, up to 70% of a typical marketing budget was dedicated to image building through the media, with the remainder going to promotions. Today, that ratio is reversed for many marketers. Driving this shift in spending is the appeal to advertisers of engaging consumers closer to the point of purchase for products. They believe that sticking a coupon in consumers' hands in the store will be a more effective motivation than conditioning them through a TV commercial. In this fashion, marketers are voting with their marketing dollars to try for a quick win with consumers. Yet this isn't necessarily a knife that cuts through either. More often, consumers get sick of the proliferation and bland nature of the constant promotional activity they find in stores. Most promotions are lost in the crowd, just like ads.

Financial requirements for a quick payback: Why are marketers sometimes willing to sacrifice the very essence of their brands — the image — in order to generate some short-term sales? The answer is almost always the need to deliver short-term financial results. Financial markets demand constant and quick payback. Therefore, marketers are pressed to make cycle times for new brands shorter since investors aren't willing to wait years for a payback. Companies often need to generate an immediate sales bump.

This pressure of the financial marketplace has led many image creators to make colossal errors in judgment. The attempt by many dot-com brands to short-circuit the brand-building process is a prime example. Flush with IPO (initial public offering) cash, many of these companies thought they could turbo-charge their efforts and achieve in months what others have labored for years to achieve. These new marketing know-it-alls decided that a burst of spending, coupled with some outrageous marketing tactics, would help them break through the clutter and get them quickly on the road to brand recognition and loyalty. They were more or less forced to take this route, because the financial markets were demanding a quick and large payback in return for the substantial amounts of money they rolled on these new ventures.

Ironically, in the end, investors were the ones who were let down because of mistakes the dot-com companies made trying to hasten the brand-building process. Investors, not just the marketing executives, had to learn the expensive lesson that simply blowing a gerbil out of a cannon in your TV commercial might get noticed temporarily, but it certainly doesn't make a brand or help you win in the Image Economy.

Future prognosis: Image creators will continue to be plagued by short-term demands that will distract them and potentially tempt them to compromise on proper image management. Image creators will come under increasing pressure to balance structural business pressures with long-term image-creation needs.

- **Challenge 4: Fame, while leveraged as an asset, can be frail. Image crises are more rampant with a scrutinizing public and press.**

The fickle public: The changing mood of the public represents a constant challenge for brands, celebrities or anybody in the spotlight. Like a flock of birds that abruptly alters direction in mid flight, public sentiment can quickly shift. Many politicians have discovered this fact the hard way. They lose the pulse of the times and suddenly find that they have overstayed their welcome with voters. The same can happen with brands and personalities, though they aren't voted out of office. Instead, the public tunes them out. The celebrity has lost the magic touch, and it becomes impossible for them to get airplay. Sometimes, these forgotten stars are "rediscovered" decades later. But, most often, they simply fade into obscurity.

If the public is not ignoring stars, then it is lusting after the gory details of their private lives. Despite the best effort of publicists and other spin-doctors, bad news almost always gets out. The ever-more aggressive press virtually assures that any mistake by a company or celebrity will be quickly and widely covered. And the public finds it irresistible — bad news helps sell magazines and gossip tabloids around the world.

What could be more riveting than the age-old story of the fall from grace, turbo-charged by modern press coverage with live feeds and TV exposés? The stories are often mythical in their quality: O.J. Simpson — a trusted, familiar and well-liked personality suddenly brought up on charges for a brutal double murder; or Elvis dying on the proverbial throne in the shag-carpeted bathroom of his Graceland mansion.[9] People today are fascinated by the carnage of public personalities' lives. They are titillated when the sexual escapades of stars like Hugh Grant or George Michael become embarrassingly public. The drug addictions of sportsmen and actors soak up pages. The star game is now like auto racing: the wrecks are too fascinating not to watch.

There seems to be no limit to the public's appetite. The bigger the image that has been built, the more intense the scrutiny and the grander the fall. Many people tuned in to watch U.S. President Bill Clinton squirm and struggle during public inquiries into his relationship with White House intern Monica Lewinsky. While many argued that they watched the proceedings because they had significant political consequences, there were plenty of people who simply couldn't resist the tabloid-like details.

The perverse public: The public is not only ghoulish at times; it can also be perverse. While some people are seeking the dirt of the stars, others are seeking to own a little piece of them instead. Want to own Gianni Versace's old pillows or Elvis's Texaco card?[10] No problem, if you can write a big enough check. Public auctions of stars' personal effects, from underwear to their most private letters, have become a public obsession.

The brand world also engenders loyalties and even obsessions that are no less intense than with celebrities. Coca-Cola fanatics collect memorabilia of all types, and some Harley-Davidson fans are happy to sport a tattoo of the company. However, this type of intense brand loyalty can also have its downsides. Once consumers have been enticed to "internalize" a brand — to see it as their own — they consider it their right to be involved in the brand. So when product companies make a mistake, consumers have genuine and sometimes violent reactions to brands. The classic case is New Coke. This miscue at re-launching the drink caused such an eruption from Coke loyalists that the company soon had to reintroduce the original under the Classic Coke name.[11]

For corporations, an incident or an accident can cause a sudden shift in public sentiment. After all the careful work that goes into building an image, a misstep or two can quickly bring it down. Tainted food, an oil spill or some other catastrophe can suddenly plunge a company into a PR crisis. How it then deals with the problem says a lot about the company, and it can guide how the company's image is seen for many years to come.

Future prognosis: The Image Economy will be increasingly unforgiving. Irrespective of the work and investment that went into building an image, image makers will suffer if they make a misstep. In this environment, there will be even greater pressure to manage public opinion carefully.

• **Challenge 5: As a result of overload and marketing burnout, some consumers are moving from being docile targets to aggressive combatants.**

Advertising avoidance: Image creators cannot ignore the basic fact that a lot of people out there simply hate ads or any attempt to market to them.

Some consumers aren't happy to let passivity and inattention serve as their method of dealing with the excesses of the Image Economy. Instead, they aggressively weed out unwanted communication. A large percentage of commercial mail goes in the trash without ever being opened. The remote control has become a favored tool for zapping and weeding, as viewers quickly flip between TV channels. Computer programs strip ads out of websites and delete unspecified e-mail. New TV services, downloaded through a computer hard drive, even enable viewers to completely skip over the ads.[12]

This all highlights the palpable anti-marketing sentiment at work today. Some advertisers are starting to realize that marketing overload doesn't help their cause and are being forced to shift tactics. Rather than assume that just because they can reach you they're going to sell to you, some advertisers are pursuing more consumer-friendly approaches. A new advertising social contract of sorts has emerged through opt-in marketing on the Internet. Only consumers who have agreed ahead of time to receive messages or information are sent messages. If consumers are greeted instead by spam — unwanted messages — they only have to hit a reply button to send back a vitriolic message.

Hostile targets: This point underscores that the consumer isn't necessarily a smiling, friendly couch potato. Today, he might be armed and ready for battle. At the farthest extreme is a lunatic fringe of people who want to rid themselves of the Image Economy altogether. These people go beyond the normal steps at avoidance and weeding. Some become anti-brand vigilantes, damning companies in chat-rooms, creating anti-brand websites and sending e-mail attacks and hateful snail mail too. They might have a legitimate beef that stems from a bad experience with a company. Or, they might be stoked by irrational motivations. Whatever the cause of their actions, aggressive consumers are another reality of the Image Economy.

Future prognosis: *The marketing standoff is likely to escalate in the future. This will put a greater onus on communicators to find ways to build goodwill and make themselves more welcomed by consumers.*

- **Challenge 6: The globalization of images i** **for ruining our social fabric.**

The fight against globalization: The social backlas]
Economy is most clearly evidenced by the violent standous ...
typical at various world trade meetings. Many protesters see the issue as a
matter of cultural and financial survival, requiring an extreme stand. With
the world moving inexorably towards common icons, some people feel
that the Hollywood and Madison Avenue hype machines have overrun local
culture, bringing about a lowest-common-denominator society. Just as the
biodiversity of life is being threatened by growth, so too is the diversity of
cultures, leading to the death of cultural distinction.

There is some clear evidence that cultural diversity is indeed under
threat. The range of languages, which serves as one of the most basic markers
of societies, is dwindling. Predictions are that by the year 2100, the number
of languages spoken in the world will have halved, from 6,000 down to
3,000.[13] Language, however, is only one marker. The greater threat is that
the spread of a common marketing culture will cause the rich textural
difference of societies to lessen or disappear altogether.

For many, world culture now translates into American-led culture.
This "McSociety" concerns many people around the world. Foremost
amongst the concerned are anthropologists who see traditional societies,
such as those in the Amazon jungle or Pacific islands, rapidly giving up
their ways of life. Globalization and the mechanisms of the Image Economy
are seen as the key instruments that are stripping people of the richness of
their cultures and traditions, creating cultural clones. Image makers and
marketers are the enemy lined up to persuade people to trade the color and
pageantry of their forefathers for a new pair of sneakers and some greasy
fast food. They wonder how in the world this can be called "progress".

Future prognosis: *Expect further confrontation over the role of the*
Image Economy in fueling a globalized culture. The debate is likely to become
more strident and polarized, with image makers having to find new ways to win
doubting consumers over. This will require communicators to understand the
way in which universal images can best be localized to cultures — a vital topic
that will be explained in later chapters.

his the Future We Want?

Perhaps the biggest challenge for image creators will be the need to strike a balance that suits consumers' wants, yet is effective at building images for their commercial goals. Otherwise, ours will be a world in which every spot is plastered with commercial images and where everyone will wear a price tag and have a spin-doctor behind them. As technology evolves, the cacophony of products vying for attention will become exponentially worse with each passing day. Consumers will be bombarded, from all directions, by images. The growth of marketing through new media such as hand-phones will ensure that the marketing machine is always on, always there, running all the time, everywhere. Big Brother will not only be watching, he will be trying to sell you a new toaster or a set of steak knives. If this is the future, what normal person won't try to reach for the off button?

The Persuasion Process

4

The Communications Paradox

So which one is it, then? Is the Image Economy a fertile field of business opportunity or an overcrowded jungle, choked with images? Is it a land of consumer choice or a patch of consumer confusion? Do consumers really enjoy consuming commercial and entertainment images or do they feel increasingly oppressed by them? The answer, in fact, is all of the above.

This seemingly contradictory prognosis is a reflection of a fundamental communications paradox that exists today. Or, rather, it reflects a collection of paradoxes. Consumers have more choice than they've ever had before, but they are now blinded by that choice. They emulate and worship celebrities like never before, but many are also jaded about stars. People seek more access than ever to information, yet they often tire of it and want an escape. Scientific advances seem to ensure a constant cycle of product improvements and innovations, yet the lack of product distinction makes it harder for consumers to discern differences between these products. Consumers are clearly torn.

Ironically, marketers too suffer from communications paradoxes. There are more marketing channels than ever before to help them reach their consumers, but clutter and competition make it difficult to actually connect with them. More marketing data is available for companies to use, but they often lack the time to glean enough understanding from it. Competitive replication now occurs with each successive marketing innovation, with no end in sight. Players will always follow others who appear to have a winning idea.

Ultimately, both sides of this communications paradox lead to the same conclusion: a strong, clear and effective image is both the key to taking advantage of the huge opportunities in the Image Economy and a fundamental requirement in order to avoid the pitfalls of clutter, consumer annoyance or eventual death from a lack of distinction. Only effective images can survive in the Image Economy.

How successful can a strong image be? One study has shown that some commercials are up to 4,000% more effective than others are.[1] This enables effective communications to act as a "multiplier", turning the millions that are spent on advertising into billions-worth of value through persuasive product and brand imagery. The best images can truly motivate people. The *Star Wars* characters, for example, are so fascinating that people were willing to camp out for a month to get *The Phantom Menace* tickets.[2]

However, this is easier said than done. Creating effective images is a demanding task. Even seemingly good images can sometimes fail to resonate with consumers. The central issue to consider at this stage then is *how* effective images are created. What are the keys to creating images that connect better than others do?

The Persuasion Process

As a first step towards identifying the answer, we need to consider how image makers go about developing a commercial image and message today. It's clear from my experience with a wide variety of clients that companies approach the issue differently and with diverse philosophies. Some leave it to a few individuals to guide the process using little more than gut judgment. Other companies employ a more scientific approach that involves a battery of people. So, it would be fatuous to claim that there is only one way companies attempt to build their image. What is clear is that there are some basic, broad principles that most companies follow.

These common elements form a process — a persuasion process — the central tenet of which is that the right message, exposed frequently to the right "target", will create habituation, interest and belief in a product. Success happens in varying degrees, creating different levels of consumer loyalty. It also happens over a period of time, with success happening quickly in some cases and more slowly in others. The goal, though, is to move the target audience constantly towards greater levels of attachment.

Simply understanding the persuasion process doesn't ensure doing it better. However, a close look at each of the key elements of the process allows for a better understanding of the theories at each stage.

The Target: Demographics and Psychographics

One of the first steps in the persuasion process is to identify with whom you want to communicate — the target audience. A message is ultimately intended to reach and persuade specific individuals. However, even with direct-marketing techniques, it is still difficult to truly tailor communications down to the individual level. Therefore, a "target audience" — a group of people who share similar demographic factors, such as age, gender, income or location — is identified. A target audience approximates the individuals who are part of the group that you want to reach through the communication, whether that's with a TV commercial, a new product, a piece of entertainment or merchandise — virtually everything that's sold is sold with a target in mind. It also provides a quantifiable basis for the persuasion process. Later, when media are being selected, media time is bought and sold on the basis of its ability to reach that target audience.[3]

The process of targeting is not just a demographic exercise. A critical link that is made in the persuasion process is the extrapolation of demographics into related psychographics in an attempt to understand how the target audience thinks. This is where a large leap of faith occurs with many marketers. There is a basic assumption that if you meet a certain demographic profile, a corresponding set of psychographic characteristics will follow as well. No doubt, there are some generalizations and assumptions that can be — indeed, must be — made in doing mass marketing. Fifty-year-old men with children, a large income and a house in the city will no doubt have some needs and wants in common. The primary purpose of considering both the demographics and psychographics is to gain insights about the common denominators of the group.

But there are also many tenuous or incorrect links that can be made between demographics and psychographics. The "target audience" is not a homogenous mass with identical attitudes, despite similar demographics. Plenty of 50-year-old men with sizeable incomes have different ways of thinking. Therefore, what will actually appeal to the individuals in a target audience is a complex issue.

The correlation between psychographics and products is often not obvious or straight. For a target audience of rebellious teenagers, the fact that their moms *don't* like the product might be the most compelling reason for them to want it. So there are substantial limitations to what advertisers or media executives can assume about the individuals who consume their products or TV programs. They can't blindly count on a psychological profile following a demographic profile in lock-step.

The Message and "Idea"

With a target audience in focus, the next step is to determine what to say and what to show. This may sound simple, but those people at the coalface creating commercial messages every day know how truly difficult this is. There are often many things that can be said about a product. A number of points are equally convincing and important in the selling process. The key, though, is to shed everything but the kernel of what must be said to make a product different and believable. The communications process, therefore, is one of distilling and simplifying, to get down to the very essence of what to say. The best communications follow this simplifying principle.

With a message in mind, the job is then to find a way to express that message creatively. The trick is to find the common denominator — the thing that everyone can understand and relate to — without "dumbing down" the message and making it pedestrian. This results in what advertising professionals often refer to as the "idea". Broadly defined, an advertising idea is how the key message about the product is put into a creative expression that will capture people's attention. An idea should enable a piece of communication to create surprise and interest so that it captivates consumers' imaginations.

The persuasion process is especially demanding at this point because of a seemingly opposing set of requirements. While there is a need for communication to create something new, it must simultaneously maintain some connection to previous communication for the brand. If it doesn't, it will be virtually impossible for a brand to build a consistent image and values over time. One of the hardest tasks in the image-creation business, therefore, is to repeatedly create messages that are fresh and unexpected, yet consistent for the brand.

A great advertising idea should expand consumers' minds; it should open them to new possibilities that have never occurred to them. Yet, communications is not art. Unfortunately, some people in the communications world fall into the pretension trap. Art's purpose is to open people's brains for pleasure and for intellectual or spiritual gain. The job of commercial communication, on the other hand, is to direct consumers' brains in a specific direction with the specific purpose of selling a product. Advertisers aren't interested in enlightening individuals; they are paying their valuable dollars to create materials which guide and habituate viewers to their product. So while communications expand consumers' minds to possibilities, they must ultimately channel their minds towards a specific end.

The Role of Exposure and Frequency

The repeated exposure of the message helps this channeling effort. With rare exceptions, messages don't take root on their first viewing. They generally require repeated showings before they sink in with consumers. So a key step in persuading consumers is to build "frequency" — the number of times the target audience is exposed to the message. In fact, the standard advertising calculation that is used to determine advertising's potential impact is based on a function of reach (the number of people in the "target audience" who will see the message) times frequency (how many times they are likely to be exposed to that message).

While the concept of exposure seems relatively straightforward, there are different psychological levels on which frequency of exposure is actually effective. "Top-of-mind awareness" is one of the most immediate results of frequency. In the rawest sense, this part of the persuasion process operates by sticking something in front of people's faces, which prompts them to think about it and, hopefully, want it. The power of suggestion can be quite strong. For example, even if you are not hungry for chocolate, you might be tempted to have some — or at least you will think about it more readily — if someone offers you a box of chocolates.

A tactic to create top-of-mind awareness is a spending "heavy-up". This is essentially an increase in spending to higher-than-normal levels, with more frequent exposure of a commercial message. Many advertisers increase their spending during peak selling seasons. Toys are usually advertised more heavily around gift-giving holidays to ensure they're on the shopping list, and cold medicines are advertised during flu season, when medicine is most in demand and consumers need to decide which one to use. The use of heavier spending can also be done around peak parts of the day that coincide with the most natural times when a consumer might consider purchasing a product. Family restaurants that thrive on dinner traffic, for example, tend to get better results advertising prior to and during the dinner hour, when people have food on their minds. They build frequency at this point in the day, rather than putting advertising on the morning news, when dinner isn't of primary concern. Even for products that don't have seasonality or day-part dependency, a general spending heavy-up can still be effective. Most companies notice some sort of spike in their sales during the periods when they advertise heavily. Indeed, they have to see some sales results if agencies expect them to continue spending money on advertising.

However, there are deeper implications of frequency than simply top-of-mind. Some advertising is rendered effective by creating frequency over a longer period of time. Take Sony billboards as another example. The billboards do more than stick the name Sony in front of you. Over time, if there are enough of them, they create a real sense of presence for the brand. This, in turn, triggers a logic sequence in consumers' heads that works like this: if you seem to be everywhere, you must be big; and you can't be big unless you're successful, and you won't be successful unless you are good at what you do. So, presence equals some degree of quality assurance. In truth, big is not always good. But people often feel that there's safety in size. As the old business maxim goes, you probably won't get fired for choosing a market leader like IBM. The weight of repeated exposures can create stature and trust for a brand.

Some professionals in the persuasion business would argue that any exposure is worthwhile. A number of new media mentioned previously, from rotating signboards to stickers on apples, operate on this principle that every opportunity for a consumer to see a commercial message contributes to building awareness for the brand. In addition to pure exposure, however, there's also the environment in which a message is shown. So, other professionals would argue that the context in which a message is seen makes a big difference in how ready consumers are to receive that message. Some advertisers love the idea of advertising in cinemas because consumers are relaxed and undistracted and possibly more receptive to a message. Overall, effective exposure usually requires some balance between pure frequency and the quality of the environment.

The issues of frequency and exposure are vital to the development of a brand in a broader sense. Brand managers struggle to maximize the amount of shelf space that stores give them for their product. They seek the greatest possible number of "facings" — rows of their product, — because of the presence it creates. Maximizing the positive exposure of a brand in every form is the key principle behind integrated communications. The extension of commercial images into merchandise and sponsorships is another way in which the frequency of exposure for a brand can be increased. Of course, integration requires more than just exposure. Each time a consumer sees a brand, it also needs to be consistent in tone and quality as well as take advantage of the benefits that are unique to each marketing channel. But assuming that the brand is presented consistently, there is a multiplying effect achieved by having the brand exposed in different marketing channels to build brand presence.

It is at this stage of exposure that consumers become participants in the persuasion process through self-selection. As much as a company has attempted to target a consumer, consumers themselves must be willing to take up the message. They must find it interesting or intriguing. The message must resonate somewhere in their minds. If the message does get through to them, then a process of habituation and bonding begins.

Repetition Leads to Habituation and Bonding

The end goal of building frequent exposure is to create familiarity and, eventually, habituation to the product. Most advertising and communication doesn't work on impulse. People don't leap from their couches to run and buy a new car because of a TV commercial. They don't dash out to the supermarket for some new detergent when they see a print ad. Rather, they select the product they want when they are in the supermarket aisle for their shopping. But how exactly they became familiar with the product in the first place isn't always clear. They usually can't trace their knowledge to a specific time or place when they saw a piece of communication. The message has simply sunk in over time through repetition.

So while frequency does build top-of-mind, it also builds depth of memory.[4] If an image is effective, consumers not only think about it in the immediate sense but also store it away in the back of their minds. In this process, consumers become familiar over time with certain products. Through the repetition of commercial messages, and also the repeated use of the product itself, consumers build a habit for the brand (provided that the product performs properly). It simply becomes second nature for them to reach for that particular brand of soap powder.

The psychological mechanisms of conditioning drive the bonding process with consumers. Do you remember the story of Pavlov's dogs? The scientist Ivan Pavlov discovered that dogs would salivate at the ringing of a bell, once they were conditioned over time to associate the ringing of a bell with their dinnertime. This same mechanism of conditioning occurs every day in the commercial world.[5] Modern communication conditions you to believe things so that you will use products. In some cases, the conditioning happens through positive reinforcement. The happy, smiling faces in advertising subtly convey that you, too, will be happy if you use that product. Just reach for a Pepsi or a Coke, and you will be part of the lifestyle you see. Advertising conditions people in a number of other ways too; it's not all smiles and thin waistlines. Advertising also persuades by conditioning you to fear things so that you will buy insurance, get your house re-roofed, and buy a new car with anti-lock brakes.

The ultimate purpose of commercial communication goes beyond persuading you about which brand to choose. Commercial activity is also intended to drive consumption. Companies condition consumers to use their products and to use them more often. Coke and Pepsi are again a good example of this. They don't simply want you to reach for their brand of cola. They want you to reach for it every time you are hot or thirsty. And the average person feels the physical sensation of thirst several times a day.

The psychological process that bonds people and brands reaches deep into our psyches as social beings. This extends conditioning into bonding. If we go back to the Pavlov example, we see that conditioning is largely an individual activity. When Pavlov rang his bell, the dogs salivated because they anticipated eating their own dinner. They weren't salivating out of sympathy for the other dogs. Yet advertising affects groups of people, not just individuals. As we observed earlier, brand recognition is dependent upon brands creating common symbols which others recognize too. So the persuasion process taps into a group dynamic, as well as the individual conditioning dynamic, to create a durable bond between consumers and the brand as a symbol.

Levels of Consumer Loyalty

It's important to note that what results from the persuasion process is not a simple *yes* or *no* decision from consumers; the choice is often not just *purchase* versus *non-purchase*. Fundamentally, what results is a spectrum of consumer interest. In some cases, the advertising will be "successful" because it makes a consumer who has never noticed the product before suddenly aware of it. In other cases, the same commercial message might move the product higher up in a consumer's consideration set. At whatever point consumers are in their relationship with a brand, the key is to move them further on towards loyalty. The goal is to reduce customer turnover and maximize repeat business from existing customers. As mentioned earlier, the reason for this is simple: the cost of acquiring new customers is often far greater than pleasing and retaining existing customers.

This is the critical aim of marketing in general and communications as a component of marketing. Consumers are not all equal: some use brands on only an infrequent basis, while others are brand loyalists who swear by the brand and use it more frequently. It is these types of users who provide the real financial payback for a brand. Therefore, loyalty must be nurtured.

However, messages are not laser bombs. So even with careful targeting, there are plenty of people not in the target group who still see the communication. Some consumers automatically de-select themselves from the persuasion process. After giving the message some thought, they determine that they don't like the product or it's not relevant for them, at least for now. They might do this unconsciously by ignoring the message altogether. In fact, all of us do this every day. We all make as many decisions about what we ignore as we do about what we observe.

But not being part of a target group doesn't automatically disqualify a consumer from potentially being interested. This is an important point to note, because it can have long-term impact on brands. Let's take the example of people who don't have children. Even though they do not have a baby who needs diapers, they still might see diaper advertising. They might also remember the message because they simply enjoy the commercial. If they do have children one day, their familiarity with the brand would then result in their trying that brand of diaper first. The long-term building of goodwill with consumers is a relevant part of the brand equity process.

Commercial communication, though, is generally focused on the short-term conversion of consumers who are most likely to have a current interest in acquiring the product. Therefore, the key measure of commercial communication is its ability to deliver persuasion that results in commercial activity and brand selection.

An Imprecise Process

The persuasion process is not arbitrary or haphazard, though it sometimes feels that way to people involved in the daily fracas of image creation and guidance. The many professionals who are paid to help sell products consider, analyze and debate a variety of issues at different stages of the persuasion process. They look for associations and insights so they can better articulate the brand positioning and message. They study and attempt to improve virtually every aspect of their creative work — the colors, the props, the look of the models, the sizing of the photography — whatever is involved in that particular type of communication. Other professionals debate and analyze the delivery process to consumers, selecting the specific media and programs that will be used. This is all done in an attempt, through applying a discipline, to ensure an ironclad result. Ultimately, the various steps in the process are intended to generate one outcome — commercial success.

When executed properly, the persuasion process is indeed effective. If it weren't, we wouldn't have the growth of the Image Economy that has been witnessed over the past 100 years. There wouldn't be the famous brands we can all name. Advertisers, though, want to take it beyond a process to find an algorithm — a consistent and repeatable set of steps that guarantees them success time after time. They want to know that if they put X amount of money behind their efforts, they can count on Y amount of sales and brand equity. Particularly with so much hinging on the performance of their image, advertisers expect consistent success. Companies desperately want a Holy Grail of the communications business. But it simply doesn't exist. Success can never be guaranteed.

The process of image creation is a guided process, but it isn't like a production process. You can't "Six Sigma"[6] your way to a better image. Despite all the best efforts to apply science and methodology to the process, there are still wide areas for interpretation, with success usually resting on the intangibility of human insights and talent. This makes the process far from perfect. In fact, more often than not images fail to connect forcefully, if at all.

Four Causes of Failure

There are some key reasons why this persuasion process often fails. These issues, which correspond to the key points outlined, are important to consider, because they represent the key communications problems that most advertisers must address if they wish to have success.

• **There's a lack of consumer understanding:** Often, basic targeting doesn't reach deep enough to provide real insights about the consumers that a company expects to buy their products. If assumptions about the target are inadequate or simply wrong from the start, the rest of the process will unravel. The message won't persuade the intended consumers.

• **Messages often fail the consumer relevancy test:** The advertiser is only one side of the equation. The persuasion process is always a combination of both advertiser and consumer factors. A successful persuasion process rests on consumers actually internalizing the message. This will only occur if there's relevancy to consumers on emotional and rational levels. Unfortunately, many images fail to connect with consumers' psyches — a topic we'll be examining in great detail later on.

- **Creativity is lacking in most messaging:** Messages must be articulated in a way that both stands out and breaks through with consumers. Everything hinges on the quality of the message and its getting noticed. Otherwise, it's a bit like flogging the consumer with a piece of tissue paper: go ahead and hit away, because they won't notice. A communicator's efforts will be futile if they don't have the right voice to reach consumers' ears.

- **It's difficult creating effective exposure:** Lastly, effective exposure is difficult to create. The Image Economy offers companies a variety of media options and outlets to reach consumers. But given the amount of clutter, most brands find it difficult to get the level of exposure that is required for messages to sink in. On the opposite end of the spectrum, some companies wear out their welcome by sticking their messages in front of consumers too much. This might sound contradictory, particularly given the point just made about the difficulty of creating breakthrough with an image. But some brands do suffer from overexposure. The result is what's generally called "commercial wear-out". The effect of frequent repetition can be consumer stress or even distress. After a while, the viewer becomes so annoyed that it results in negative brand equity.

Most often, though, images are simply ignored. There are a lot of dud images out there. Nothing shows this more clearly than a simple advertising test called a clutter reel. The test simulates a typical commercial break, which includes several commercials. Placed in the group of commercials is the one commercial to be tested. The purpose is to see how that commercial stands out against the others. Even image professionals are amazed to see how many details of the commercials consumers can't recall just a few minutes after people watch them. We're not talking hours or days here — we're talking minutes. Images that were seen when a person lights a cigarette are gone from their mind by the time they stick the butt in the ashtray. Images can disappear that fast, at least from conscious memory. This isn't the exception; this is the norm.

The Search for the Consumer Code

For many companies, this persuasion process is increasingly failing to deliver the goods. It might have sufficed in the past, when the media and brand worlds weren't as competitive as they are today. But particularly now, given all the challenges of the Image Economy, a deeper understanding is required. Only the best-crafted images will manage to cut through the growing mound that is dumped on people daily. Success rests on figuring out better ways to create images and fundamentally improve the persuasion process.

Image mastery is vital, not optional: it is a prerequisite for success today and tomorrow. Given the high stakes, companies invest heavily in professional advice to "crack the code" of how to create and nurture brands, manage personalities and create cut-through communications. Marketing and research gurus offer a variety of techniques to help them uncover a better way to communicate. They search for new consumer insights — nuggets that will help them connect with consumers. They use focus groups, interviews and statistical analyses. Some product companies have even taken to filming in consumers' homes to view their daily habits in an attempt to unearth new insights.[7]

The great shortcoming, though, of many of these techniques and so-called experts is that they do little more than regurgitate the basics of the persuasion process. They focus on what people do or think in relation to a product or lifestyle, without making new, critical connections to consumers' deepest psychological workings. They don't get far enough into how people fundamentally think and feel. Instead, marketing and advertising folks often turn to more spending or spurious new methodologies that don't get to the core issues of what will create the vital connections with consumers. They fail to get to the code level.

The next challenge to consider, then, is how to get to the source code to find the keys to better consumer connections. And, indeed, the source is there, grounded in the deep reaches of our psyches. We all have it. We all use it. Without much digging, you can bring its power to the surface.

Section II
The
Mythic
Connection

Archetypes:

The
Source
Code

5

Searching for the Source

Most things can be traced back to a source or basic elements. This is true of virtually everything that is part of our physical, biological and intellectual world. The multitude of life forms that populate the Earth, for example, stem back to simple, prehistoric plant and animal life forms — the Adam and Eve of the natural world.[1] The elements, whether seen in the Western chart of elements or the Oriental interpretation of the five elements (Fire, Water, Wood, Earth and Metal), are the building blocks of our physical world. Math, science and philosophy all rely on their respective tenets and laws. It is important to understand all of these types of sources because they often provide the key to a greater comprehension of the things they help to engender.

This principle holds true for communications as well. If we dig far enough into the human psyche, we reach the origins of what enables people to communicate and connect. There are basic mechanisms and a primary "source code" at work in every instance of human communication and interaction. To understand this process of connection, we must look much deeper than language, which facilitates communication at a conscious level. In fact, we must understand the process of connection at a rudimentary, subconscious code level in our psyches.

This should come as no surprise, since our bodies are built to interpret codes buried deep within us. At the microscopic level, for example, the code of our DNA is spinning a story within each of us every day. What makes the source code of communications unique and particularly fascinating, however, is its ability to accommodate the unpredictability of the human mind and our daily experiences. Unlike the DNA source code of our body, which programs us to grow and change according to some sort of approximate plan, the source code of communication must function in a fluid environment. People's thoughts and interactions are not programmed. So this communications code must be flexible enough to cope with the spontaneity and randomness of the world around us, while still enabling us to make some sense of it all.

An Introduction to Archetypes — The DNA of Communications

At the root of our ability to communicate is a concept known as archetypes.[2] This comes from Carl Jung's pioneering psychological studies in the first half of the 1900s. Archetypes are interlinked with a second and equally important theory that Jung developed — namely, the collective unconscious.[3] An understanding of both concepts, starting first with the collective unconscious, is vital to ultimately understanding the underlying dynamics of the Image Economy.

Prior to Jung, psychologists and theorists had postulated the existence of some form of unconscious portion of the mind. What Jung added to the canon of the psychological understanding was a much richer appreciation of the role of the unconscious. First, he saw the unconscious as an active agent in our lives. Jung asserted that the unconscious isn't some sort of "closet" or "attic" in the mind, where old or useless objects are simply stored away.[4] He also argued that the unconscious should not be relegated to the position of an inferior or less-important part of the mind. Rather, Jung defended the unconscious as a potent, dynamic force in shaping people's actions, although — by the very definition of the unconscious — we cannot have a direct experience of it.

Second, Jung theorized that, in addition to each of us having our own, individual unconscious, there also exists a so-called collective unconscious, which we all share by virtue of being human. Jung described this collective unconscious as "identical in all men and thus constitutes a common psychic substrate of a suprapersonal nature which is present in every one of us".[5] This collective unconscious acts as a communal well in the mind, filled with psychic content that we all share.

This is where archetypes play their role. Jung postulated that archetypes are the critical content of the collective unconscious. The simplest explanation of archetypes is that they are primary forms. They are the original patterns or prototypes in the human mind.[6] These forms cover a range of concepts — for example "evil", "mother" and "happiness" — which are basic elements of our human psyche. All of us have these same primary forms in our collective unconscious. Indeed, archetypes are not learned or acquired — they are with us from birth and are as natural and embedded in us as our own DNA.

Archetypes: Fulfilling Key Requirements as a Source Code

The notion of archetypes was revolutionary in the study of psychology at the time and it expanded the understanding of the human mind. To many people, the notion that the human mind isn't purely personal is, at first, a strange concept.[7] But archetypes have profound relevancy today as the heart of the communications source code. Archetypes provide the keys to understanding the power of images and why they create strong human connections.

As we will examine, archetypes deliver on all the requirements of a code. Archetypes are flexible, yet enduring; they are universal, yet personal; and they create both instant impact and a lasting effect. When we look more thoroughly at archetypes, not simply as a theory but also later when we observe examples of how they are utilized for commercial purposes, it becomes apparent that they are the ideal building blocks for enabling human connections.

As unconscious matter, archetypes are both unseen and can never be directly experienced. However, as we'll shortly observe, they are expressed through conscious forms that can be observed. Also, there is a clear logic to the way they function in the communications process. So we can glean some clear insights that can later be used for harnessing their power in commercial images.

There are two critical implications — related to the broader topic we are examining — that stem from the role of archetypes. These should be noted since both points have substantial implications for the remainder of this book. First, human motivations often start below the rational and conscious level of the mind. People's dreams, ambitions, desires and wants originate in the depths of the psyche, making it impossible for people to pinpoint the genesis of why they have certain desires and wants: they simply know they do.[8] So any effort to communicate with and motivate people should recognize that the persuasive power of communication must work in the far recesses of the mind where people's emotions reside. The role of the subconscious and unconscious mind, therefore, is a key to communication. Anyone seeking success in the Image Economy must understand how the communications process relates back to the human psyche.

This leads to the second key point. Since communicators are dealing in things that are invisible and irrational, there will always be some uncertainty. Archetypes do not provide a formula. They provide the basic building blocks that enable the process of human connection to occur. However, as we will see, a myriad of combinations can be fashioned from the primary elements that originate in our subconscious. So the fact that there is a basic code at work in communications does not imply that the process of communication can ever be made formulaic. This second point is critical in framing up communicators' expectations of how much they can control the communications process. It will always involve some trial and error. However, a deeper understanding of what gives power to communication should make the process of connection much more intelligible for you and should improve your chances for success in the Image Economy.

The following maps the basic traits of archetypes, with some specific implications noted for how these traits apply to the communications process.

Archetypes: A Universal Basis

The first point in an examination of archetypes is their universal nature. Philosophers and assorted wise men throughout the ages have said that people are basically alike. Exactly how alike we are, at least at a genetic level, has been one of the interesting findings from the human genome project. According to early results of the mapping of the human DNA strand, all human genetic codes are about 99.99% alike.[9] There's an awful lot that we all share in common at the most basic level of our DNA. Further, the project has shown that this genetic similarity crosses all racial boundaries. In fact, there's every likelihood that your neighbor — whatever his/her race — will have as much in common with you genetically as a random person from your own race.

It's ironic that it took medical science almost a century to further "prove" in biological terms what Jung and others argued in psychological terms — that even at our most elemental levels, we share a common, primordial base that makes us human. This biological finding is nevertheless meaningful to our topic because it emphasizes, once again, the universality of our existence.

Since archetypes serve as primary forms within all of us, they are a common denominator — we are all equally "qualified" when it comes to archetypes. Despite the babble of language and divisions of nationality, race and religion that often cause strife amongst people, archetypes provide a form of unconscious glue that binds us all. In fact, archetypes cut across all societies and cultures; they span all nationalities, races and age groups; and they bridge the gender gap. Male or female, tall or short, Asian or Western, irrespective of where you grow up and what language you speak, the same archetypes reside in everyone's psyche.[10]

Universality is the basis of the communications code. For the code to work effectively it must be equally understood by all and it must apply to all. Otherwise, it would work like a secret code, keeping certain people out, rather than enabling universal connections.

Key implication for the communications process: *The universality of archetypes is what allows for universally appealing messages that can cross cultures. This will be important when we look at how to create effective transnational communications.*

Archetypes: Expressed in Society as Mythology

The next point in our map is the way archetypes are expressed. A basic tenet of Jung's theory is that archetypes are the content of our collective unconscious. Jung described archetypes as "those psychic contents that have not yet been submitted to conscious elaboration and are therefore an immediate datum of psychic experience."[11] According to Jung, there is no *direct* experience of archetypes. However, he and others recognized that archetypes do find their way from the unconscious into various forms of conscious expression. Indeed, they must or they wouldn't be able to make the impact they do in our everyday lives.

A number of influential thinkers, most notably Joseph Campbell and Bruno Bettelheim, have asserted that mythology, folklore and fairy tales provide the most natural expressions of archetypes in society. Campbell, in particular, described the symbols of mythology as "spontaneous productions of the psyche" which burst forth from the unconscious.[12] Consequently, mythologies often don't have clearly identified origins. They are seemingly organic creations of a culture.

For most people today, mythology conjures up images of ancient gods and goddesses, strange monsters and magical powers — subjects that are amusing but distant from real life. But mythology in the broad definition includes the stories, traditions and icons that are meaningful to a culture. In this wider sense, mythology does indeed touch people's lives. In fact, mythologies throughout the ages have always connected easily with contemporary audiences. The stories and figures that populate mythology take root and become meaningful symbols because they strike deep, natural chords within us all. The characters become relevant icons in a culture.

It is at this conscious level of articulation through mythology that archetypes create universal connections.[13] We can all relate to characters involved in stories of love, jealousy, heroism and loyalty. We see part of our deeper selves in the characters — both their bravery and their stupidity — and realize that their story is really the story of Everyman. The labors of Hercules represent our struggles and labors. These stories work largely because they bring archetypes to life in conscious form through the various characters.

The characters and stories we find in mythology also illustrate universal lessons we know viscerally: the bad guy is dangerous; the wise old man can be trusted; and the joker is unpredictable. We can often anticipate the actions and attitudes of these characters because we already have a deep, intuitive comprehension of their nature since the archetypes on which they're based reside within us all. Consequently, although the stories of societies are told in different languages, featuring heroes and villains with different names, there are recurring themes that can be found across most cultures.

The role of mythology in society is ultimately to do more than amuse or provide bedtime stories. The stories and mythic characters of mythology give voice to our basic human nature. People see and relate to the stories, which express what they already feel on some deeper level. The stories also provide important morals and lessons which people use to guide their lives. So, through characters and icons, archetypes from the unconscious are expressed in our conscious lives and shape our beliefs.[14]

Key implication for the communications process: *This role of mythology as the means for conscious expression of archetypes is critical when we look shortly at how archetypes are expressed in commercial images today.*

Archetypes: Individuality and Diversity

For archetypes to be truly useful, they must create a personal relevancy and connection as well. This fact is not as contradictory as it may seem at first. The universality of archetypes doesn't preclude them from being "personal" too.[15] As we've just observed, archetypes aren't vague forms devoid of personal consequence. Instead, since they are within us all, archetypes must also have personal and meaningful expressions.

To help understand how this happens, think for a moment about the following analogy that has been used to describe archetypes. An archetype has been compared to an empty glass — a generic, universal form that has the same approximate shape and contours for us all. The liquid that fills that glass, however, is our own, individual experiences in life. While we all share the same archetypes as primary forms (the glass), we ultimately experience that form on a personal level (the liquid). This brings meaning and individuality to the form.

An example of this is the archetype of "mother". As humans, we all start life with that primary form within us. It provides an innate under-standing of what "mothering" means.[16] Somewhere deep inside us, there are expectations that the archetypal mother provides warmth and love and nourishment. Ultimately, though, our individual experiences of our own mother shape and personalize our understanding of that archetype.

We don't live for a vague notion of warmth and love; we are motivated by the specific examples of it in our lives. Through our own experiences, we come to have a personal understanding of all these universal forms. However, the archetype — and its universal associations — never vanishes from our collective unconscious. For this reason, people continue to recognize the deep symbolic importance of mothering, even if their own mothers are far off the archetypal mark.

Archetypes allow for the diversity of individual experiences. The human genome project again provides an interesting biological parallel to this point. Even as the genome project neared completion of its first phase, most scientists expected to find anywhere from 50,000 to 140,000 genes. One of the great surprises from the actual findings was that the number is closer to 32,000 genes. In fact, humans have only about 6,000 more genes than the *Arabidopsis thaliana* — a weed.[17] Yet humans, from a smaller set of genetic codes than expected, still vary greatly in their shapes, colors and attitudes.

Similarly, from a common set of archetypes, the complexity and diversity of our individual personalities and experiences can be accommodated, while maintaining some degree of common understanding. Archetypes are not a straitjacket, requiring that everyone think or feel the same things. Rather, they have the flexibility to allow for personal expression while maintaining universal consistency at a deeper level.

Key implication for the communications process: *People's personal connections with archetypes are vital when we later consider how individuals relate to different commercial images and form brand affinity.*

Archetypes: Instantly Recognizable and Useful

In order to be useful, a basic code must also be instantly recognizable and understandable. Otherwise, the process of recognition would take too long. Activity would grind to a halt during the hiatus while the codes were being interpreted. This makes immediate recognition the next key feature of archetypes to consider in our mapping exercise.

Essentially, we are hardwired as human beings. Archetypes are automatically built into every human's unconscious as part of our human "operating system".[18] As primary forms, they are the first content that fills our heads. So, from the moment of birth, archetypes are functioning, helping us interpret our world. As innate content, archetypes also make almost-immediate connections within our brains.

This immediate connection is instrumental since archetypes are put to use in the mind; they do not sit idly. In the case of communications, archetypes help enable us to make sense of the images we see and the symbolic relationships that things represent. We derive fast and often powerful "gut" reactions from these innate forms.[19] Also, they help play an interpretive role, which gives them real usefulness in our lives.

Archetypes power the process of interpretation because they provide stationary points, deeply embedded in our psyches, against which we then measure the world. The process of learning is a constant exercise of comparing and contrasting new experiences against previous experiences and stimuli. In increasingly complex ways throughout our lives, we use the process of comparison against a standard. Archetypes provide the primary forms we use as that unconscious base for sizing up and interpreting the world. They provide a universal and instantly recognizable starting point from which we all unconsciously measure and assess our surroundings.

Key implication for the communications process: *The instant connection that archetypes create enables commercial images to quickly connect with consumers. This is a particularly beneficial trait of archetypes, given the difficulty of breaking through the clutter of the Image Economy.*

Archetypes: Persuasive and Motivating

Archetypes serve as powerful and persuasive motivators.[20] In the depths of our unconscious, the universal images of archetypes mingle with our personal unconscious to help create personal ambitions and dreams. People connect with particular icons and often seek to emulate those icons in their lives. Some people wish to be powerful and strong — to be successful business powerbrokers. Others choose to be writers or sculptors, teachers or firemen. So, while archetypes are universal, individuals tend to gravitate to particular archetypes that motivate them and help determine which callings they choose to follow.

Everyone goes through some process of discovery as they seek meaning in their lives. The journey is not only outward — characterized by what they choose to do with their time or how they behave; it's also an inward journey.[21] People have a visceral need to find or create things in their lives that give expression to their inner desires. Dreams — both the nighttime visitations from our subconscious and the waking dreams and aspirations that direct the energies of our lives — are fueled by archetypes. This ensures that they are powerful and persuasive motivators for all of us.

Key implication for the communications process: *The motivating aspect of archetypes plays a key role in creating persuasion in commercial messages. The strongest commercial images use archetypes to connect with people's deeply founded dreams and aspirations.*

Archetypes: Enduring and Timeless

The last characteristic in our mapping of archetypes is their timelessness. In describing archetypes, Jung wrote that, "As far as the collective unconscious contents are concerned we are dealing with archaic or — I would say — primordial types, that is, with universal images that have existed since the remotest times."[22] Archetypes are not a fad or a theory of the month from the latest management guru. They are enduring, timeless forms. This too is an important characteristic of archetypes and has a couple of major implications.

The first is that archetypes have not only been around for ages, they will also be around for ages to come. Human nature is not likely to undergo a sudden change, and archetypes are not about to evaporate from the human mind. Consequently, it's worth any communicator's investment to understand these forms, since they provide a lasting basis for creating effective communication.

Second, archetypes are the source of durable, eternal images. The most powerful images have tentacles that reach back to the archetypes deep within us. Cutting-edge images often have ancient underpinnings.[23] Consequently, powerful images can resonate and connect for years and years. Just as people today are fascinated by the enigmatic look of the Mona Lisa — hundreds of years after it was painted — people in the future are likely to feel the same about the painting. They will also look at the best contemporary images from our time and share the same feelings we feel. Basic human images are, by their very nature, timeless. The image of a mother cradling her child, for example, is universally understood and connects with all people at some instinctive level. And, I would venture to argue, thousands of years from now, people's basic, human reaction to the image of a mother and child will be the same.

Key implication for the communications process: *Archetypes provide an enduring foundation on which to create lasting images, because archetypes are timeless. This gives well-crafted commercial images longevity. This last point is especially important. While the initial focus of many image makers is a quick breakthrough, it is the ability of an image to create an indelible, meaningful mark in consumers' psyches that is perhaps the most important measure of success.*

Archetypes and the Image Economy

With this grounding in the fundamentals of archetypes, we are now ready to turn our full attention back to the task at hand: determining how to connect better with consumers. To achieve this, we next need to consider the role archetypes play in creating modern commercial communication and, in particular, examine how they underpin the Image Economy.

Making Modern Mythology 6

Mythology: A Vital Link

As we've already examined, the content of the Image Economy —
entertainment, advertising, stars, personalities and brands — are familiar
fixtures in many people's lives. Indeed, they are potent shapers and
motivators in many contemporary societies. People of all ages follow and
emulate stars and athletes — the dominant icons of our day. Brands create
badge appeal and play a major role in the way people exhibit and define
themselves in society. Advertising influences what people choose to buy
with their hard-earned money. And entertainment provides the engrossing
material with which people amuse themselves.

If we go back to the broad definition of mythology as encompassing
the stories, traditions and icons that are meaningful to a culture, we realize
that the Image Economy fits this definition. The material of the Image
Economy generates a *modern mythology* that is as meaningful and active
with people today as previous mythologies were with contemporary
audiences in the past. Indeed, for any mythology to resonate with people,
it must be symbolic of something real and meaningful in their daily lives.

Some people might dismiss modern mythology as simply pop culture,
filled with transient, hollow symbols. Certainly, many of the images today
do fail. But on closer analysis, it is clear that the successful images create a
modern mythology that has a basis in the same subconscious elements that
powered past mythologies. And while individual brands and personalities
do come and go, modern mythology creates many symbols that are enduring
and that form powerful belief systems.

Archetypes and Artifice in Modern Mythology

Archetypes play a central role in this modern mythology, just as they powered previous mythologies. Archetypes are effective motivators today when expressed in contemporary terms. Jung acknowledged the power of archetypes when he said, "That people should succumb to these eternal images is entirely normal, in fact it is what these images are for. They are meant to attract, to convince, to fascinate, and to overpower."[1] As we will see in the next section, the exact same archetypes that have powered mythology, art, literature and folklore throughout the ages are functioning right now. These primordial building blocks, via contemporary expression, provide the root power supporting the material of the Image Economy: brands, personalities, advertising and entertainment.

While there are many fundamental parallels between modern mythology and its ancient counterparts, there is also a critical difference. Modern mythology is not the spontaneous creation of a society, but rather a by-product of images that are consciously and meticulously crafted daily by professionals paid to sell. Brands and other commercial images are not natural to the world — they are fictions built up over time. They must be created and cultivated. Therefore, companies and personalities in today's Image Economy make very conscious choices about the values they want their image to stand for and how to present themselves to the world. They then set about habituating consumers over time to the symbols they have chosen in an attempt to make a connection and a durable bond with the public. Whether it is the figure of the Singapore Girl or Obi-Wan Kenobi, these images and symbols are specifically designed to connect for commercial, rather than spiritual or societal, gain.

It is critical to note here that the notion of purposefully manipulating symbols and images is a timeless practice. For millennia, kings, queens, despots, hucksters and the clergy have all relied on symbol-laden propaganda and the basic mechanisms of communication to influence and persuade the masses. But in no previous time in history have people been able to reach the masses so readily, nor has the living environment been as fast-paced as it is today. Therefore, companies have mammoth pressures on them, like never before, to develop the ability to make fast decisions about how to create and actively manage their mythology.

Mythology takes them into a rich new space of consumer involvement, enabling them to stand for more than a balance sheet and set of products. Broadly, this entails developing the right image that will connect with consumers at the deepest emotional and sub-rational levels. More specifically, this requires an understanding of how to harness archetypes so that those symbols reach the depths of consumers' psyches and tap their power. *The ability to choose the right archetypes and maximize the dynamics of mythical story-telling are the pivotal issues that determine success and failure in the Image Economy.* Effective images must be grounded in something fundamental in the human mind in order to be truly persuasive and lasting in the form of customer equity. Indeed, the most powerful images in the Image Economy are always those that rest most squarely on the existing foundation of archetypes.

This basic point is misunderstood by a large number of people involved in the Image Economy today. Most people think the process of persuasion is about putting messages and images *into* people's brains. Indeed, the job of marketing is to create wants in order to get consumers to buy a product. However, the most effective way to do this is to attach a product to symbols and stories that tap the unconscious codes that are *already there* in people's heads. That is the essence of creating consumer connections. Persuasive images reach the existing reservoirs within consumers' psyches in order to motivate them.

The Key Components for Making Mythology

Tapping consumers' psyches takes careful planning and attention to detail. As a professional who has been in the business of creating communication for many years, I can tell you that every detail counts. Most things around us carry some form of symbolic meaning. Even seemingly trivial details can communicate on some deeper level. So, irrespective of whether you're an aspiring entertainer, a product manager or a news anchor, you must carefully consider every aspect of how you project your image. Everything must work.

Modern mythology is created by specific elements that help breathe life into it and reinforce it every day. The persuasion process, which we examined earlier, is the broad description of the way in which companies attempt to get their message across. In addition to this macro process, there are a number of elements commonly involved in both mythical stories and modern communication at a micro level. These elements, which we will consider next, are mythic figures, story plot, symbols and mnemonics, rituals and moral lessons. Each of these elements contributes in some way to making modern mythology both more memorable and convincing. Further, it is the combination of these critical elements that allows images to work. We will next examine each element, noting how the most effective communicators employ these elements today to strengthen and reinforce their images and generate a modern mythology.

Mythic Figures: The Incarnation of Archetypes

For archetypes to play their central role in modern mythology they require some shape or form that allows them to have conscious expression. Mythic figures provide that form.[2] As we'll see later, they are the incarnation of a variety of archetypes that underlie virtually all entertainment and all types of commercial messages. John Wayne, for example, is an incarnation of the Hero archetype. Darth Vader is an expression of the archetype of Evil. Each of these mythic figures has deep roots that go back in history and that touch parts of our subconscious, since they serve as the conscious expressions of subconscious elements — archetypes.

Mythic figures are just like character actors in a movie, who play a specific role. Each archetype is expressed as a figure that has attendant characteristics. Similarly, each has a consistent dynamic to how they behave and react. In fact, mythic figures must represent a consistent set of values and traits for them to be "true to character" and reflect the archetype on which they're based. This has a very practical purpose in mythology. The nature of each mythic figure provides an easy shorthand in stories. It takes little more than a glimpse of the archetypal "bad guy", for example, to understand volumes about him. Ultimately, mythic figures are not people per se as much as they are representations of different universal characteristics and emotions with which people can relate.

There's another critical point about mythic figures that must be noted. The outward "look" of a person can sometimes be deceptive. The deeper, underlying traits that define his or her character might take some time to emerge. All heroes, for example, don't look like the David who slew Goliath. A Hero figure could just as easily be a young girl or perhaps an old man who prove themselves as heroes. Sometimes, one has to see a bit more of a character before his or her deeper nature — or mythic character — becomes apparent. Although mythic figures can sometimes have initially diverse outward manifestations, if they operate from the same underlying archetypal roots, they are considered to be the same type of mythic figure. The deeper dynamics of the figure are what is important — not the way they're dressed. This point will be especially important when we look later at 12 of the most prominent mythic figures in the Image Economy.

Lastly, every culture has a range of mythic figures. Classical Greek and Roman mythology, for example, was populated by a number of gods, each of whom had a distinctive character. Cultures need this diversity of figures, since each represents and relates to a different part of our complex human nature. Figures of heroism, evil, goodness, friendship and sexuality all connect with different aspects of our psyches. As we shall see shortly, modern mythology is no different in its inclusion of a range of mythic figures that touch different aspects of the way we think and feel. However, since modern mythology is focused on commercial gain, the critical issue for us to consider will be how these various mythic figures and their attendant traits and dynamics relate to different types of marketing messages and forms of entertainment.

Archetypes and Contemporary Expressions

In the Image Economy, we frequently see that a multitude of expressions can draw their source power from the same archetype. Take, for example, a Sumo wrestler in Japan, the movie figure The Terminator, and the late karate star Bruce Lee. All three have their roots in the same archetype — the Ultimate Strength — that symbolizes physical supremacy and challenge. They exhibit many of the same core traits and dynamics, enabling them to serve as potent symbols of power. Yet these expressions obviously don't look exactly the same, despite having a common archetypal basis. In the Image Economy, messages and entertainment can be tuned to different cultures, by allowing for culturally relevant expressions of mythic characters, which all relate back to a common, underlying archetypal heritage.

Not only can archetypes be expressed in various ways across different cultures, they also receive new expression over time. Every generation anoints its heroes and villains, sex bombs and playboys. Today's Hollywood stars follow in a long line of leading ladies who have captured the hearts and imaginations of audiences for years. While Marilyn Monroe titillated a generation of young men in the '60s, stars such as Pamela Anderson and Jennifer Lopez have similar appeal to many contemporary viewers. Equally, the heroes and other mythic icons of today will eventually give way to new heroes in future generations. This process is as natural as human evolution, since societies turn to contemporary figures in order not to fossilize.

The need for contemporary symbols stems from the basic role of mythology in a society. A mythology not only amuses people; it also guides and influences them. Mythic figures play an active role in people's lives, serving as guideposts for the way they think and what they aspire to. People turn to contemporary figures because they feel a connection with them. Through these connections with — and emulation of — mythic figures, people also find expression for their deep desires. This is not to say that people can't equally feel inspired by great figures of the past — the poets, statesmen and heroes who stand out as the great icons of history. But there will probably always be a need for cultures to generate contemporary expressions of mythic figures that reflect both the spirit of the times and the timeless dynamics of archetypes.

Mythic Stories: The Dynamics of Transformation

Mythic figures are not intended to be still portraits — quite the contrary. Mythic characters in stories must take action, because it is through their action that their nature and attitudes, not simply their appearance, becomes clear. The hero becomes a hero through heroic deeds.[3] Similarly, evil figures must do evil acts, and mythic figures of kindness must have the opportunity to prove their kindness to those around them. Every mythic figure must take some form of action, which is the real proof of their mettle and nature. Through dramas, tragedies, sagas and trials we come to see what we already instinctively know — the deeper nature of each mythic figure.

Mythology revolves around story plots in which different mythic figures compete and interact. It is the combination of characters in stories that adds depth and fascination to these figures. David needs his Goliath to fulfill his role as a hero. Romeo needs his Juliet to suffer the love and eventual tragedy with which people connect. Even the Three Little Pigs must have the menace of the wolf, or they would simply sit idly in their houses. Just as mythic figures are instantly recognizable for what they are, the various combinations of mythic figures interacting also communicates instantly recognized dynamics.

The instant recognition of mythic characters, especially in certain combinations, allows advertisers to quickly establish the situation and dynamic in a commercial. Modern mythology relies heavily upon this to work, since an advertiser rarely has more than a few seconds to get a complex message across. The classic advertising setting of two friends in the kitchen, for example, instantly communicates a dynamic of congeniality and familiarity between old, trusted buddies. The sales message for the product that's then featured in this situation evokes subliminal feelings of the trust that two friends share. These immediate, subliminal associations play a big part in making advertising and entertainment effective at connecting with consumers. In the next section, we will examine a number of archetypes, illuminating how the unique dynamics and innate expectations attached with each of them power different types of sales pitches in the Image Economy.

On a deep, symbolic level, the process of interaction between mythic characters usually involves some form of transformation for at least one of them. Their character often doesn't manifest itself all at once but through an evolution throughout the course of the story. A hero, for example, often doubts his ability to achieve a great task until after he has emerged victorious. Mythic characters of kindness are not always bubbly and cheerful, simply waiting like a boy scout at a corner to help an old lady. Instead, their kindness usually becomes evident when they've been put to the test. In still other mythic situations, we see a homely girl transformed into a princess, or an ugly duckling emerge as a swan.

This dynamic of transformation figures heavily in the most successful messages of the Image Economy since it helps make them more persuasive. A good example of this is the classic marketing approach called problem/

solution. On the surface, this approach seems like a fairly straightforward way of showing how a product works. A shirt is dirty and stained, you wash it with this wonderful soap powder, and now it's amazingly clean. What could be simpler? But at a deeper level, problem/solution also communicates to people a very potent message of transformation about the users. Products ultimately connect with the people that use the products. So the message is not simply that the washing powder will be successful at fixing this situation. Inherently, it provides a message that the user will be empowered to transform the situation, using the product.

Particularly in advertising and marketing, what follows on from this transformation is a sense of resolution and the peace of mind that comes with it. Transformation, followed by satisfaction, adds a further emotional payoff. In numerous examples of soap-powder advertising from all over the world, the harried housewife or mother is depicted as feeling relieved when the stained, dirty laundry comes out clean. While the challenge might pale in comparison with David's battle with Goliath, it nevertheless relies on the same mythic message of overcoming a challenge. At some level, we can all appreciate when her problem is resolved, and her "trial" is over.

By connecting product efficacy with the users' sense of transformation and resolution, the modern mythology of selling subtly gets to the deeper depths of consumers' psyches. The most effective marketers offer solutions. This approach is almost always more potent than simply highlighting ingredients or basic product features, since it provides symbolic messages of assurance that products will make their users more potent at mastering their surroundings. It also provides positive reinforcement that helps the conditioning process. In this manner, the modern sales pitch connects back to timeless images and the subconscious, primordial soup in consumers' brains.

Mythic Symbols: The Link to Modern Mythology

In addition to mythic characters and the dynamics of a story plot, mythology and its modern counterpart utilize symbols to help communicate on deeper levels with consumers.[4]

Symbols play an important role because, like an altar in a church, they have the function of focusing attention while also adding deeper meaning to the surroundings. Symbols also serve to provide extra points of reference to both clarify the situation and add new layers of significance. A royal coat of arms, for example, is a symbol that gives a frame of reference to viewers and instantly connotes the importance of the situation. In a similar manner, symbols often become connected with countries — chocolate with Switzerland or kangaroos with Australia, for example — which then act as shorthand for triggering recognition. Mythic figures too usually have specific, defining symbols and visual cues associated with them that trigger recognition. Cupid, for example, has his bow as his defining symbol. It acts as both a visual reference about his identity as well as a cue to how his power is manifested. In modern mythology, symbols play a similar function. Crocodile Dundee and Indiana Jones, for example, would seem a bit naked without their respective trademark hats. Nike wouldn't be Nike without its trademark swoosh.

Modern mythology frequently appropriates existing symbols to help in the selling process. Some of these symbols have universal values. A stop sign or a peace sign, for example, are recognized in most places today. Similarly, there are forms of body language, such as the arm extended with the palm held up to mean "halt", that most people would recognize. Universal symbols are used in much of the Image Economy, particularly in multinational marketing.

However, in addition to universal symbols, there are many subtle variations of body language and mannerisms that are specific to cultures, or at least require someone to be familiar with the culture in order to comprehend what's going on. Communicators must be sensitive to local symbols, since they are often even more meaningful as societal markers. From the universal to the local, and from the overt to the subliminal, symbols of all types help further the communication power of stories at different levels of awareness.

But modern mythology doesn't just use symbols; it also manufactures them. A lot of symbols associated with modern mythology are the product of the Image Economy itself. A key goal of modern mythology, in fact, is to attach timeless values to specific objects in order to transform those objects into potent symbols that have durability and meaning. Product logos are the most prevalent example of this.

Consider McDonald's golden arches as a specific example. Those arches didn't have to be yellow — they could have been green, they could have been blue. McDonald's didn't have to have arches at all. However, after creating that logo as it did, the company set out to imbue that visual reference of the company with great meaning. Each time that logo is shown, it is in combination with messages such as the high quality of the food, the friendly atmosphere or the warmth of a family meal. As a result, those arches are now easily identified as McDonald's by hundreds of millions of people around the world. They are not only recognized, they are associated with a variety of positive feelings for many consumers. McDonald's has created a proprietary bond with a symbol that sticks with consumers' brains. Via this symbol, it triggers deeper psychological associations every time a consumer sees the logo. In this manner, it "owns" a space in consumers' psyches.

Diamonds are another example of symbol creation, although in this case the symbol is not a logo but the product itself. Over decades, through consistently associating that product with the eternal and universal feelings of love, manufacturers have transformed diamonds into a symbol that represents love.[5] As a result, people use diamonds as their own symbol to transmit their feelings. Giving diamonds has become a symbol of one person's love for another, so diamonds are used in engagement rings in many markets and hold a special meaning as a gift. This wasn't always the case. It was through this process of attaching values directly to the product that people were habituated to recognize and believe the modern mythology of diamonds.

The Mnemonic Value of Symbols: The Link with Commercial Recall

Symbols provide another simple but important function in modern mythology: to help people remember. Except in a few, freakish examples, people's memory doesn't allow for total recall. Instead, visual, auditory and olfactory triggers connect with more complex feelings and thought sequences in the brain. Mnemonics leverage the associative powers of the brain to help trigger memories. The scent of a former lover's perfume, for example, can evoke strong feelings and trigger detailed memories of a romantic evening stroll from long ago.

Through an associative process, symbols not only connect with memories, they also connect back to the unconscious portions of the brain, to archetypes and their associated dynamics. The symbol of a crown in a commercial, for example, might trigger the image of a king or queen. On a deeper, often unconscious level, it also associates that product with power, authority and status in society — the dynamics associated with the archetype of the Powerbroker. It's no wonder that Rolex uses a crown as the prominent visual in its logo. It's often these seemingly small details that begin the process of memory and association. As a result, the subliminal message is strengthened and the appeal of the product can be dramatically increased. This potentially gives great value to details in a story that might otherwise seem extraneous.

For this reason, symbols have immense commercial relevance. Because of this capacity to trigger memory and connection to deeper elements of the brain, mnemonics are used extensively in modern mythology today, particularly in advertising. They come in many familiar forms that most viewers don't even recognize as mnemonics, including theme music, logos, characters and mascots. There are abundant examples of all of these in the brand world. Mascots such as Mr. Clean, Tony the Tiger, Ronald McDonald, Charlie the Tuna, Felix the Cat, and the KFC Colonel are just a few of them.[6] Each of these mascots serves to jog the memory and also connect consumers back to a deeper set of associations that the brand has embedded in their psyches.

Mnemonics are necessary because in today's Image Economy people are exposed to a constant flood of visual images. There's simply a lot of stuff vying for their attention. Their function, therefore, is to act as cognitive markers that will quickly jog people's memories and create mental pathways back to products.

Myth and Ritual: The Link to Familiarity in Commercial Messages

The goal of most communicators in the Image Economy is to move their image from users' short-term memory into long-term memory — to become embedded parts of people's thoughts. But this is where the challenge of the persuasion process comes in again. Even if a consumer remembers an image, it doesn't ensure that it has positive associations for them. After all, we can point to many things that we both remember and dislike. So something more is needed.

In mythology, symbols are often imbued with greater meaning through those symbols being the centerpiece of rituals. Various types of rituals are commonly found in most mythic stories. Whether it's a troll demanding three wishes of each person who crosses a bridge or a god that visits a mountain each day, there are usually symbolic actions repeated consistently in myths. Rituals, though, are not just for stories; they are also a regular part of our lives. Soldiers salute their flags every day and go through the formal process of raising and lowering them out of respect. People regularly get on their knees to pray to images of the Buddha, to crosses or to other religious idols they choose to use in worship. Bells ring as teachers call their young pupils to attention each school day to sing anthems or pledge allegiance to their flag.

Rituals form something more important than a casual habit. Through the process of rituals, people reconfirm and renew their belief and commitments. In very practical terms, rituals also ensure that symbols stay in the forefront of people's memory, rather than receding to the background, where they risk being forgotten. Thus, reaffirmation helps maintain the potency of symbols. Additionally, rituals can be therapeutic because they provide comfort and familiarity. People often find solace in ritual, whether it is a religious ritual practiced by many or the small personal or family rituals that are particular to individuals.

Again, this general aspect of mythology is also active in creating modern mythology. People become familiar and comfortable with products because of the subtle rituals that are associated with them in advertising. Consumers become habituated over time to seeing both the product and the specific rituals attached to each. Whether it's a storekeeper squeezing a roll of toilet tissue in every TV commercial[7] or orange-soda drinkers always sticking their thumbs up after a drink, companies use the power of repetition to associate certain actions with a product. These specific actions ultimately generate a vital sense of familiarity that helps the connection process.

Morals to Mythic Stories: The Link with Commercial Persuasion and Beliefs

Audiences generally don't sit and dissect mythology, as we are doing here for the purpose of understanding the mechanics of how it works. Rather, people take on mythic stories as a whole. Therefore, all of the elements of mythology — the mythic characters, their interaction in story plots, and the symbols, mnemonics and rituals associated with them — must integrate seamlessly. The inclusion of all of these elements, however, doesn't guarantee success. To be effective, the story must subtly create some sense of magic.

The intended outcome, though, is not subtle: great stories and myths make real impact. Over time, the mythic stories that we consume have had to survive the natural weeding process of images by maintaining their relevance to society. Those stories that ring true to generation after generation remain; those that don't simply drift away. For a myth to continue to attract an audience, it generally must impart some form of powerful and enduring lesson. In childhood fairy tales and various folktales, this usually happens in the form of a moral to the story — an overt statement of the intended lesson of the tale. Even in less overt form, mythology provides enduring lessons. Thus myths are beacons of meaning about human nature and the many situations that confront us in our lives.[8] It is these lessons in life which enable stories to sustain their role in society, with readers returning to them repeatedly. The great stories don't lose their appeal or power.

Similarly, the stories of modern mythology are intended to direct consumers towards specific, enduring beliefs. The goal is to create more than a message to buy. They must culminate in a bigger promise, which will bring consumers back to buy, watch, consume and reaffirm their interest repeatedly over the years. The beliefs this modern mythology is intended to create can be found in the brand and entertainment messages of our time: if you drink a Pepsi, you will be young at heart; if you buy a Volvo, you will be safe on the road; your Cartier watch will bring you admiration and make you elegant; and your shiny new motorcycle will make you one cool dude. The morals of modern mythology might seem simplistic, but they've been built up through the combination of subconscious elements that we've just examined. And, when marketers do a good job of it, it works.

The Image Economy revolves around people readily buying its manufactured dreams every day.

The images that succeed in connecting are those that best exploit the deeply rooted dynamics of stories and mythic figures that people become familiar with from their earliest days. Effective modern mythologies tap the source power of archetypes to fuel fascination and dreams. So with the end goal of learning how to create more effective images, we will examine further how archetypes are brought to life in the Image Economy.

Section III
Mythic
Profiles

The following section provides profiles of 12 archetypes most commonly found in the Image Economy. The profiles are intended to explain the unique traits and dynamics associated with each archetype and demonstrate how those dynamics can be attached to products, entertainment and personalities, allowing for the frequent cross-pollination of images in the Image Economy.

The archetypes profiled by no means constitute a complete list of all possible archetypes. Additionally, each profile offers a snapshot, rather than an exhaustive study, of each of the figures. As elements of the unconscious, archetypes don't lend themselves to strict classification or formulations. Rather, they have approximate contours that become recognizable only through their conscious expression. Therefore, each profile contains a number of examples that provide a good start at understanding the general shape of each archetype and the manner in which the source code of archetypes is powering a wide variety of messages in the Image Economy today. The inclusion of numerous examples from the Image Economy is intended to provide clear demonstrations of how others are tapping the dynamics of these archetypes to build effective images.

Also, please note the following point regarding the textual treatment of these profiles. Most of the mythic figures can be unisex. However, for ease of reference, their masculine form *his* has been used instead of *his or her*. The two exceptions are the Siren and the Mother of Goodness — singularly female forms. This is not meant to confuse the key point that archetypes drive universal messages that motivate consumers of both genders as well as cutting across cultures.

"We confide in our strength, without boasting of it; we respect that of others, without fearing it.

Thomas Jefferson[1]

Mythic Profile

The Ultimate Strength

An Introduction to the Ultimate Strength

Whether it's Samson pulling down the pillars of the temple of Dagon, The Terminator snuffing another cyborg, Xena the Warrior Princess crushing a dangerous foe, or Ken Shamrock body-slamming a WWF opponent to the mat, the mythic figure of the Ultimate Strength has an awesome and indomitable presence. Yet this mythic figure's strength is not a given; it must be proven by overcoming adversities and adversaries. In this profile, we'll see how the various dynamics of testing and proving make the Ultimate Strength a favorite of both Hollywood and Madison Avenue.

•   **The universal messages associated with this figure:** The Ultimate Strength represents the universal messages of strength, performance and endurance.

•   **Timeless dynamics in summary:** Few words capture the spirit of strength as aptly as George Mallory's answer to the question why he wanted to climb Mount Everest: "Because it's there."[2] This statement reveals the essence of the Ultimate Strength. When an obstacle is there, it must be overcome, since strength must be proven in its use.

Of course, there are no guarantees for those who try to pass great tests. Some fail. George Mallory is a tragic, real-life example of this point. His corpse was discovered on Everest some 75 years after his disappearance, his hands still clinging to the rocks.[3] Despite his brave words, Mallory didn't succeed in conquering Everest. There was some speculation that he might have actually made it to the top and then died on his return. However, one of his relatives put the issue in context when he said that it doesn't matter if he made it to the top, because what makes a successful climber is making it back to the bottom as well. The lesson is simple: the Ultimate Strength's conquest must be complete.

In the process of overcoming challenges, deeper aspects of this mythic figure's character are revealed. The Ultimate Strength must be capable of performing under pressure, and he often must struggle and suffer in order to prove that he has mettle and endurance. The 12 Labors of Hercules provide a classic example of this mythic figure proving his strength through suffering and trials.[4] Since ancient times, people have become habituated to seeing various figures of the Ultimate Strength put to severe tests. However, the suffering is not in vain, since the process of testing validates and sometimes revalidates the superior might of the Ultimate Strength, making these figures credible.

In some cases, the Ultimate Strength is mighty in a general sense. But, more often, expressions of the Ultimate Strength have their own, distinctive sources of power. Samson, for example, has his hair, Achilles has his armor, and even Popeye has his spinach. Therefore, specific objects often come to symbolize strength in conjunction with various figures of the Ultimate Strength.

Lastly, this mythic figure is sometimes forced to face another figure of the Ultimate Strength. The climax of *The Iliad* is a classic example of this clash of the titans. On the one side stood the greatest warrior of the Greeks, Achilles. On the other side was Hector, the great warrior of the Trojans. Their single battle determined the ultimate fate of Troy — no small trophy. In the end, Achilles slew Hector, signaling the downfall of Troy. Achilles then dragged Hector's body behind his chariot for several days straight.[5] The clash of figures of Ultimate Strength has captivated audiences ever since.

All of these dynamics and traits of the Ultimate Strength archetype, which have been communicated over millennia through various stories, are at work connecting subliminally with consumers in today's Image Economy.

The Mythic Figure in Advertising and Marketing

•   **Torture tests and performance messages:** The dynamic of the Ultimate Strength facing challenges figures prominently in the creation of modern mythology for brands. Contemporary advertising and marketing frequently highlight strength proven through testing to convince consumers of the quality or durability of a product. This happens in a variety of ways, most notably through product torture tests and performance messages.

In torture tests, a product is put to the test against the elements or perhaps head-to-head against the competition. The subconscious dynamics of the Ultimate Strength being tested are instantly familiar to consumers. However, where there's normally a person as the Ultimate Strength, a product is inserted instead. In this manner, modern mythology appropriates the recognition and impact of the timeless qualities of the archetype and transposes them onto products.

A well-remembered example of this comes from the 1960s' advertising campaign for Timex. Over the course of many years, Timex's "Takes a Licking and Keeps on Ticking" campaign showed its watches enduring the most unbelievable tests.[6] In one commercial, a Timex was strapped to the bottom of a powerboat, which viewers then saw skipping full-throttle across a lake. The end of the commercials always featured a shot of the product still working — clear proof that the product had withstood its Herculean test. The advertising left consumers astounded with the product's ability to endure such a torturous test and therefore convinced it could withstand the minor challenges of daily life.

Decades later, another watch campaign, from Tag Heuer, provides a more contemporary example of a similar approach. However, in this case, the torture test shows people wearing the watches in situations of extreme testing, jumping between buildings and balancing on a beam suspended precariously in the air. The message this approach imparts about the product is more than just *surviving* the test. In this case, consumers see product *performance* under extreme pressure. Just as the mythic figures of Ultimate Strength gain their credibility through performing when they're under the gun, products gain credibility by coming through when put to the test. Products such as car batteries or tires often rely on similar approaches to build consumer confidence in their reliability.

•   **Using obstacles to convince:** In modern mythology, there are often many layers of communication at work at one time. Both the Timex and the Tag Heuer advertising utilize symbols to help communicate the magnitude of their challenge. In order to help dramatize what a product must overcome, props that serve as obstacles are often featured in performance messaging.

Pinnacles and mountains, in particular, are potent symbols that occur repeatedly in association with the Ultimate Strength in advertising and marketing.[7] There are a couple of key reasons for this. First, on a physical level, mountains are a sign of both power and challenge: they are huge and dangerous and hold within them volcanic eruptions, rock falls and avalanches. So conquering a mountain is used as a metaphor in advertising that enables products to communicate the struggles and challenges that they must overcome. Second, ascending a mountain has age-old mythic value in the process of the Ultimate Strength validating and reinforcing his strength. A Biblical example of this is Moses climbing Mount Sinai to receive the Ten Commandments — an act that also gave him new strength in the form of the laws for mankind.

Therefore, advertisers frequently appropriate mountain symbolism to help dramatize the testing and proving that their products must undergo. This is a particularly popular approach in automobile advertising. Sticking a car on a mountaintop provides images that people instantly recognize on subliminal levels. There's no need to tell people the background. When they see a Jeep or Rover conquering a mountain, consumers can fill in much of the inherent, unwritten message about the brand personality and performance ability for themselves. No more needs to be said.

•   **Symbols of unique strength and brands:** The dynamic of mythic figures having unique sources of strength and attendant symbols is also important in modern mythology. These symbols work on two levels. First, specific objects help to outwardly signify strength. Wonder Woman, for example, has her headband, and Superman has his cape. For ages, emperors, kings and queens have utilized the power of specific objects, such as a crown, crown jewels, and a throne — which serves as a symbolic mountain — to be specific representations of their might.

We also see that the absence of this symbol of strength is a cause of temporary or fatal weakness. Popeye is always in trouble until he gets his spinach; Samson was easily subdued once his hair was shorn; and Achilles, the mightiest of all the Greek warriors, was eventually slain by an arrow shot into his heel — the one place his armor didn't cover. The fact that such figures of strength can be brought down by the absence of this symbol actually helps to reinforce the potency of the symbol.

Whatever the object symbolizing strength, other people want to possess it in order to appropriate the power. For example, once Achilles was slain, Odysseus and Ajax, two other heroes of the Trojan War, struggled over who would possess his armor. When an assembly of the Greeks awarded it to Odysseus, Ajax went mad. Achilles' armor had that much symbolic importance. Brand power was born.

There is a direct link between these symbols of strength and the role that power symbols play in the modern mythology of brands today. Take, for example, a Rolex watch. Beyond the obvious functional benefits it has as a watch, a Rolex has intrinsic brand value as a symbol of power. This is no accident. The Rolex brand has built its mythology as a symbol of power by associating itself directly with various people who embody the Ultimate Strength. Rolex has had a long-running ad campaign that highlights the various adventurers, explorers and sports victors — symbols of strength — who wear a Rolex. So while ancient mythic figures may have worn magical armbands, modern consumers aspire to wear a widely recognizable symbol of strength and status on their wrists.

This raises a general point that's worth noting here, which is the link between brand personality and the target user. The reality is that most of the people who choose to wear a Rolex are no closer to being the Ultimate Strength than Kermit the Frog is. The same is true of a brand like Marlboro, since most users definitely aren't cowboys. In fact, Marlboro often appeals to women.[8] So why do Rolex and Marlboro still connect with these consumers? Simply put, brands define a brand "personality" that they think will attract people. They are not trying to reflect who users actually are. If they wanted to do that, they would simply hold up a big mirror so that consumers could see themselves. Instead, they build a mythology around their product based upon what they think will tap into consumers' fantasies. They then link their product with those archetypes of aspiration. In the process, they make a connection with consumers. The result is that the actual user who puts on a Rolex might be old and dumpy, but he feels the surge of confidence of having a symbol of power on his wrist. He has bought into the brand mythology lock, stock and barrel.

There is also a corollary between the unique aspects of strength in the mythic figure and the advertising message of special ingredients. Just as the Ultimate Strength is powerful in a specific way, so too are products. Consumers look for credible pieces of evidence to support why they should believe in a product. So even simple, mundane products call upon special or specific ingredients that allow them to support superior performance claims. Dishwashing powders, for example, frequently have specially formulated crystals that are attributed with providing superior cleaning capability. And cookware is made from special types of glass that make it more durable and capable of withstanding the incredible heat of microwave ovens. The trait of the Ultimate Strength's having unique sources of strength plays a subconscious role in making these types of messages believable and effective with consumers.

The Mythic Figure in Entertainment and Popular Culture

• **The clash of the titans:** While the dynamics of testing and proving are effective at convincing consumers about products, they are also highly entertaining. In particular, the clash of titans — two figures of strength pitted against each other — has been an engrossing public spectacle since ancient times, when gladiators fought for their survival. Today, the interest in the modern gladiators is no less intense. Audiences love the seesaw battle of two extremes of strength pitted against each other, whether it's two boxers or two Sega game characters. Just as consumers have emotional connections to brands as symbols of power, fans are also emotionally connected with "their" warrior as they watch the spectacle of the two foes battling it out.

This basic fascination with the clash of titans exists in a variety of sports. Nothing in the boxing world, for example, generates as much genuine excitement as a world heavyweight bout. People want to see Lewis and even Tyson — the heavyweights, the true titans. In Japan, Sumo wrestling taps into this same mythic appeal of the clash of titans. Filled with symbolism and ritual, Sumo captures the same essence of confrontation and challenge. Professional wrestling might seem like a hokey fix to many people. But it, too, has many devotees, since some people love to watch the pantheon of wrestlers matched against each other in varying combinations. Can the Undertaker beat Dr. Death? Which of these titans will triumph?

Consumer fascination with the clash of titans extends well beyond sports. Videos such as *Mortal Kombat* and *Doom* capture the public's imagination by offering up an endless variety of titans who battle it out daily on LCD screens.[9] Kids simply hit a few buttons and a new clash begins. No wonder the video-game business is now a multi-billion-dollar industry. Programs such as *Survivor* also connect with viewers' innate fascination with people being pressed to the limit.[10] It's part of our human chemistry to find it fascinating to see which contestants can withstand great tests and which cannot.

An important sidebar is that this dynamic of clashing, which is so prevalent in entertainment, plays a part in brand-building as well. The best-known example of this is the global cola wars. The battle of Pepsi versus Coke has spread to virtually every corner of the Earth. Both brands have made it newsworthy. The truth, too, is that Coke and Pepsi have both gained as a result because increased awareness generally translates into increased soft-drink consumption for both of them. This serves as an example that competitors fighting it out for supremacy creates consumer fascination even in the brand-building world. Regardless of whether it's a David and Goliath match up, or a war of equals, the clash of brands can create news because of the underlying dynamic of the clash of titans. In this manner, commercial activity works its way into popular culture and is also highly entertaining.

• **The personality business — Muhammad Ali:** Entertainment is driven by personalities who personify the various archetypes at work in consumers' psyches. The most resonant personalities are often those who capture the essential spirit of these primary forms.

Muhammad Ali is a stellar example of a personality built on the foundation of the Ultimate Strength archetype. Ali possessed amazing skills as a boxer, but his keen sense of self-promotion and his colorful tongue were as well noted as his skills in the ring. It wasn't aimless self-promotion though. Muhammad Ali was a master mythology-maker who truly understood what makes images tick.

Ali started by breaking all of the rules. That made him hated by some at the time. But he knew that thrusting himself into the public eye by challenging norms was the way to build his image. So he said things you just weren't supposed to say. When Ali pronounced "I am the greatest"[11], he was seemingly challenging the Fates. Mythology conditions us to believe that braggarts are usually punished for too much zeal. This is something others are supposed to say about you: you don't say it yourself. But Ali did. He knew how outrageous it was to taunt his opponents by predicting, in rhyme, the exact round in which he would defeat them. But Ali not only got away with it, he was often right about his predictions! Consequently, his mythology continued to grow.

Beyond the bombast and the bravado that went along with his well-hyped clashes with other titans, there was something fundamentally mythical about Ali. There was real, hard-earned substance to his image. During his years in the ring, Ali suffered a broken jaw and won the heavyweight title three times, proving himself time and again — as all figures of Ultimate Strength must. His bruising fights with his greatest opponent, Joe Frazier, were truly epic. Ironically, Frazier helped build the image of Ali as the Ultimate Strength when he said he had hit Ali with blows that would have knocked a building over.[12] Ali had withstood Frazier's great challenges, just as he had beaten the unbeatable Sonny Liston and outsmarted the ferocious George Foreman. On many levels, "The Greatest" truly is one of the greatest sporting figures of all time, and a great mythic figure. Because of this, while other boxers have faded into obscurity, Ali still captivates the public, years after his retirement.

Mythic Highlights to Note

- **The roots of universal appeal:** This figure represents the warrior in all of us — the need to challenge, prove and endure.
- **The proving process:** History is an important component for creating the mythology of the Ultimate Strength. Effective mythology-builders highlight trials and challenges that they withstood in the past.
- **Adversities:** Adversities can often work in your favor in building mythology. Don't hide challenges — *highlight* them and how you overcame them. Admitting to overcoming problems actually builds credibility and character.

- **Specific sources of strength:** Identify and build on specific sources of strength. If you are creating a product, is there something specific that you can point to as evidence of power or performance?
- **Identify a challenger:** Great warriors need great foes to build their fame, since the battle of titans interests the public. This principle is true in the world of brands, too. So identify your competition clearly. Don't be afraid to utilize the power of PR to play up on the struggle.

"A light broke in upon my brain —

It was the carol of a bird;

It ceased, and then it came again,

The sweetest song ear ever heard."

Lord Byron[1]

Mythic Profile
The
Siren

8

An Introduction to the Siren

Throughout the ages, the Siren has had the consistent and defining trait of attraction.[2] This provides the Siren with a power to which even the Ultimate Strength frequently succumbs. It is no surprise, then, that sexual attraction is so often and effectively used in modern mythology. This profile will show how the Siren's powers of attraction have become the main motivating force behind a variety of commercial messages and entertainment.

•   **The universal messages associated with this figure:** The Siren represents the universal message of the power of attraction, linked with the possibility of destruction.

•   **Timeless dynamics in summary:** The power of the Siren has its roots in our basic instincts as human beings. Innate sexual drives and sexual attractions are some of the strongest motivations in our lives. Most adults can relate to the intoxicating experience of walking into the room and seeing Mr. or Ms. Right before them. Call it what you want — animal magnetism, animal attraction, or animal drive — the power of our animal instincts is hard to resist and almost impossible to ignore.

Although sex is tied to procreation, the mythic figure of the Siren is unrelated to the role of women as the bearers of offspring. That is reserved for the Mother of Goodness archetype, which will be covered later. Rather, the Siren revels in the power of her sexuality, which has hypnotic and immediate effect, as her tool of control and seduction. Because the Siren has the ability to seduce, domination is a key driver of this mythic figure.

Ultimately, attraction and seduction involves some degree of risk, which frequently leads to destruction. In classical mythology, the Sirens weren't harmless, pretty birds. Rather, their seductive call led people to their ruin. This attraction-seduction-destruction cycle has its origins in the original story of mankind — the story of the Garden of Eden. God sent Adam and Eve from the Garden because Eve led Adam to temptation. As a result, they both became suddenly aware of their nakedness and sexuality.[3] Eve, as the destroyer of the bliss of the Garden of Eden, is the original temptress-destroyer icon. The mythic link of sexuality and destruction was formed forever.

The Mythic Figure in Advertising and Marketing

These dynamics connect with contemporary consumers in the Image Economy. Sexual power, and the sense of risk that accompanies it, creates both consumer fascination and commercial persuasion.

•   **Sex sells:** It's difficult to pinpoint any logic to the human libido — we just know when ours is turned on. But marketers are both logical and, often, calculating in exploiting sex in the sales process. They know that attraction is not a delayed or intellectualized feeling — it works right away. So sex is an effective way to grab the consumer by the … well, you can figure it out. Simply put, sexual attraction works. It leads people to buy clothing they don't need, stand in movie lines to see stars and heartthrobs, and spend increasing amounts of money to look their best. Given the difficulty of getting consumers' attention, the immediacy of the Siren's appeal is a tantalizing option for communicators.

But this doesn't imply that you simply sprinkle some sex into your ad and it works. Not everyone gets it right. The old advertising ploy of sticking a sexy woman in a short skirt in the ad to attract users is the most brutish use of sex to create persuasion. Typically, marketers of "guy" products — beer, auto parts and the like — have used this route, and many still do. But some have discovered the hard way that simply showing flesh is not an infallible method for attracting consumers *and* creating an enduring belief around a product. In a lot of cases, consumers are interested in the tits and ass but not so much in the product. For sex to work effectively in commercial persuasion, it needs to effectively tap the appropriate psychological triggers that link the advertising to the user's self-image. It's one thing to notice a sexy woman in a print ad. It's quite another thing, however, for the ad to make the critical, subliminal link to *users* so that they think they will become more attractive because of the product.

When advertisers misunderstand or ignore this critical connection, the marketplace is likely to punish them with indifference. Archetypes do not provide guaranteed success for advertisers, even when they use a well-known Siren figure in their advertising. A case in point is a campaign of TV commercials created by Burger King using the sultry voice of Kathleen Turner. The commercials showed close-up shots of Burger King products, such as their quarter-pound burgers, accompanied by a tempting voiceover from Turner that contained a variety of sexual double-entendres related to the products. Turner might have sex appeal for many male consumers, but this type of approach failed to use sex to make the vital link between the product and the *user's* sex appeal. What consumer in his right mind is going to feel more attractive because he regularly tucks into a burger? Given the poor marketplace results, Burger King eventually pulled the commercials.[4]

The connection of archetypes and users is particulaly important when we think about how archetypes are tapped in order to appeal to women. The Siren can be used effectively to motivate either side of the attraction equation. Imagine, as an example, a print ad featuring a sexy woman, assuming that the ad is for a female product such as eyeliner. The ad might get male viewers' notice, but it is meant to convince the *female* viewers to buy the product. Although the female viewers don't necessarily share the male viewers' sexual attraction to the woman in the ad, it works because female consumers subconsciously wish to possess her power of attraction. The woman in the ad serves not as a sexual object but as an icon of envy and emulation.

Furthermore, this type of advertising is not intended to simply inspire envy. Marketers are in the business of generating actions that lead to sales, not jealousy. So marketers seek to bind people subliminally to their products by positioning them as enablers that give viewers greater attractiveness. In the case of the print ad with a sexy woman, female viewers see her and subconsciously believe that if they use the product they will be more attractive. There is a transference of power from the person in the print ad to the viewer, with the product serving as the link. This might seem pathetically simple, but modern mythology is full of these types of promises: use the facial soap that the beautiful model is using, and you'll have beautiful skin (and you'll be more attractive); buy these jeans that a sexy model is wearing, and you'll have an irresistible bottom (and you'll be more attractive); and wear this new lipstick, and you will have more luscious-looking lips (and you'll be more attractive) — all just like the Sirens in the ads. The examples go on and on. This commercialized version of the Siren's song is hard for people to ignore. After all, who is going to pass up an opportunity to be more attractive?

The use of the Siren archetype is particularly common for products that lack rational product features to hang the advertising on. Fashion, cosmetics and perfume all fall into this category. The advertising that's done for these types of products tends to be amongst the most mythic that you'll find, rich in the use of imagery and without the boring hard sell. The packaging and naming of a product can be equally important in creating attraction for the product. Just look on the shelves of any airport duty-free shop and you'll find plenty of examples of this at work in creating a modern mythology — *Allure* from Chanel, *Envy* from Gucci, and *Pleasures* from Estee Lauder. These marketers know that everything counts in building an effective modern mythology and aren't afraid to go for the short and curlies to achieve it. After all, the product itself — a scent — is meant to attract and serves little other purpose if it fails to do that.

• **Hair as a symbol of sexual attraction:** Like the Ultimate Strength, the Siren has attendant symbolism that ultimately links her to commercial activity. Hair acts as one of these key symbols. The reason is simple: the growth of body hair is one of the most overt ways in which the onset of puberty — the beginning of our adult sexuality and the biological changes that allow it — is manifested. Consequently, hair features frequently in both folklore and mythology, with a similarly strong symbolic presence in the modern mythology of brands and products.

Starting in childhood, we are conditioned to recognize symbols that are attached to different archetypes. Children's fairy tales are full of the use of hair as a key symbol of sexuality. The Grimms' fairy tale of Rapunzel is a classic example.[5] Rapunzel, a beautiful girl, is endowed with extremely long, blond hair. At the age of 12, the approximate age of puberty, the Old Witch locks her in a doorless tower (symbolic of the witch's desire to lock up her chastity).[6] To let the Old Witch in and out of the tower, Rapunzel must let her hair down. As the story goes, a young prince hears her singing and then goes to the tower and uses Rapunzel's hair to climb up and enter her room. The Old Witch becomes enraged when she learns that Rapunzel has used her hair — a symbol of her newly found power of attraction and sexuality — to let the young prince in. Effectively, the Old Witch is no longer in control of Rapunzel and cuts the young woman's hair in order to eliminate the source of Rapunzel's power. She then uses the hair — now a symbol of her desire to usurp the power of sexual attraction from Rapunzel — to lure the young prince to his destruction.

Symbols don't lose their effect or associations, even when they're used years later to connect in advertising and marketing. Thus, in the world of brands and marketing, hair maintains its symbolic significance. The link of hair and attraction is particularly obvious to the makers of shampoo, who essentially sell the notion that beautiful hair is a key to attraction. The next time you're in a supermarket, just spend a few minutes in the shampoo aisle and you'll realize how successful these modern mythologists are. It's quite amazing to consider the proportion of total shelf space that's dedicated to the vast array of products that help consumers simply look after their hair. Shampoo marketers do more than sell the notion of hair as a symbol of beauty. They rely on the underlying, transformative message that if you possess beautiful hair, you will possess the power of attraction. This point is not buried in the frequent scenes from shampoo advertising that show hair swishing and men's heads turning in admiration.

The earlier point about the Siren connecting with both genders is relevant here, too. Beautiful women in shampoo advertising are often used for women's shampoo products, since female consumers hope to emulate the Siren. But you probably wouldn't see all those late-night TV commercials for men's hair transplants if men didn't equally buy into the belief, on some level, that their hair serves as a symbol of their sexuality. Today, more and more personal-care products are directed to a long-overlooked male segment. This is emblematic of a broad point about modern mythology, which is that archetypes can easily cross the gender divide in modern commercial messaging.

The Mythic Figure in Entertainment and Popular Culture

•　　**Animal attraction in images:** The power of animal attraction — the root power of the Siren — is also evident in many subtle and not-so-subtle anthropomorphic connections in both marketing and entertainment. Language is the most common means through which things in our conscious surroundings are connected to and trigger the rich substrata of our unconscious. So slang terms such as "sex kitten", "chick" and "bird" through to some racier terms (which you can fill in on your own) are a prevalent way in which the Siren's subconscious animal-sexual link is expressed. In advertising and entertainment, women are often linked with visual cues and animal imagery, such as a tiger skin, the Cat Woman motif, and — in a literal animal-human mix — as the Mermaid, an age-old figure of allure. Perhaps one of the best-recognized examples in modern mythology of this human-animal-sex link is the Playboy bunny. The celebrated bunny logo came to define not just the men's magazine but an entire lifestyle built around more open sexuality in society.

The drawing power of sexuality and its link to our animal nature can also clearly be seen in the popularity of the catwalk. Fashion modeling is big business. And some of the most frequently covered personalities in today's tabloids are the sleek runway models who grace fashion magazines all around the world. The public's fascination with fashion and, to a lesser degree, beauty pageants is due to the connection back to the power of the Siren. Sexiness is a currency of power. As today's top models prance and prowl down the runway, this fact is evidently not lost on any of them. They are the center of attention. The Siren's power is in full force.

•　　**The call of the wild:** Mythic symbols are not necessarily all visual, of course. Music, for example, can be an equally effective trigger. In the animal world, the call of the wild — the mating call — plays a key role in initiating sexual attraction. On subconscious levels, this link also applies to humans. Music and singing touch our animal instincts deeply, since the rhythm of music and singing links us to the rhythmic nature of sex. You only need to spend a night out in a club or disco to be convinced of that fact.

There are numerous examples of music, particularly in the form of a serenade, serving as the subtle trigger of sexual attraction. Nowhere is this more prevalent than in the world of entertainment and personalities. Regardless of whether it's Marilyn Monroe singing a sultry rendition of "Happy Birthday" to JFK, the hip-swishing musical scenes of India's countless Hindi films, or the sizzling moves of Jennifer Lopez, the same timeless and universal mechanisms of enticement are at work. As a result, many of today's pop music divas — such as Madonna, Mariah Carey, Jennifer Lopez and Britney Spears — are as much an embodiment of sexual power as they are great singers. They are modern Sirens, and the subject of their music itself is often love and sexual attraction. But let's not forget that songs also frequently tell of the heartache and pain that love can wreak. The Siren's song is often the signal of the dangers that lie ahead. This leads us back to the critical issue of destruction and the Siren archetype.

If attraction leads to possible destruction, a logical question to ask is why the Siren still holds such appeal. Are men really such fools? Clearly, logic and reason frequently give way to our instincts and sexual desires. The Siren has the ability to cast a spell over men — to bewitch them with her charms. Sexual attraction pulls some people inexorably into folly and disaster, despite the fact that, on an intellectual level, they know of the dangers.

This ever-present potential for the Siren to seduce and destroy is one of the most tantalizing stories around. The young Kathleen Turner as the seductress-destroyer in the movie *Body Heat* is a steamy example.[7] So too is Sharon Stone in *Basic Instinct*, with the famous scene in which she sits smoking, legs spread for the entire world to see, while police question her about a murder.[8] Over the years, sex symbols such as Sophia Loren, Raquel Welch, Ann-Margret, Michelle Yeoh or Pamela Anderson have been the centerpieces of countless movies and TV stories. The Siren makes a compelling focal point in entertainment. Sex symbols are a key to box office drawing power and will therefore always be a central fixture of the Image Economy.

• **Symbols of attraction — sun, fire and gold:** A profile of the Siren would be incomplete if we didn't touch upon another set of tangential symbols associated with the Siren. Intertwined with sexual symbolism is the symbolism of mankind's eternal lust for riches. Sex and money often go hand in hand.

This is no surprise, since mythological symbols throughout the ages have banded the two together.

The sun, fire and gold are all used interchangeably in mythology to represent an irresistible attraction. The story of Daedalus and Icarus, his young son, serves as a fitting example.[9] Daedalus fashions wings so that he and Icarus can fly like a bird (note again the animal imagery) to escape captivity. But despite his father's warnings, Icarus can't resist the temptation and flies too close to the sun, which melts the glue of his wings and sends him plunging to his destruction. In many stories and myths, gold serves as the irresistible object that, like sexual attraction, leads people to folly and destruction. The myth of El Dorado, the city of gold, was powerful enough to inspire great efforts to find it. Fire, too, as a sort of junior version of the sun, has a hypnotic effect that is too great for people to resist, until they get burned. Therefore, in modern mythology, too, fire, gold and the sun often feature in advertising to create a symbolic link to temptation.

Two dominant symbols of the Siren — hair and gold — converge in the form of blond hair, which has held a mystique throughout the ages. This is found in various mythologies from the around the world. The German tale of the Lorelei is a particularly fascinating example.[10] As the famous poem about this German folktale goes, the Lorelei sits on a cliff above the Rhine, combing her beautiful, golden hair with a golden comb and singing a song. The captains of ships who see her or hear her song become so entranced they forget to watch where they are steering and meet their doom as they crash into the Rhine's steep, cliff-lined shores.

The symbolic power of blond hair still figures in the modern mythology of entertainment and brand-building. The next time you flip through an international women's magazine, take a moment to notice the high proportion of blondes that are used in ads. Or look at the video-rental section to see the frequent presence of blondes and movie titles featuring blondes, particularly as sexually attractive figures.[11] These are a testament to the enduring mystique around blond hair, which was perhaps best captured by Marilyn Monroe's famous quip, "I want to feel blonde all over".[12] Few understood the mythic power of blondes and of the Siren, or used it so well, as Marilyn Monroe.

Mythic Highlights to Note

- **The roots of universal appeal:** This figure represents the sexual being in all of us — the need to attract and be attracted to others.
- **Animal attraction and symbols:** Animal symbolism is common in modern mythology since animal attraction is part of the selling process.
- **The spell:** The Siren figure has a unique ability to hold and transfix her audience. The Siren's voice — singing — is often the way she casts this spell.
- **Role as destroyer:** Linked to the ability to cast a spell is the role of the Siren as a force of danger and destruction. Her sexual power is always linked to her potential to sway and even destroy those around her.
- **Hair, fire and gold as a key symbols:** Hair, the sun and gold figure as key subliminal symbols associated with the Siren.

"See, the conquering hero comes!

Sound the trumpet, beat the drums!"

Thomas Morell[1]

Mythic Profile
The
Hero

An Introduction to the Hero

The Hero is a classic figure who has played a prominent role throughout history. From David who slew Goliath in ancient times to figures such as Amelia Earhart, Joe DiMaggio, Neil Armstrong, Cathy Freeman or Ichiro Suzuki in more modern times, the Hero has always been a defining icon of the day. This mythic profile will show how the very fundamental appeal of the Hero puts him/her center stage as the protagonist in entertainment and in the sales process via endorsements and the "product-as-hero" approach.

• **The universal messages associated with this figure:** The Hero represents the universal messages of fortitude, courage and victory.

• **Timeless dynamics in summary:** Heroes aren't born as Heroes. While it's true that some enjoy noble birth or have the mark of greatness from the start, a Hero must go through a process of struggles and challenges before he can emerge triumphant.[2] The story of the Hero, therefore, is the story of a journey and transformation.

The road to heroism is usually a bumpy one. Heroes often face surprises, dangers and setbacks along the way. These challenges are a prerequisite to an ultimate triumph, since the Hero's struggles are analogous to the Ultimate Strength's process of testing. However, in the case of the Hero, his ability to overcome obstacles is based more on courage than on overpowering physical strength. So, irrespective of whether the Hero is of strong or weak body, he is able to overcome great challenges through bravery.

In some cases, a Hero is an underdog who faces a long, uphill climb. But he ultimately proves himself in moments of crisis or challenge. At critical points, real heroes take decisive steps. They marshal their resolve to proceed with purpose, even in the face of uncertainty. The Hero doesn't turn and run from the challenge. Therefore, the Hero is a symbol of steadfastness. He reminds us that common people can *become* extraordinary in their heroism.

The Hero must often make sacrifices along his journey. He commonly gives something of himself to others or helps others through his deeds. By making sacrifices, the Hero learns to shed what is not important to him. But this process equally brings into focus those things the Hero won't sacrifice — the core of his beliefs and his ideals. Often, when the Hero is pressed to the breaking point, it might seem easier for him to abandon these ideals to save his skin. But the Hero finds — or somehow creates — new reserves of strength that enable him to see the challenge through. This process of transcendence reveals the deeper essence of his heroic character. The Hero's journey is representative of an internal transformation that results from his challenges. The Hero not only succeeds in overcoming adversity; he also grows in the process. The heroic journey brings about his coming to awareness of his inner strength.[3]

The Hero cycle is never really over, because the Hero is frequently subjected to multiple trials. Heroes must maintain their heroic character by showing ongoing fortitude and conviction. Consequently, heroic figures become trusted for their ability to repeatedly overcome challenges. This is an important point that relates to the Hero's role in the Image Economy, as we'll see shortly.

Joseph Campbell explained in his seminal work *The Hero with a Thousand Faces* that the story of the Hero is ultimately the story of Everyman.[4] We can all relate to overcoming challenges in our lives and the process of inner transformation it brings about. The Hero figure is, therefore, the basis of stories that have broad appeal and universal connection, with the Hero serving as an aspirational icon for the masses. Through watching the Hero, we come to realize that the Hero lies within all of us. Like the Hero, we can all be winners.

The Mythic Figure in Advertising and Marketing

•   **The Hero as endorser:** Advertisers often seek to take advantage of the Hero's broad appeal in order to connect with a wide group of consumers. One of the most popular ways to do this is through an endorsement. The logic is simple: if heroes appeal to a broad group of people, and a product has a Hero associated with it through endorsement, then many people will find the product appealing. This is the basic equation behind star endorsements. When product companies pay Michael Jordan or Tiger Woods tens of millions of dollars in sponsorship deals, they are banking on this associative process to work and pay dividends.

Endorsements frequently do work because they tap into the mechanisms of Hero emulation. People often wish to be like their favorite Heroes in what they do, how they behave and what they wear. This emulation of idols is the reason kids — and even adults — wear athletic gear with their favorite sports Hero's name on it. But consumers often have a subconscious dream that goes beyond simply looking like a Hero; they want to *be* the Hero and be capable of doing the things their heroes do. When kids lace up their Nike shoes — the shoes that Michael Jordan uses — for a pick-up game, they often have the fantasy of floating and jamming just like Jordan. Sponsorships and endorsements use Hero figures to provide brands with a "rub-off" effect that motivates consumers, through this fantasy mechanism, to purchase products to be like their Heroes.

Emulation goes well beyond the equipment that sports Heroes use to achieve their greatness. It can extend to what they use in their daily lives, such as the food they choose to eat for breakfast. Wheaties is an American breakfast cereal that became an icon brand as a result of its long-running campaign as the "Breakfast of Champions". Over the years, dozens of sports stars have appeared on the cereal box, enticing consumers to eat the same thing their heroes eat. For many of the athletes, appearing on the box is not simply a product endorsement — it's a symbol that they have "made it" as champions. Similar to being invited to appear on Larry King, having your picture on a cereal box is a sign of success for America's athletes. On the consumer side of the equation, the cereal provides people with a way to feel on some deeper level that they are cut from the same cloth as their Hero.

It's also important to note that, similar to the Wise Old Man — a figure we'll see shortly — the Hero lends credibility to products through his endorsement. Since Heroes are reliable figures, their recommendations are often considered reliable too — one of the many bonds of trust connected with mythic figures. Because they are trusted, Hero endorsers can be effective at building consumer trust in a wide range of products, including those with which the Hero has no logical association. Who, for example, would normally link Joe DiMaggio and coffee? Nothing in the Yankee Clipper's career would have suggested an expertise in this area. Yet, since consumers viewed DiMaggio as a Hero figure, he was a credible and effective endorser for Mr. Coffee for many years.[5]

• **Product-as-hero:** The process of building bonds of trust extends to another popular advertising approach, which is known as "product-as-hero". In this approach, the product itself is the center of the action, just like a Hero. But the product-as-hero entails more than just putting a product in the center of a print ad. The product must come through at the crucial moment to help solve a consumer's problem or challenge. This is the ultimate proof point of a product's efficacy, so the approach is frequently used to highlight a product's reliability.

The example cited earlier of washing powder that transforms a situation by cleaning even the dirtiest laundry is a typical example of the product-as-hero. The washing powder overcomes the seemingly insurmountable filth to make the user feel like a winner. It solves a problem that the consumer couldn't solve on his/her own. When a product proves itself in this manner, it can build trust effectively, even without a star endorser attached to it.

The product-as-hero approach is used more frequently than consumers recognize. While it's suited to hard-sell advertising, it can even be present in TV commercials that consumers find humorous or light-hearted. Soft-drink advertising frequently positions the product as a Hero. It's common to see situations in which a scorching sun beats down on sweaty, thirsty people. Invariably, the soft drink comes to their rescue to slake their thirst. Although people typically don't think of soft drinks in terms of *efficacy* in the same way they'd associate that word with washing powder, this type of advertising approach nonetheless reminds consumers that the product will work at quenching their thirst. The soft drink is transformed from a simple treat into a reliable solution to their challenge.

The Mythic Figure in Entertainment, Sports and Popular Culture

As we've just seen, the figure of the Hero can be a potent commercial force in the marketing process. But the Hero archetype is a powerful motivator in other parts of the Image Economy as well. In particular, entertainment and sports provide the public with icons of heroism that fuel people's basic dreams. Consequently, countless numbers of boys and girls spend hours dreaming of growing up to be their favorite sports stars or TV heroes.

• **Sports — the breeding ground of modern Heroes:** If you think through the list of popular personalities that people would call Heroes, many emerge from the world of sports. Wayne Gretzky, Stefi Graf, Hermann Maier, Jackie Joyner-Kersee, Pete Sampras, Pele, Derek Jeter and Tiger Woods come easily to mind as heroic idols. One reason for this is that sport is big business today. Between promotional deals and TV rights, billions of dollars a year are spent on promoting the popularity of various sports. With professional leagues often cramming many games into a regular season, the frequency of coverage results in top-of-mind awareness for many sports stars.

But frequency of exposure alone doesn't lead to heroism, just as a sportsman's playing time on the field isn't the most important measure of his contribution to the team. On a basic level, sports are popular because they are a natural breeding ground for heroism. Sports provide a very public stage on which players and teams struggle to triumph over others. They also provide millions of viewers, whose day-to-day lives are divorced from the drama of matches under the stadium lights, with a chance to live out their dreams vicariously through heroes on the pitch. Sports are full of drama since games or matches sometimes come down to crucial moments, where a miraculous shot or save turns the tide or even wins the match team. Potentially any player on the field could become a Hero of the match if he or she rises to the challenge at the right moment. Consequently, sports hold a particular fascination and entertainment value.

International sporting events such as the Olympics or the World Cup provide the greatest stage of all for these sports Heroes. These events generate natural appeal, since consumers automatically understand that the stakes of the competition are high. People tune in around the world, irrespective of the time, to see if their Heroes have the courage to come through when it really counts. Regardless of who wins, the events themselves create an aura of heroism — a further reason why companies are willing to pay millions to be involved as sponsors of these events.

• **The action Hero:** While some are Heroes on the athletic field, others are heroic figures on the battlefield. The Heroes of TV, movies, books and comics are equally potent entertainment icons. John Wayne, for example, became a legend for his portrayal as a gutsy fighter in war movies and westerns such as *The Alamo*, *True Grit*, and *The Sands of Iwo Jima*.[6] He played characters that had a sense of purpose and conviction, that could be relied on to get the job done, even if it meant huge personal risk or sacrifice. Like all Heroes, Wayne's characters didn't flinch when the moment of greatest challenge was upon them. Both off stage and on, The Duke became an American classic — an icon and role model that defined heroism for an entire generation.

Today, a new crop of stars has taken on the mantle of Heroes of the silver screen. Actors such as Harrison Ford, Mel Gibson, Jackie Chan and Tom Cruise provide bankable box-office appeal playing heroic roles. They frequently star as characters that must overcome immense challenges, facing down danger in the process. Like John Wayne in the past, they provide role models for the current generation of moviegoers because they exhibit the Hero's archetypal values. And true to heroic form, they remind us all of the difficult road the Hero travels before he is able to transcend the moment and triumph.

Tom Cruise, as the ace pilot Maverick in *Top Gun*, is one example of the lonely road of the Hero.[7] Despite his talent, Maverick must battle self-doubt and lingering memories of losing his co-pilot in an accident. But when the time of real need calls him to battle, he finds the inner reserves of strength that enable him to save the day. Just like Luke Skywalker as a Jedi in *Star Wars*[8], Maverick ultimately realizes he is the one who must make it on his own — to fly solo against self-doubt. He discovers that the process of becoming a Hero is really a process of self-discovery that occurs in the heart.

From an early age, children learn these key dynamics of heroism, and the Image Economy is right there playing a prominent role in shaping and fueling young children's dreams. Comic-book action heroes, GI Joes and childhood characters such as the Power Puff Girls provide potent icons for young minds. The story of Woody and Buzz Lightyear in *Toy Story* is a fitting example of heroic icons in entertainment.[9] Despite the fact that they're just toys, both Woody and Buzz display the classic traits of the Hero. In the original *Toy Story*, Woody overcomes his initial jealousy of Buzz to become his rescuer. At the end of the movie, when Woody can slip away from Sid — the wretched kid who destroys toys — he turns back for Buzz. Woody has found both the inner light of courage and the willingness to sacrifice. When children delight at this story, they are reacting to more than the wonderful Pixar animation; they are delighting in the subconscious scripts of the Hero archetype that are already at work in their young heads.

• **Underdogs and unlikely Heroes:** Lest we think that the Hero always appears in a uniform or has Buzz Lightyear's rock-solid chin, we must not forget the unlikely or uncommon Hero. As Woody Allen films have repeatedly reminded us, the wheezy, scrawny guy with a drippy nose can be the protagonist and Hero, like anyone else. Unassuming figures might emerge as the centerpiece of courage. And when they do, their tale symbolizes that Joe Everyman can be heroic if he takes action at a decisive moment — plunging into an icy river to save someone from drowning or racing up a burning skyscraper without flinching. In less dramatic fashion as well, everyday heroes stick to their beliefs and make sacrifices for others. Their stories connect the Hero figure to the common struggles we all face in life.

Erin Brockovich, with Julia Roberts starring in the title role, is a well-known entertainment example of an unlikely Heroine.[10] Brockovich is a single, unemployed mother with a turbulent home life. She is not the figure viewers would initially expect to succeed, let alone champion a cause. Yet fate and her sense of justice catapult her into the role of the Heroine ready to fight against Pacific Gas and Electric. Her resolve and perseverance result in the largest class-action suit in history. And on a personal level, the process changes Brockovich, transforming her into a new woman.

Erin Brockovich highlights the underdog dimension of some Heroes. The fact that she is an unlikely Heroine accentuates the enormity of the challenge she faces. Audiences love to see stories of the Hero from the wrong side of the track or one who has hit upon hard times. These types of Heroes have to crawl even farther to reach success, giving audiences a message of hope in the process. This is the key to the appeal of screen figures such as Rocky Balboa in *Rocky*[11] or Russell Crowe's character in *Gladiator*.[12] By persevering and succeeding, the underdog gives viewers a sense that anything is possible. Russell Crowe's Academy Awards acceptance speech for his role in the film further built upon the heroic aura of the film. Mixing real life and art, Crowe said that the award proves that even someone from the "downside of advantage" can make it big.[13] This is a message that fuels many dreams — and brings people into theaters.

A final example from the world of entertainment provides a fitting summary of the Hero. *Forrest Gump* incorporates many of the resonant Hero dynamics we've just seen.[14] Blessed with only a low-watt bulb, Forrest has a gift for being in the right place at the right time. He is not only an unlikely Hero; he is an accidental Hero as well. How could a guy like Forrest ever make it? Yet he goes from being a brace-wearing youngster to star high school athlete, decorated war veteran and international sportsman. Forrest overcomes enormous challenges to span the heroic spectrum in the process, which is one of the reasons for the film's great popularity. But Forrest, as a rather simple-minded guy, provides a poignant reminder of yet another aspect of the Hero. Like all great heroes, he doesn't gloat. A true Hero is glorious in victory, yet he is also humble and thankful because he understands the difficulty of overcoming adversity and challenges. And although a Hero often receives adulation, that is not his goal. Instead, the Hero is focused on the path of decency. The Hero is positive proof that good guys can win.

• **A dying breed?:** Some people question whether the notion of real-life Heroes is dead. In today's free-for-all press environment, many public figures have become like our troubled neighbors, dirty laundry and all, rather than simple representations of values and attitudes that people can admire and emulate. To some, the knight in shining armor is an anachronism. "Sure that actor looks good on screen, but he beats his wife in real life," they say. This type of cynicism is one of the unfortunate by-products of the Image Economy.

Some people want to know gory details about stars' private lives because they're a reminder that even the rich and famous have concerns and problems, too. Yet deep down, the public really doesn't want to demystify its Heroes. People are surrounded daily by mere mortals and need icons whom they can hold in high esteem. They want Heroes that truly embody the courage that lies within everyone — Heroes that inspire us to take on challenges and to go through the journey of life. To lose faith completely in heroic accomplishments would mean to lose faith in the potential to triumph over our own challenges.

And if one looks at "real life", there are indeed genuine Heroes out there, on both the international and local stage. Figures such as Nelson Mandela and Burma's Aung San Suu Kyi are true Heroes. Despite being under house arrest for several years, Suu Kyi — like all true Heroes — has remained unwavering in her commitment. Nelson Mandela also suffered years of imprisonment without relinquishing his beliefs or losing his resolve to pursue racial equality. And as the September 11th attacks on the World Trade Center reminded us, Heroes exist amongst us each day. We just don't know who they are until the critical moment of sacrifice comes. Then, real Heroes show what they're made of.

Mythic Highlights to Note

- **The roots of universal appeal:** This figure represents the champion in all of us — the need to strive and succeed.
- **Transformational journey:** The story of the Hero is that of a transformational journey. The Hero must become the Hero through overcoming obstacles.
- **A representative of "Everyman":** The Hero is a representative of everyone's struggle to overcome adversity and challenges.
- **An icon of emulation:** Given his universal appeal, the Hero is often the icon of emulation.

"When the people of the world all know beauty as beauty,

There arises the recognition of ugliness.

When they all know the good as good,

There arises the recognition of evil."

Lao-tzu[1]

Mythic Profile
The
Anti-
Hero

10

An Introduction to the Anti-Hero

The Anti-Hero is a symbol of mankind's dark side. While the Hero represents hope and belief, the Anti-Hero symbolizes faithlessness and the lack of repentance. Figures such as Darth Maul[2], Hannibal Lecter[3] and Lucifer are Anti-Heroes that remind us of the human potential for destruction and evil. This dark side, though, has always had a certain appeal, and probably always will. Sometimes it's fun to be the bad boy — the cowboy in black. Indeed, recognizing that there is a dark side working in all of us is key to understanding this mythic figure. As we'll see in this mythic profile, the Anti-Hero's appeal translates into ringing cash registers and packed seats. In the Image Economy, the dark side too can be an effective commercial motivator that sells, sells, sells.

•   **The universal messages associated with this figure:** The Anti-Hero represents the universal message of destruction and the attraction of evil.

•   **Timeless dynamics in summary:** The yin and yang of human nature reflect the inextricable linkage between good and evil and between creation and destruction. In fact, evil is a necessary opposite to good, with each relying on the other to give it definition. Therefore, the dark side is an undeniable part of our human chemistry. We all have the capacity — and sometimes the desire — to do harm. And we all must battle the urge to be cruel and unkind at times. The function of the Anti-Hero archetype is to give voice to these negative and destructive emotions that work deep inside all of us. So while most people attempt to resist the negative pull of this archetype, the Anti-Hero nevertheless makes strong and universal sub-conscious connections. The story of Jekyll and Hyde provides a classic study in this duality of human nature and mankind's eternal struggle to come to grips with its less-savory side.[4]

If we accept that evil is the counterbalance to good, then it's logical that the Anti-Hero should so frequently be locked in battle with good. In mythical stories throughout the ages, the Anti-Hero is pitted against the Hero or Ultimate Strength. Consistently, the Anti-Hero is of equal or even seemingly superior strength to the Hero, since an opposite force must be strong in order to fulfill its role as a counterweight. In fact, evil is frequently in a position of temporary control and seems likely to emerge as the victor.

But, in most stories and mythologies, evil loses out in the end. That's because, in the heat of the struggle, the fatal flaw of the Anti-Hero is exposed: the lack of faith and repentance. Thus, while the Hero is saved by his beliefs, the Anti-Hero is not saved from the destruction he wreaks. Yet the Anti-Hero, true to form, remains defiant and unrepentant, waiting to fight another day. There are no apologies from the forces of evil and no regrets from the Anti-Hero about his actions.

The fundamental flaw of the Anti-Hero translates further into the lack of mercy or empathy for others. The Anti-Hero is not compassionate and cannot be trusted. In fact, he often has a wanton disregard of others. At best, he is selfish, uncaring and unsympathetic. And, in the most extreme cases, the Anti-Hero is demented, devious and deadly.

Yet despite the litany of bad character traits, the Anti-Hero has his appeal. The forces of destruction can indeed be enticing and awesome. Virtually all religions around the world recognize this seductive quality of evil. Silver-tongued devils have managed to attract more than one victim. The Anti-Hero works like the Siren, creating a powerful and hypnotic appeal that even breeds its own form of sexual attraction, making it so easy to give in to temptation.

The Mythic Figure in Entertainment and Popular Culture

The magnetic appeal of our dark sides is a mainstay of popular entertainment, since entertainment provides one of the least harmful ways to give our bad sides an airing. The Anti-Hero in entertainment can range from mischievous bad boys on TV and in music to true icons of darkness and evil.

•   **Bad boys and "trash-talk" as great entertainers:** The Anti-Hero is the ultimate contrarian — the one who chooses to go against the grain. With more and more people vying for star status, a common entertainment ploy today is to use this contrarian stance of the archetype to shock the public in order to break through to them. This has led to the growth of radio shock-jocks and "trash-talk" from people such as Howard Stern and Jerry Springer.[5] These two American entertainment personalities exemplify how to harness the innate appeal of the Anti-Hero to build commercial potency by breaking taboos. Both have built their fame by challenging expected and accepted norms of behavior.

Like Oprah Winfrey, Howard Stern has spun his image into a one-person multimedia empire. But rather than listening attentively to the guest on the sofa, Stern has done it through crank calls and talking a lot about his private parts.[6] The popularity of smash-mouth TV is also built on the foundation of Anti-Hero behavior. It is proof that audiences today connect with this archetype. Consumers have varying levels of attraction to the different archetypes, so there are plenty of people to whom this type of entertainment doesn't appeal. But there are some people who wouldn't dream of starting their morning any other way than listening to some trash-talk on the radio. Again, it is tempting to make value judgments about this fact. Yet this is simply the nature of the Image Economy. The important thing for readers is to understand *how* and *why* different archetypes connect with some consumers.

The Anti-Hero archetype's traits of defiance and the lack of repentance are also effective commercial motivators, especially for teen audiences, who often relish a chance to give the finger to society and everyone in it. This is particularly true in the music industry, where Anti-Heroes ironically are the idols and "Heroes". Heavy-metal icons of doom and death, such as Marilyn Manson, follow in a long tradition of music figures who represent the defiance of this mythic figure. Music Anti-Heroes are popular because they enable listeners to give vicarious expression to their dark side.

Gangsta rappers, such as Dr. Dre, Eminem, Tupac Shakur and Snoop Doggy Dogg have taken the Anti-Hero to new lows in the music business, much to the glee of their fans. With little numbers like "Hit 'em Up" and "I Just Don't Give a Fuck", rap stars serve as Anti-Hero demigods.[7] They've turned "livin' in the 'hood" into something fashionable for a certain segment of consumers. And the mixture of violence and vulgarity is a potent brew for selling records — just ask the good folks at Death Row Records. Given the growing image web and commercial spin that is so prevalent in the Image Economy, consumers can also play the part with their own Eminem logo visor, dog tags or caricature figurines available for purchase on his website.

Even sports exploit the commercial appeal of this archetype. The Oakland Raiders, for example, have long worn black and cultivated their image as the bad boys of the NFL. "Iron" Mike Tyson, though, stands out in the sports world as a defining personality built on the Anti-Hero archetype. Indeed, his "bad-seed" image stems from a string of real-life incidents, some resulting in prison time, that have marred his life and boxing career.[8] However, promoters have also carefully cultivated Tyson's image as the Anti-Hero, because it generates crowds. Although Tyson is possibly beyond his best years in boxing, as a figure of menace and danger, he continues as a magnet for exposure. The fighter, like the tattoo of Che Guevara on his abdomen, is a potent commercial symbol of rebelliousness. And if he continues to bite off bits of other people's ears, his reputation as a bad seed is likely to continue.

• **The opposite of good:** The core dynamic of the Anti-Hero as the opposite of good is also a potent commercial motivator. What all movie executives, authors and scriptwriters know is that the Anti-Hero, in the form of a villain or devil, is a key ingredient in stories. The Anti-Hero is the quintessential enemy, which places him in a central role in stories. He is also the object of very strong feelings. Sometimes the appeal of rooting *against* the bad guy is as strong as rooting *for* the good guy.

Since good and evil are linked as opposites, we often see the fate of characters of good and evil intertwined. Thus in movies, books and plays, story plots frequently involve the good guy trying to locate the bad guy or the bad one trying to hunt down and kill the good one. Inevitably, this leads to a showdown of the two. And when it does, we see that good and evil — the Hero and Anti-Hero — are not total strangers to each other. Their confrontation is eternal. Thus the words "So, we meet again" are a common refrain.

Yet while the Anti-Hero is the opposite of the Hero, it doesn't mean that figures of evil can't share some of the same skills or powers as the good guy. Often, one of the key characteristics of the Anti-Hero is the attribute of intelligence. The evil genius is a particularly popular figure. We've seen him as the brilliant, psychopathic cannibal Hannibal Lecter. He is also a recurring figure in most of the vintage James Bond films. Evil geniuses are fascinating to audiences for two reasons. First, they usually have some sort of major destructive power. Evil geniuses in movies always seem to be trying to blow up the world. This taps into the audience's morbid fascinations with destruction and death. Second, the mix of evil and genius poses a moral dilemma of sorts for the audience. How can people of such great intellectual gifts still choose the path of evil rather than good? It is hard to reconcile, thereby making the evil genius intriguing.

Lastly, the duality of our nature comes through frequently in entertainment to create audience interest. The character of Harry Angel from the movie *Angel Heart* is a particularly fitting example.[9] Angel is put on the case to find a man who is the key to a string of murders, only to discover in the end that unknowingly, he has been chasing himself. He has forgotten the pact he made with the devil when he sold his heart. The inclusion of the Anti-Hero in entertainment, in a variety of forms, ultimately reminds us of the potential for evil that lies within us all.

The Mythic Figure in Advertising and Marketing

• **The "bad seed" and brands:** This mythic figure is also a potent force that connects for the building of brands. As we've observed, mythology — ancient and modern — gives conscious expression to innate, subconscious portions of our minds. So the vicarious pleasure of emulation that we saw in relation to the Hero in brand-building is also at work with the other archetypes, including the Anti-Hero. Thankfully for society, though, most people give expression to this part of themselves through buying a leather jacket or a motorcycle, rather than robbing banks or knifing people in the park.

For some, the Anti-Hero archetype becomes a key lifestyle driver and part of their self-definition. Harley-Davidson has often been cited as a brand that creates very strong brand affinity amongst its users. One of the reasons for this is that Harley has tapped into a strong consumer desire to express an alternative side to their personality. For some users, their Hog gives them a chance to play the part of the renegade — to be a bad dude. There is something both liberating and enjoyable for users when they do. For them, the brand personality gives them a vicarious way to feel bad to the bone — even if, as with the Rolex, the real user doesn't exhibit the traits of the archetype.

Given that the dark side also has sex appeal, the Anti-Hero archetype is a frequent fixture in the fashion business. Again, the transference of power from the object in advertising to the viewer is critical. When most people look at fashion advertising in which the clothes on the models make the model look like the bad seed, their reaction is not simply that they want to look that way too. Rather, the underlying archetype communicates that these models have the power and appeal of the Anti-Hero. Thus, the clothes are linked to a greater motivator — the power and sexual attraction of the Anti-Hero — that reflects how the consumer wants to be. The clothes become part of a bigger, more powerful fantasy that drives consumers' consumption. While most brands use positive icons and various techniques of positive reinforcement, a contrarian route can also be an effective strategy for winning in the Image Economy.

Mythic Highlights to Note

- **The roots of universal appeal:** This figure represents the evil in all of us — the need to deal with our dark side.
- **The ultimate contrarian:** The contrarian nature of this mythic figure is one of the keys to its commercial potency.
- **The evil genius:** Figures of evil are often known for their cunning. The fact that they choose the side of evil doesn't make them stupid. In fact, portraying brilliance in this evil figure makes him seem even more sinister.

•   **Unrepentant and defiant:** This mythic figure is characterized by being unrepentant and defiant. It's not enough to do evil — the Anti-Hero must proudly choose to do so.

•   **A figure of attraction:** This figure represents another facet of attraction that comes from the depths of our psyches.

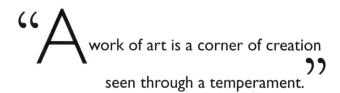

"A work of art is a corner of creation seen through a temperament."

Émile Zola[1]

Mythic Profile
The
Creator

An Introduction to the Creator

In modern mythology, the Creator is expressed in many forms, ranging from the moody artist to the wacky inventor. Figures as diverse as Karl Lagerfeld, Steven Spielberg and Yoko Ono all draw their source power from the archetype that underlies this mythic figure. These Creators are often held in high regard, since they produce things of wonder and fascination. In this profile, we'll see how the Creator archetype is behind the modern mythology of new products and the adulation that people have for many contemporary entertainment personalities.

*   **The universal messages associated with this figure:** The Creator represents the universal message of creative inspiration and the potency of the imagination.

*   **Timeless dynamics in summary:** The Creator is an icon of the potency of invention and creativity. Whenever this mythic figure is involved, viewers instinctively understand the possibility for new things and ideas to burst forth. And because the imagination has no boundaries, there are virtually no limits to the opportunities associated with this mythic figure.

Since the activities of the Creator are quite diverse, particularly in today's commercial environment, the Creator can be manifested in many forms. This mythic figure has been expressed throughout the ages as the manic, fevered artist — Michelango chiseling away at his Carrara marble or, in more contemporary form, as Jackson Pollack splattering paint on canvasses. But the Creator can equally take the form of the inventor of new products or the computer genius who devises new operating systems. Regardless of how different these manifestations of the Creator might appear on the surface, they all tie back to a consistent set of dynamics of this archetype, with creativity and the imagination serving as the epicenter.

Inspiration is another key element that binds all types of Creators. Irrespective of the specific nature of their creative activities, Creators possess a connection to forces that give them creative energy and propel them forward. This generally comes in the form of an idea, which is a seed of virtually all artistic and inventive endeavors. Mankind has often wondered at its own ability to generate ideas — a defining trait that separates us from the animal kingdom. For this reason, people have long attributed the spark of creative inspiration to the divine. The Creator's ability to fashion, build, mold and invent symbolically connects him back to the God-like act of creation — bringing forth something new from the ether. All forms of human creativity, therefore, serve as an emulation of the divine force that has created us. This does not imply, of course, that artists are gods (though some might think they are). Nor is every creative output considered worthy of being called divine. However, people who are creative are often considered gifted, as if specially blessed. Consequently, talented artists, musicians and writers are accorded a particular type of respect for their connection to the invisible font of inspiration.

While Creators are often respected and even revered for having this gift, the gift actually comes with a price tag. Frequently, the Creator is a volatile figure. Since art and invention serve as expressions — and extensions — of a Creator, he is vulnerable and racked by a certain degree of doubt. After all, there's the real possibility of rejection, with the world failing to understand or appreciate his creation. Consequently, the Creator is a mythic figure who is both powerful and vulnerable at the same time.

This reflects the creative process itself, which can be random and disjointed. Creative inspiration does not come to people in consistent, predictable patterns like an assembly line stamping out widgets. Rather, the creative process has its ups and downs, with long stretches of barren times as well as sporadic bursts of ideas. These barren times can be long and painful for the Creator. Often, too, Creators are not fully satisfied with the things that they create. Their nature is to make the work of perfection — the perfectly written book, the perfect painting or the perfect song — their goal. Consequently, they are forever chasing the unattainable, and feel anxiety about their shortcomings.

The Mythic Figure in Advertising and Marketing

These symbolic dynamics of the Creator might appear ethereal and of little commercial use. However, when we look at modern mythology, there are important links between the inherent mythic power of creation and the underlying messages found in marketing and entertainment. We will consider both, with a look first at how the traits of this mythic figure are involved in generating powerful beliefs in support of new products.

•   **The potency of new products:** As we observed in an earlier chapter, tens of thousands of new products are launched each year. Successfully establishing a product can be a daunting task for some companies. After all, new products are unknown, unproven and have yet to establish emotional bonds with consumers. So in this launch phase, the power of archetypes can be vital in establishing credibility with consumers. The right selection of symbolism and subliminal ties is vital to giving them a fighting chance for survival.

If we look carefully at commercial messages for new products, it's apparent that language plays a central role in both initiating and supporting a set of beliefs that are established around the "newness" of products. The key message is usually that *new* equals *better*. This would seem to follow basic logic, because why would companies bother to create new products that are inferior to existing ones? Imagine how absurd that message would be: "Try our new and vastly deficient product!" But just because products are new doesn't necessarily mean they are better. New products sometimes result from companies simply attempting to improve their flagging performance with new items in the hope of bolstering sales.

The language of new products is intended to create confidence and positive associations with newness. Companies achieve this by surrounding new products with words that will build an underlying promise of improvement. Advertising frequently touts that products are "all new", "never seen before", "the next generation" or are the result of "a revolutionary breakthrough in technology" — all of which are intended to build a sense that newness is a positive benefit. Substantiating promises are made in the form of claims that the new products involve new formulas, new materials and new production processes, resulting in superior features. Products also make the simple, direct link through the commonly used advertising phrase "new and improved". Finally, "new" in modern mythology infuses products with energy and a sense of new opportunities associated with the Creator. They promise to fix problems and provide pleasures for consumers like no other product before. The end goal is simple: to tie new products to a promise of creating a better life for consumers.

This messaging tactic has worked on consumers for decades. Most market economies, in fact, basically rely on the potency of this message. Otherwise, consumers wouldn't feel induced to trade in old cars for new models, ditch their old razors or try new types of electronic gadgets. The deep-seated belief in modern mythology that "new equals better" generates economic turnover. It works since people believe, on some subliminal level, in the power of creation and the wider halo of inspiration.

•   **The message of originality:** Of course, products don't stay new forever. And companies are forced by law in many countries to abandon the term *new* after a set period of time. But the mythic power of the Creator can work on an ongoing basis, even once the newness is over, through the message of "originality". Many marketing experts talk about the importance of brands being category leaders and benefiting from building a dominant position that comes with being the first brand in a category. In some cases, brands then become the generic term that's used to represent the category, such as saying "Kleenex" to refer to facial tissues. What most of these experts fail to note, however, is that being the first in a category makes a deep mythic connection with consumers. Fundamentally, it enables brands to take the high ground of being the Creator, with all the attendant subliminal benefits.

Coca-Cola is a prime example of how resonant this type of message can be. Coke has repeatedly used its position as "The Real Thing" in its protracted cola war against Pepsi. It understands that being the original means more than just being first — it confers authenticity and superiority on the product. Creators are frequently perceived to be in a unique position to understand the deeper genetic code of the business, since they gave it life. Furthermore, brands such as Coke also leverage the aspirational aspects of this message to appeal to users who want to be associated with originals.

This is yet another example of the transference of power from products to users — a key strategy for creating consumer relevance and persuasion. This doesn't imply that users will become more inventive as a result of using an original product. However, it often does enhance the product's badge appeal, since consumers feel that by using original products, they show their appreciation for authentic things. This provides a positive reflection on the consumer. Marketers avidly promote this belief, too, because if consumers didn't buy into this belief, there would be very little separating their brands from generics and cheap knock-offs. Brands would then fail to command their premiums. So we see that both for new products and for long-established products that have invented categories, the mythology of the Creator translates into the commercial messages of superiority and authenticity — necessary belief systems in the Image Economy.

• **The message of invention:** Many of the items we use daily, such as computers, hand-phones and cars are the result of a manufacturing process. Since they are not like a painting or a song, where creativity is so evident in their creation, these types of products might seem quite removed from the notion of the spark of creativity. But, in fact, they too can benefit from the underlying mythic dynamics of the Creator by associating "inspiration" with "invention".

Connecting these two achieves a couple of important things for products. First, on a subliminal level, it humanizes even mechanical products, since invention is more than a soulless by-product of a computer program or manufacturing process. This leads to the second benefit, which is the positive rub-off of "superiority" that comes with the divine inspiration of creativity. Together, they impart a message to viewers that the product isn't the result of a sterile process; there was something special — inspiration — involved in its inception.

Hewlett-Packard's "Invent" campaign is an excellent example of this approach. The campaign, which features different people at the company's labs, highlights the way the new technology products they are inventing will help people. As the copy in one of its print ads reads, "Your eyes never take a bad picture. This simple fact is the inspiration behind the next generation digital cameras Ross is inventing." Again, the principles of transference of attributes from the product to the users, as well as the transformation of the user, play a central role in the communication. Products that highlight invention frequently give consumers the subliminal hope that they will fuel their own creative and inspired endeavors when they use the product.

The Mythic Figure in Entertainment and Popular Culture

•   **The potency of Creator personalities:** There is a romanticized image of the artist as a loner, toiling in obscurity and semi-poverty for the purity of art. The reality, though, is that even Creators in the past, such as Leonardo da Vinci and Mozart, were frequently famous or rich during their own lifetime. Some even enjoyed the equivalent of mega-stardom in their day. So it would be incorrect to assume that the public's fascination with Creators is purely a contemporary phenomenon. But the Image Economy has certainly elevated creative stardom to a new level through exposure in the mass media. There is also an increased element of commercialization in all forms of art.

This exposure has enabled artists, more than ever, to step from behind their art. As a result, Creators are engrossing figures in their own right, and the public today is curious to know more about them. The authors, directors, musicians, actors and others who create the entertainment we consume through the media are often focal subjects of the media. Being a Creator today means being a media figure as well. By necessity, then, many Creators today are media savvy; they know how to use the media and the right symbolism to build their image as a Creator. Some personalities have moved mythology to a new level of self-cultivation and self-consciousness. The artist Prince, for example, dropped his name for several years and was simply known by the archetype "The Artist Formerly Known as Prince" and a written symbol that could not be pronounced.

Further fueling the public interest in Creators is their often erratic behavior. Creators, particularly artists, have a long tradition of being odd and sometimes bizarre. Salvador Dali, Picasso and Van Gogh are amongst the most fabled examples of this artistic temperament. Van Gogh in particular is seen as an archetypal artist — brilliant, tortured and disturbed. The belief that Creator figures have a special source of creativity is perhaps the reason that the eccentricities of Creators are not only tolerated but even celebrated. Eccentricity serves as a source of the creative mystique. Indeed, it is often a badge of authenticity of sorts. The public almost expects artists, musicians and other Creators to be racked with troubles that somehow fuel their creativity. Consequently, their tribulations and their twisted lives are of as much interest as their actual work.

Eccentricity is often the case with inventors as well. Whether it's the eccentric inventor Doc Brown, who builds the time-travel machine in which Michael J. Fox traverses decades in *Back to the Future*[2], or the nutty inventor Professor Tinkerputt in the *Barney*[3] videos for children, the figure of the wacky inventor is a recurring motif in entertainment. Inventors don't necessarily put paintbrush to canvas. Nor are they expected to suffer the same mania as artists. But they nevertheless have this underlying dynamic of eccentricity that stems from their creative nature.

• **Builders of the image economy:** Creators are more than just the subjects of fascination; they are power figures in the Image Economy — the dominant icons in the business of creating icons. Creators make the images that power the marketing and entertainment mill and keep the Image Economy from stagnating. Their creative ability is the source of profits.

Just as products use newness to fuel consumer interest, personalities leverage their image as potent Creators to keep the public eager for their latest creations. The public stays interested because the Creator possesses the ability to repeatedly produce things that are new and fascinating. This fascination is the essential ingredient for generating mass attention. It also leads to a perfectly symbiotic and reciprocal relationship between Creators and the public: since Creators create things that amuse and fascinate the public, the public is fascinated with Creators. This relationship is the key to understanding the cult of personality that has grown around stardom, with mass media fueling the interchange.

Sometimes Creators in the Image Economy are the nameless producers, media executives and advertising executives who drive the Image Economy from behind the scenes. But increasingly they are also the front men that drive the labels and products they produce. Consequently, Creators such as Versace, Donna Karen, Tommy Hilfiger, Giorgio Armani and Issey Miyake have become household names, with cult-like followings. Creators are also today's master storytellers and directors: Steven Spielberg, Woody Allen, Francis Ford Coppola and assorted Hollywood biggies, as well as a growing cadre of international directors who are receiving worldwide acclaim. All of these people have a deep and profound understanding of the mechanisms of creativity, which acts as a valuable currency around the world.

Perhaps the master of them all, though, was Walt Disney. He made film history with movies such as the 1928 classic *Steamboat Willie*, the first "talkie" animation film, starring Mickey Mouse. But Disney was much more than simply a filmmaker. He understood the potential for the Creator archetype to expand the Disney name in many directions, such as the theme parks that can now be found around the world. What Disney built was a franchise for creativity and imagination.[4] Even many years after his death, the Disney brand name continues to captivate the public's interest because of the quality and the spark of creativity in everything the corporation does. Consumers expect nothing less than fascination from the Magic Kingdom.

What Disney further exemplifies is that, in many respects, the public's fascination with the power of this mythic figure has become detached from Creators themselves. The creativity business — show business — is an obsession in its own right. Hollywood, India's Bollywood and Madison Avenue are defining, potent icons of the business of creativity. Consequently, they have grown beyond any of the individuals who contribute to it. They endure and thrive, while individual Creators come and go. Ironically, Creators have become subsumed by the wider appeal of the Creator business which they've helped engender.

Mythic Highlights to Note

• **The roots of universal appeal:** This figure represents the creative spark in all of us — the need to fashion and create things in our lives, using the inspiration that taps into an invisible power that enables us to generate ideas.

- **Inspiration and the divine:** Great ideas are also often attached to the divine through inspiration. The most effective mythology-makers utilize the concept of inspired creators to instill greater confidence in their products.
- **The role of perfection:** The Creator is forever seeking perfection. Using the notion of perfection provides a strong link between modern mythology and implied superiority of products.
- **Eccentricities:** Ironically, these often add credibility to Creators and act as a stamp of authenticity. Effective communicators are not afraid to let products be a bit quirky, offbeat and eccentric, since they ultimately add to the pedigree of the product or personality as being creative.

"The basic fact of today is the tremendous pace of change in human life."

Jawaharlal Nehru[1]

Mythic Profile
The
Change
Master

An Introduction to the Change Master

As a figure that represents the power of change and self-transformation, the Change Master[2] is one of the most prominent mythic images in modern mythology. If any of the mythic figures could be considered in vogue today, this one is it. Change Masters come in many forms, ranging from Madonna to Superman to GE's former boss, Jack Welch. New industries that sell the potency of change, particularly business re-engineering and the personal self-help industry, are also led by their own Change Masters such as Michael Porter and Stephen Covey. This profile will show how the allure of the Change Master archetype has made the promise of transformation a driving force behind both our business and social lives.

• **The universal messages associated with this figure:** The Change Master represents the universal messages of transformation, self-improvement and self-mastery.

• **Timeless dynamics in summary:** While the Creator symbolizes creativity, the Change Master archetype represents self-creation and the ability for self-fashioning. In addition, the Change Master often has the ability to control the seemingly uncontrollable. This mythic figure is the master of transformation.

Mythologies and stories through the ages have often reflected people's deep subliminal wish to control change. Figures such as the wizard Gandalf, who can snap his fingers and vanish, or ancient gods who could suddenly morph into new forms, are symbolic of people's desire to posses the power of rapid transformation. They also reflect the sense of magic that most people feel about the process of change. Childhood fairy tales initiate young readers into the wonders of metamorphosis, which stems from this archetype. Cinderella, for example, is enthralling to children because she undergoes the dramatic transformation from a pathetic girl to a glowing princess. Similarly, the ugly duckling is a classic childhood manifestation of the Change Master archetype, emerging as a beautiful swan.

Inherent in this transformation process are the positive aspects of change. Ultimately, the figure of the Change Master is symbolic of the promise of rebirth, since stories of transformation are often an allegory for inner blossoming, not just external change. The Change Master represents the potential that lies within all of us.

The Mythic Figure in Advertising and Marketing

•　　**Products as Change Masters:** Products commonly use the Change Master archetype to position themselves as the instigators of consumer transformation. Every day we are conditioned by modern mythology to believe in the transformational power of products: "Look what a hassle it is to cook with that old oven. Voilà! Now look how easy it is with your beautiful, new microwave!" This mythic power of the Change Master plays a central role in advertising for a vast array of products.

Some products overtly wrap themselves in the mantle of the Change Master in order to achieve success. Viagra, a medicine for erectile dysfunction, serves as a particularly vivid example, since it activates a fairly dramatic and significant physical transformation in its users. The product literally gives potency to men by helping them achieve erections. But despite this, there was no guarantee that the product would link properly to the symbolism of the Change Master. It required calculated and purposeful brand-building efforts, such as the sponsorship of a NASCAR team, to make Viagra a well-known symbol for mastery and control.[3]

Most products don't make as swift or dramatic a change in people's lives. This doesn't, however, diminish their potential to leverage the dynamics of the Change Master. Evian water would seem to be on the opposite end of the spectrum from Viagra. Water is a tasteless, colorless and odorless product with few real differentiating or distinguishing features to set the various brands apart. But this didn't stop Evian from becoming a defining symbol in the U.S. market in the late 1980s by using the subconscious power of the archetype. Evian achieved this by associating itself with the aerobics and workout craze that was hitting new heights at the time. Sleek, stylized ads showed highly toned nudes alongside the product, positioning Evian as a key ingredient in the quest for the perfect body. As a result of this strategy, which leverages consumers' innate desire for self-fashioning, Evian became a defining icon of the workout generation. Moreover, it was highly differentiated in consumers' minds, despite the fact that water is essentially a basic commodity.

• **The Change Master in the form of the brand re-launch:** Another way in which the Change Master archetype figures prominently in the product world is one of the mainstays of brand management — the rebirth of existing brands through a re-launch. Most brands try to avoid having to re-launch — the equivalent of re-booting a product — opting instead to change incrementally over time. These incremental changes allow brands to evolve and stay contemporary. However, this approach sometimes fails. Brand managers awake one day to discover that their product has lost a lot of its appeal somewhere along the way. In these types of situations, product-makers frequently turn to a re-launch strategy, in which the product receives new packaging, a new positioning, new advertising and (hopefully) a new lease on life.

The re-launch process leverages people's willingness to accept that a brand can be re-created. This usually isn't done through relying on their good faith. Instead, substantiating proof is required to help support the claim. As is the case with purely new products, re-launched products point to different ingredients, new processes and technology to substantiate their claims. This last approach promises not only to make a difference but also a dramatic improvement, since technology increasingly serves as the most believable support for rapid transformation. Technology is one of the main factors contributing to the belief that "change" equals "good".

- **Science and technology in transformation:** The frequent use of science and technology to support re-launches and product claims in general connects back to a major issue in the way corporations think and behave. While most commercial organizations attempt to foster change, viewing it as part of their lifeblood, they also inherently avoid unpredictability and irrationality. Both are anathema to corporations, since they are expected to provide steady, predictable earnings and apply rational planning and process to get there. While companies want the benefits of change, they also want it to come with an airtight and predictable process — just like they want with their communications. Consequently, they often turn to science and engineering as the rational means for generating product changes.

They also use it to build bonds with consumers, since people today commonly put their faith in the power of science and technology. Or, to be more precise, they believe in its ability to bring about progress. Scientific advances build our expectations that the resulting change will be positive. Moreover, science seems to be gaining in its omnipotence, with new developments allowing for the improvement or enhancement of almost everything, including nature. Thus we see mechanical hearts, *in vitro* fertilization and synthetic low-fat ingredients. Engineering, too, is seen as contributing to constant advances. Concepts such as Moore's Law — a key tenet in the computer industry which stipulates that computing power doubles every 18 months — adds positive proof of this assumption.[4] In general, there is a palpable sense of scientific and technological acceleration. Some brands capitalize quite directly on these beliefs in building the mythology of their products. Audi, the German car-maker, serves as a good example. Its campaign tagline "*Vorsprung durch Technik*" (literally "advancement through technology") turns a latent belief into a potent sales pitch for its cars.

In addition to representing advancement, technology is also frequently linked to the pursuit of perfection. Techniques such as Six Sigma or quality circles are utilized by more and more businesses. These approaches propagate the notion that through continuous, rational improvement, the imperfections in manufacturing can be eliminated. Products from Mercedes-Benz cars to aircraft engines are touted as approximating perfection through stringent engineering discipline. And engineering is subtly introduced into the way products present themselves in order to instill greater confidence that they are cutting-edge Change Masters. The use of numbers — Gillette's Mach 2

Razor or the Porsche 911, for example — conveys the idea that these products are the outcome of a logical, calculated engineering process.

Technology has become increasingly pervasive in the language of modern mythology, further bolstering the implicit belief in technology as a driver of change. Advertising language — "scientifically proven" and "space age" — connects products to technological and scientific advancement.

The Mythic Figure in Entertainment and Popular Culture

•	**Change in entertainment:** Mastering change is not just serious business — it's also entertaining. Audiences find it refreshing to see rapid transformation, rather than watching characters suffer through the long, hard slog that reminds most people of their own daily lives (despite all the self-help promises). People have long enjoyed watching Superman, for example, burst from a telephone booth, instantly transformed from the bookish Clark Kent into the man from Krypton. The Change Master archetype in entertainment reminds viewers of the potential for metamorphosis and transformation that lies within them as well.

Successful personalities in entertainment understand consumers' deep interest in watching fictional characters undergoing transformation on screen, and they also realize the need to master it themselves if they hope to stay in the limelight. The ability to transform has become a prerequisite for most successful celebrities today as they attempt to ensure that the fickle public doesn't leave them in the dust of yesteryear.

Few stars have mastered the art of transformation as well as Madonna. When Madonna burst onto the music scene as the hot, writhing young singer with a cross around her neck, few in the audience could have imagined the future incarnations that would accompany each new album. What became evident over time though was that Madonna was not only fresh, brazen and sexy — she was a Change Master. As she'd later admit to *People* magazine, she had nobody guiding her image, so she had to do it herself.[5] But there was a purposefulness with which she built her public persona, and she instinctively understood the need to continue to evolve and change in order to maintain her position in the public's eye. Over time, she became known less for any specific persona than for her ability to master her own self-fashioning to transform herself, almost at will.

Dorothy from the film classic *The Wizard of Oz* provides a different but equally cogent example of the Change Master.[6] Just think of her tale in simplified form: Dorothy, who wishes to get away from Kansas, suddenly finds her life turned upside down when she awakes in Oz. She then tries to find her way back home by seeking the help of a Change Master — the Wizard of Oz. However, she eventually discovers that the power she has been seeking so desperately has actually been there inside her all along; she already possesses the power of the Change Master. Dorothy simply had to believe in her own ability to catalyze change and click her ruby shoes to transform her situation and transport herself back home. Run the motivational tape!

• **The Change Master and the business of self-help:** The story of Dorothy and the Wizard of Oz encapsulates central aspects of the self-help industry, which is now a booming, multi-billion-dollar business.

First, the ultimate payoff of all the searching for the Change Master wizard is the promise of personal transformation. Today, people believe they can learn to control those things that have traditionally been uncontrollable. Do you need to control time? No problem — the Change Master helps you with time management. Do you want to control your weight? Again, it's a piece of cake (or not) — the Change Master can help you learn to control your hunger. You want to know how to become a millionaire? Easy — there are methods and advice to help.

Second, despite the term "self-help", gurus play a pivotal role in helping people to change. If Dorothy were around today, she wouldn't need to look further than the local bookshop to find a host of wizards to help her with her situation. People like Stephen Covey, Anthony Robbins, John Gray and Deepak Chopra are amongst the upper echelon of those offering to share the secrets of self-transformation. Whole sections of bookstores today are stacked with their recipes for change and self-mastery, and a variety of videos, audiotapes and infomercials have turned the self-help business into a multimedia experience. This also includes revival-like events held by many of these Change Masters, costing hundred of dollars to attend. For most of the attendees, the outlay seems worthwhile, since these gurus are beacons for how to structure their time and even how to organize their view of the world.

Given the frequent media exposure that many Change Masters now command, self-help gurus have joined the ranks of today's popular personalities. Meanwhile, entertainers too are increasingly mixing show business with the business of self-transformation. Oprah Winfrey is one of the new high-priestesses of self-help. This should perhaps be expected since celebrities already command the pulpit of public exposure. Almost 20 years ago, Jane Fonda showed how effective this pulpit is when she transformed herself from an actress, best known at the time for her support of social causes, to a workout diva, via an exercise video that became a beacon of the aerobics craze.[7]

• **The growing business of changing business:** Rapid change and transformation is not just big business for individuals, it's also big business for business. Mastering change is a common prescription for most corporations today, with a litany of buzzwords used to describe it and elevate it to a sacred science. Today, people "network" and "interface" where they used to just "meet", and companies are "re-engineered". A lot of the language of business is the language of technology and, thereby, of change-mastering. Like the self-help boom, it has its own priests and priestesses, such as Michael Hammer, Rosabeth Moss Kanter, Michael Porter and Ken Blanchard. What's interesting about the corporate transformation boom is that the gurus are not just management consultants and academics — external wizards — though there are plenty of them as well. Many corporate practitioners as well, particularly CEOs, have gained fame as business Change Masters. They follow in the footsteps of people such as Henry Ford who, a century ago, popularized change-mastering with the introduction of mass-production car plants. But the Change Masters of business today can use the reach of the media like no other corporate chieftains before them. Similar to entertainers, they are leveraging the mechanisms of the media to share the gospel of corporate change and the secrets of how they have revolutionized the workplace. Consequently, people such as GE's Jack Welch have become well-known business personalities and the rock stars of the corporate world.

• **The gurus' transformation formula:** To be effective and believable, the modern Change Master of both business and self-help must rely on more than a desire to control destiny: he must have a plan to show people the way. This plan includes elements that are meant to imbue it with certainty and credibility. While most Change Masters wouldn't call it a "formula", that is nevertheless what it is intended to be, since a formula is predicated on having a consistent, predictable outcome if some critical steps are followed:

Control: The key message that the change guru preaches is the ability for his subjects to learn how to control things ("Dorothy, you can go home anytime you'd like"). In order to be credible, the Change Master must profess to be in control himself. Therefore, the Change Master cultivates this image of having already mastered the practice in his life. This often happens through promotional literature that shares details of the Change Master's private life, which invariably includes stories of how he achieved change.

Confidence: The Change Master also preaches confidence ("Dorothy, it's easy — you only have to believe"). After all, who is going to follow a master who doesn't already know the trail ahead? The wider message, though, is not just belief in the Change Master. What's required is a fundamental belief that self-mastery can be achieved. This is a big hurdle to overcome, since most people doubt their ability to control their destiny in a world surrounded by uncontrollable variables.

Methodology: Change Masters always follow specific steps and a framework to achieve change ("Dorothy, just close your eyes and click your heels three times"). Most self-help and business-transformation books offer a number of specific steps or "laws" to follow. The process of change is simplified into bite-sized pieces that the public can digest, and packaged in a framework that seems to provide a guarantee that it will work, if you just follow the steps. Ultimately, the Change Master's methodology is intended to confer the power of pseudo-science onto his or her beliefs in order to "prove" and rationalize why change should be considered something clear, objective and logical, rather than internal, subjective and unmanageable.

Rapid results: The central message of the gurus and products of change is the ability to effect rapid change ("Dorothy, you can go back home *now*"). The short time scale is vital because it again helps to "prove" the potency of the promised transformation. Otherwise, the public might doubt its efficacy and get bored before the magic kicks in. The promise of rapid results gives people what they want — controlled revolution, rather than slowpoke evolution, and the hope of having a nice, flat tummy in just a few weeks.

Mythic Highlights to Note

• **The roots of universal appeal:** This figure represents the godhead in all of us — the desire to be the master of our own destiny and have some control over our lives.

• **The transformation formula:** People and companies who sell change as a service often have very similar components that support the efficacy of what they offer. This "transformation formula" includes a clear, disciplined methodology, which is critical to its believability.

• **Products rely on change:** Successful products focus on more than their own benefits and features; they relate to change and how they can help consumers change.

• **Technology and change:** Technology is frequently positioned as an enabler of change. It provides a rational, scientific and objective reason to believe that the change will work, and is therefore a critical element to consider in messaging.

• **The language of transformation:** The naming of products and the language that surrounds products imparts a great deal about the transformational power of the product.

"**P**ower tends to corrupt and absolute power corrupts absolutely."

Lord Acton[1]

Mythic Profile
The
Powerbroker

13

An Introduction to the Powerbroker

The Powerbroker is the consummate insider. Powerbroker figures such as Rupert Murdoch, Li Ka Shing, Donald Trump and the late Kathryn Graham are usually people in positions of influence, wealth and authority. They are clearly "in the know" with the right people. For this reason, Powerbrokers are respected and admired. But some are also feared and sometimes even hated. In certain cases, this is warranted, since the Powerbroker's influence can be used to dominate and destroy others. The mandarins of politics and the godfathers of the underworld — also Powerbroker figures — are renowned for this. In advertising and brand building, this dominance is used frequently by companies to leverage their leading market positions. In entertainment, Powerbrokers are figures of great intrigue and sometimes seduction. This mythic profile will examine the mechanisms of power, with a cautionary tale about its limits.

•	**The universal messages associated with this figure:** The Powerbroker represents the universal message of authority, influence and domination.

•	**Timeless dynamics in summary:** First of all, it is important to recognize that the Powerbroker is quite different from the Ultimate Strength, although the defining trait of power is common to both of them. While the

Ultimate Strength manifests itself through overt physical prowess, the Powerbroker exerts enormous force by using personal influence and persuasion to get his way. A lot of what the Powerbroker does occurs behind closed doors, far from public view, as he works his network of contacts. Yet the Powerbroker has an aura of importance, making him unmistakable in a crowd. Those who don't know him quickly realize they should.

A key to deciphering this figure is to understand three underlying elements that are commonly part of the Powerbroker's great influence. First, he has connections and a great deal of personal sway over others. The Powerbroker knows the people worth knowing, including both reputable and unsavory characters. Second, the Powerbroker possesses knowledge and information. His ability to gather and utilize information makes him aware of things that others don't know (or don't know that he knows). Third, the Powerbroker has a vision for things to come, since he is an authority who is helping to shape the future. Given his position to make things happen, people frequently seek his advice about the future course of events.

The Powerbroker can be highly effective and inspirational as a leader. But part and parcel of the Powerbroker's influence is an element of danger. The Powerbroker is not warm and fuzzy. He plays for keeps, and he isn't afraid to use extra pressure and even intimidation to get what he wants. Whether he's a CEO, a corporate raider or a gangster boss, he can twist the knife when needed. Consequently, Powerbrokers tend to dominate the scene, leaving their imprint on everything as they go.

Each of these aspects is manifested in the modern mythology of brands and entertainment.

The Mythic Figure in Advertising and Marketing

•	**Dominant-leadership advertising:** The Powerbroker archetype plays an influential role in brands and in advertising, particularly in advertising that leverages a company's leading position in a business category. This approach can be called "dominant-leadership advertising". It is characterized by strategies that give consumers a sense of a company's unassailable position. Powerbroker brands engender respect for their authority, and people don't doubt that they know their stuff. This plays an important role in the Image Economy, since consumers often support brands and use products from companies they feel are winners.

One way that dominance is communicated is through specific language that helps build an aura of invincibility around products. Phrases such as "the world's leading", "the best" or "number one" are common in this approach. Some professionals in the communications business might argue that claiming to be "number one" has become a bit of a parity claim since so many advertisers now use it for their respective categories of business. There's the number one airline, the number one auto-maker, the number one vacuum cleaner — the list goes on and on. But despite a plethora of such messages, consumers still continue to respond subconsciously to the assurance of leading brands.

Companies can take leadership messaging a step further by emphasizing that they're more than number one — they're number one by a long shot. This portrays them as a dominator as well as a leader. The inherent message in this approach is "How could you possibly choose to use an inferior competitor (which we're going to crush anyway) instead of us?" The intention of this type of advertising is to inspire awe in, and even intimidate, the market with their unassailable position. The company wants consumers to feel that it's inevitable that it will win in its category, so they might as well go with it from the start. While advertisers generally seek to entice consumers, dominant leaders know that by creating a bit of concern, such as the worry about choosing an inferior competitor, they can often persuade consumers better.

In some cases, dominant leadership is established through smash-mouth competitive advertising — by making direct and strong comparisons that show how much one product outperforms another. Software giant Oracle has been using this approach to build an aura of domination for its products. In one of its print ads it claims simply that "Oracle runs SAP 4 times faster than IBM". This type of approach, while straight and factual, can also be an effective way to build a brand's mythology at a deeper level. The claim awes consumers and seemingly proves that Oracle's leadership is not a case of small degrees. It is a statement of dominating capability. The advertising, therefore, effectively positions the company as the undisputed authority in the field. After all, who is going to doubt the capability of a company that makes such a claim? And, by taking IBM on in such an overt fashion, it also seeks to jar consumers' expectations, since consumers are used to seeing IBM itself as a dominant leader.

In certain markets, advertising regulations or social customs might not permit such comparative and competitive advertising. But dominant-leadership advertising can work in non-competitive forms as well. A second, more inwardly focused, Oracle ad reads "Using our own E-Business Suite, Oracle saved $1 billion in 1 year". On the surface, this would again seem to be a simple, factual statement. Yet this approach can be equally effective at building Powerbroker mythology. Even the simplest of messages can indeed communicate deeper values and touch the recesses of our psyches. In this example, there are actually a few implicit messages. First, there is the basic implication of corporate size and strength. After all, if they could save $1 billion, they certainly must be a sizeable, resource-rich company. Second, the statement implies mastery and control. If they can save this much for themselves, imagine what they can do for you. Lastly, the tone of the ad — definitive and straight — is pure Powerbroker imagery. It's strong, direct and in control: exactly what you'd want from a company you're going to rely on to help you save big bucks. So we see that from a simple statement, deeper messages and images can be created.

• **Advertising of influence:** Advertising that builds upon the Power-broker archetype needn't always focus on domination. Other approaches use different aspects of the mythic figure, such as the role of knowledge and influence. CNN's advertising campaign "Be the First to Know" leverages the first of these points. The advertising, which highlights people who know the news first, reflects both the key benefit of a leading news channel — delivering the news before anyone else — and consumers' desires to be Powerbrokers by having information first. This type of message plays on the transformational aspects of modern mythology by implying that consumers will become Powerbrokers because of the knowledge they get from CNN.

An old advertising campaign from the U.S. investment firm E.F. Hutton, which disappeared in one of the many mergers in that industry, is a fitting example of how influence can factor into building a brand name. The campaign featured situations in which people in public places would stop in mid action and cup their ear towards two people talking privately about investment advice from the company. This was followed by the still-memorable tagline, "When E.F. Hutton talks, people listen". This is vintage modern mythology using the Powerbroker archetype for brand building. Hutton placed itself squarely in the shoes of the Powerbroker — the one in the financial know. It planted a powerful seed of an idea that consumers should seek its advice as a financial Powerbroker, even at the drop of a hat.

This type of authoritative demeanor is effective in communication since consumers aren't always confident when they make decisions. How should they pick a mutual fund? How can they tell if a particular brand of refrigerator is really better than another? There is, in fact, a lot that weighs on consumers' minds, even for seemingly banal products. So the confidence and authority of this mythic figure can provide important, subliminal guidance when consumers make decisions.

• **Powerbroker products:** As we observed earlier, products play more than a functional role in people's lives. They also serve as important cultural markers. Consequently, there is a symbiotic relationship between brands and contemporary culture. The more prevalent a social marker becomes, the more people want to acquire it, which further drives sales, resulting in increased visibility of the product as a well-known social symbol. This point is particularly relevant to the Powerbroker, since popular culture today is full of products that serve as symbols of power. Luxury goods, such as sexy sports cars, expensive suits and fancy pens all use the mythic symbols of power to build their image. As a result, these items have become the trappings of power in consumer society; they provide an outward mani-festation for people who wish to be seen by others as Powerbrokers. Much of what are generally called "luxury" goods are really "power" goods, which communicate the users' social status.

Powerbrokers have moved on from the days when they were old men in three-piece suits, sitting behind mahogany desks and smoking cigars. Today, knowledge and information are keys to both wealth and power. Indeed, many of today's moguls and business titans, such as Larry Ellison, John Malone, Bill Gates and Rupert Murdoch, have built their wealth and reputation around their mastery of technology and information. So the social status of some power goods today, such as sleek net-enabled hand-phones, super-lightweight laptops or Palm Pilots, relate back to this core trait of the archetype. These items of information technology couple function and form in a way that is vital to Powerbrokers staying at the bleeding edge in today's Image Economy.

• **The anti-Powerbroker message:** As we'll examine later, purposely using the antithesis of an archetype can sometimes be an effective way to get a sales message across. This is the case with the Avis car-rental company's longstanding marketing campaign "We try harder".[2] While the Powerbroker has its attractions for some, it also has its negatives: the Powerbroker can be overbearing, ruthless and rude. Therefore, dominant-leader products sometimes fail to build empathy with consumers. The Avis approach is appealing to those who seek a company that's more in step with how they feel. The "We try harder" campaign clearly communicates that it is *not* a dominant leader. Instead, it's an underdog who will try harder to win consumers' trust and affection. Further, it uses this underdog status to contrast itself with insensitive market leaders who simply want to gobble up more market share. So, by using the inverse of the Powerbroker, it is able to subliminally leverage our innate associations with that archetype.

The Mythic Figure in Entertainment and Popular Culture

• **The fascination and seduction of power in entertainment:** Audiences often have a voyeuristic interest in Powerbrokers. This is understandable since Powerbrokers have a powerful presence. Because audiences know inherently that the Powerbroker works his influence behind the scenes, they are eager to get a backroom glimpse they wouldn't otherwise have of these powerful figures. Film classics such as *The Godfather*[3], and the TV hit *The Sopranos*[4], take people into the inner circle of La Cosa Nostra to see the intrigues and potentially lethal dynamics of underworld power-broking. Similarly, popular TV shows such as the American hit *The West Wing*[5] give viewers an up-close view of power, through a fictional portrayal of a very different Powerbroker — the President of the United States. Viewers are fascinated with the glimpse they get into these rarefied inner sanctums.

For some, power is more than a fascination — it becomes an inducement that overwhelms them. Consequently, the seduction of power is an equally entertaining subject. The movie *Indecent Proposal*[6], which stars Robert Redford as John Gage, a multi-millionaire Powerbroker, provides a good example of this. In the movie, Gage proposes to sleep with the character played by Demi Moore for $1 million, despite the fact that she's already married. As a sort of modern morality play, the movie reflects the appealing yet dangerous nature of power. In the end, Moore's character has to resist more than the money; she has to overcome the broader seductive power that Redford represents as the Powerbroker. Most people in the audience can relate to the temptations at work.

There is often a point of no return with power. Consequently, the seduction-of-power story often goes further and becomes a story of the lust for power. After a few sips from the chalice of influence, some people become intoxicated and uncontrollable. Gordon Gecko, the Powerbroker figure in the movie *Wall Street*[7], is typical of the result. Gecko becomes the symbol of the unbridled lust for control and domination — the Powerbroker run amuck. This, too, touches a deep chord in viewers, since they know that Powerbrokers sometimes succumb to megalomania. In such cases, the Powerbroker goes from being respected and feared to being loathed. He tips over the edge and becomes the arch antagonist and a menace to society. It is at this point in the Powerbroker's hyper-kinetic lust for more power that society normally steps in to put a check on his power. Ironically, the Powerbroker's archetypal ability to control and destroy gets turned upon himself to keep him in check.

Mythic Highlights to Note

• **The roots of universal appeal:** This figure represents the master in all of us — the drive to have authority and influence.
• **The Powerbroker and the back room:** How the Powerbroker gets things done isn't always clear. This is part of his power. He works through persuasion and influence.
• **Symbols of power and technology:** The Powerbroker does, however, have overt symbols of power. These are increasingly symbols of technological savvy.
• **Domination as the modus operandi:** The Powerbroker is not afraid to use his overwhelming presence to dominate the situation.

"The more wise and powerful a master, the more directly is his work created, and the simpler it is.

Meister Eckhart[1]

Mythic Profile
The
Wise
Old Man

14

An Introduction to the Wise Old Man

In many respects, the Wise Old Man is the alter ego of the Powerbroker. Instead of seeking to dominate others, the Wise Old Man nurtures others by offering his advice. He is the venerated teacher and advisor — the Confucius or Obi-Wan Kenobi[2] — in the crowd who has the wisdom of experience. Given the respect and trust he engenders, the Wise Old Man is another archetypal force behind endorsements. In entertainment, the Wise Old Man figure plays a key role in guiding and aiding young Heroes. As we'll see in this profile, the Wise Old Man represents the wisdom gained from having been there himself.

• **The universal messages associated with this figure:** The Wise Old Man represents the universal messages of experience, advice and heritage.

• **Timeless dynamics in summary:** We have to look back in time to truly understand this mythic figure, because the Wise Old Man wasn't always wise or old. At some point earlier in life, a sage was once a young novice who had to struggle. He was the new student or inexperienced fighter who had to earn his stripes. This point is easy to forget, particularly for the next generation of young initiates who weren't privy to the Wise Old Man's past. But it is a key point for readers to remember about this mythic figure, since the vital dynamics of the Wise Old Man stem from his accumulated experience.

This experience is the basis for the Wise Old Man's wisdom. In fact, it's often the prerequisite for wisdom, rather than raw intellectual power. The Wise Old Man has been through it all before and has passed difficult tests. The valuable lessons that the sage has learned have come the hard way — by making mistakes and discovering what *not* to do. This gives him a base of real credibility from which to speak and advise others.

Given the fact that the Wise Old Man has "been there", he is the ideal figure to serve as an initiator to young novices.[3] The Wise Old Man is often involved in helping budding Heroes begin on their own personal journey, and he serves as the vital advisor who helps them deal with the tribulations throughout. This is a natural role for him to play since the Wise Old Man is the older incarnation of the Hero. Out of empathy, the Wise Old Man usually tries to help them avoid the type of mistakes he made. However, the young often take time to understand or truly appreciate the wisdom that the Wise Old Man has to offer.

The Wise Old Man is prepared to act as the teacher and advisor for others because his battles are done. His past experiences — the source of his wisdom — can never be taken away from him. Consequently, the Wise Old Man has an aura of complete confidence. He has fought his rounds and has nothing further to prove, except through influencing others for the good.

Finally, the Wise Old Man often helps others out of a sense of reciprocity for the guidance he once received in his youth. He recalls the value of the teacher-pupil relationship from which he once benefited. Therefore, the Wise Old Man is a symbol of the continuity of wisdom from earlier generations. He is the embodiment of tradition.

The Mythic Figure in Advertising and Marketing

•   **The initiator and endorser:** The key traits of the Wise Old Man lend themselves wonderfully to the sales and advertising process by helping to prompt people to try products and by engendering trust in those products through endorsement. Let's consider each of these points, which have an interlocking effect.

As just mentioned, the Wise Old Man is often part of the initiation process for the young Hero or protagonist. We've seen this in stories and myths throughout the ages. For example, as a young prince sets out on a journey, he often turns to his father or a trusted advisor for words of wisdom. Through mythology, people have become conditioned to the notion that, when they embark on something new, seeking advice from those who are more experienced is invaluable. This makes a direct link to the modern mythology of consumers sampling products for the first time.

The basic premise of the sales cycle is that after consumers try things for the first time, they will hopefully become loyal users. The trick is to figure out how to get them to buy it the first time. In some cases, if the items have low emotional involvement or low cost, the inducement to try might be less difficult. If consumers don't like the product, they're not greatly out of pocket. But other types of products are more expensive or might simply have a greater degree of anxiety involved in the selection process. The stakes are higher when you're choosing medicine or spending thousands of dollars on a new car than they are when you're buying shoe polish. Therefore, consumers look to factors that will give them confidence. This is where the endorsement value of trusted figures comes into play. Endorsers frequently play an effective role, similar to that of the Wise Old Man, in introducing consumers to brands and products. They also provide an extra degree of assurance in the form of an endorsement.

Endorsements work at getting consumers to try new products because a trusted figure puts his or her personal stamp of approval on it. Endorsers carry weight since their names and reputations often connote a depth of experience. They are "proven", just like the Wise Old Man. This creates a transferral of credibility from the trusted figure to the product itself. The implicit message is that if this wise figure, who has the benefit of experience, believes in the product, then it must be good. Also inherent in the endorsement is the idea that consumers will avoid mistakes if they just follow the advice that's being offered. Plus, the endorser vouches for the product through the endorsement and also provides an implied personal guarantee, based upon his or her credibility. The desired outcome is that people will feel extra confidence to try products.

The longer-term goal, though, is more than just getting consumers to try a product. The ultimate aim is to get them to believe deeply and become loyal to it. To achieve this, the endorser also plays on the archetypal Wise Old Man power dynamic of the instructor-pupil relationship. At a deeper level, the endorser is not just recommending a product; he's instructing you that it's the right selection, with which you'll be happy on an ongoing basis. The Wise Old Man's accumulated experience, and the stature it accords him, provides the basis of credibility for this mix of recommendation and instruction.

American Express provides an excellent example of the power of endorsements. Key elements of its image-building campaign over the years have utilized these mythic values. In one example, Karl Malden, an actor who played a detective in a popular U.S. TV program[4], was featured in a famous commercial in which he told consumers, "American Express Travelers Cheques — Don't leave home without them". This was not a slight, timid recommendation. Rather, this was the voice of experience at work, instructing the audience about something they should know. And because Malden's character on TV had stature and expertise, there was a direct transferral of authority and respect to his endorsement of American Express.

A second point from the campaign might seem like a minor detail but, as we've already observed, seemingly small details can have a big impact on the effectiveness of modern mythology. The mention in each ad that the endorser is a "card member since [a given year]" adds a very important touch to the underlying dynamic of the communication. It clearly shows that the endorser has the experience they're recommending, that they too have experience of the brand. This detail adds vital credibility to the endorser's advice.

• **The many faces of endorsement:** In some cases, endorsers in commercials are actually old men. Any late-night TV viewer in the U.S. will probably have seen ads and infomercials starring the likes of former U.S. football player Fran Tarkenton or the talk-show sidekick Ed McMahon. However, there are also numerous examples of women and younger people who are endorsers. The Image Economy is littered, in fact, with an array of pitchmen and pitchwomen who are ready to raise their hand to pledge their trust in products.

Mythic figures are simply representations of an archetype that has deeper universal values. So when we refer to the Wise Old Man, it reflects a given set of universal dynamics and values that can be portrayed in a range of expression. Consequently, the Wise Old Man archetype can indeed be portrayed in female form, utilizing the exact same mythic dynamics of wisdom, trust and experience as their male counterparts.

Another interesting effect of the Image Economy is that celebrity status now confers upon stars an aura of achievement that equates with experience or expertise, irrespective of their age. The implicit belief is that if you're famous, you must know something. Since Tiger Woods is so great at hitting a golf ball, for example, he is considered to have exceptional skills of concentration. The follow-on from this is that this skill or prowess makes well-known figures worthy of dispensing credible advice. There are some limits to this effect, of course. It's doubtful whether most consumers would turn to their favorite footballer to decide which medicine to use for their heart disease, for example. But one of the reasons that we see stars endorsing such a wide range of products is the basic belief that stardom equals mastery, which in turn equals superior knowledge that makes them credible advisors. So when a star or popular personality endorses a product with a message that's basically saying, "If I were you, I'd buy this product", people do listen.

A final point to note about the mechanics of endorsement is that consumers frequently trust endorsers because of the subconscious connections we have to the Wise Old Man as a benevolent teacher who provides advice for our own good. Thus, people generally extend some degree of trust to endorsers, rather than viewing them all as money-hungry rogues. Of course, there are more-cynical consumers out there. But even in the highly marketed world of today, where virtually any caliber of public personality can find sponsorship and endorsement deals, much of the public still seems willing to believe in endorsers' authority. In some senses, how could consumers *not* believe them, particularly their favorite stars, since consumers spend lots of time watching stars on TV or in the movies each week? It would seem almost hypocritical for the public to like them so much and then not believe endorsers at all. So we should not be surprised that consumers succumb to the invisible connections of the Wise Old Man in the form of endorsers. Just think of all the Ginsu knives Socrates or Confucius could have sold!

• **Heritage in selling:** Endorsements can sometimes dovetail with another effective approach based on the Wise Old Man archetype — namely, heritage messaging. In this approach, old masters lend credibility to a brand or product. They might be master brewers, master craftsmen, master chefs or master mechanics — it all depends upon what's being sold. Thus we see Chef Boyardee featured on cans of food.[5] And in numerous beer commercials, brew masters lovingly tend their beers. These old masters might be fictional characters or real. All of them, however, are meant to convey the confidence of knowing their craft because they've been practicing it a long time. They are the Wise Old Men of their respective fields.

In most cases, these old masters don't have fame or stardom to draw upon. Yet old masters still provide an implicit and credible endorsement for the product because their recognized expertise in a given field gives them credibility. So they are able to provide the stamp of approval that the product has been created the "right way". Over time, some of these old masters even become famous as quasi celebrities in their own right.

The Wise Old Man, in the form of the old master, often builds a second layer of credibility by referencing his use of centuries-old recipes, processes or traditions in creating a product. In some cases, he claims to follow the original recipe that perhaps came from the founder of the company. This approach is meant to further invoke experience as a proof point that supports the quality of the product. Having a special recipe or process also implies that there was enough wisdom in the process, and valuable experience built up over time, to make it worth preserving this knowledge. Just like a teacher codifies his teaching in order to share it with others, the old master maintains the valuable knowledge of the product. Thus, there is an unbroken heritage from which some brands draw their power and credibility.

What this shows is that, despite the trend towards worshipping newness and youth in many consumer societies around the world, both experience and heritage do still count for something. This is one of the reasons that many companies fall back on their heritage as a source of strength. Even a brand focused on the young, such as Levi's, touts its heritage. Just look on the back of your jeans and you'll see that Levi's were patented in the U.S. on May 20, 1873. Of course, people, don't run out and buy blue jeans because the company is over a 100 years old. But it is nevertheless a powerful component of a company's efforts to build its modern mythology.

Brands gain the public's respect for having stood the test of time. Heritage messaging implicitly communicates to consumers that a product has quality, which gives it staying power. It also implies that a company has deeper values and beliefs that it has retained. Particularly in a day and age when so many products quickly come and go, the staying power of a product can be another important source of confidence for consumers. Plus, it taps into the way consumers function as social beings. Some products are recommended from generation to generation, whether it's a mother sharing baking tips with her daughter or a father sharing his power tools with his son. So a company's heritage messaging subconsciously connects with consumers' desire for continuity.

The Mythic Figure in Entertainment and Popular Culture

•   **Trials and tribulations in entertainment:** Like other mythic figures, the Wise Old Man must take action for his deeper character to show. He doesn't simply sit in the corner looking wise. Often, we see the strength of his character via his interaction with pupils, whom he counsels through tough situations. This dynamic has resulted in some of the most memorable relationships in entertainment history.

A young Hero must overcome initial frustrations and challenges. Whether he's a budding Jedi or a top-gun pilot, the pupil must struggle and make his own mistakes. The Wise Old Man is there to help. However, rather than listening to the advice of the Wise Old Man, the young pupil usually rejects and perhaps even fights against the advice — at least initially.

Inherently, then, in the early stage in the young Hero's trials and testing there is tension between the young initiate and the Wise Old Man. The Wise Old Man attempts to show the pupil the way, but the pupil fights back. This conflict is often precipitated by the sage, who presses the pupil to his limits, for the Wise Old Man knows that it is only through testing that the Hero will forge a sufficiently strong character to succeed. Challenge and testing is the source of great drama and character tension. In the movie classic *Rocky*, the grizzly old boxing trainer, Mickey, tells Rocky he's a bum who will never make it. Because he can see Rocky's potential to be a great fighter, he chides Rocky for not being more than he is. So Rocky and Mickey initially have a confrontational relationship. But when Rocky gets a title shot, he knows deep down that he needs the veteran's wisdom if he hopes to stand a chance against Apollo Creed.

During the darkest hour of challenge, the pupil often has a crisis of confidence. But when times are the worst, the Wise Old Man is at his best. This is when the Wise Old Man usually steps in and proves the worth of his experience.[6] His knowledge and composure help him stay levelheaded, even as others buckle. The sage can truly help the young pupil over the hump of the challenge because the Wise Old Man remembers "how it was". Indeed, the relationship usually arises because the pupil has a quality that reminds the Wise Old Man of himself. He therefore builds a sympathetic relationship with his pupil that finally blossoms when the young Hero starts to listen to the inner wisdom of the Wise Old Man.

As the relationship moves to a higher level of trust and reliance, the Wise Old Man helps the novice across the threshold to mastery. Ultimately, what the sage possesses and imparts to the pupil is not a specific piece of knowledge but, more importantly, a broader and deeper sense of understanding and confidence that comes through experience. This culmination of the relationship, like the initial tension, is a great winner in entertainment. Thus, audiences are drawn in as Obi-Wan Kenobi helps the young Jedi, Luke Skywalker, to finally feel the force within him and realize his full power as a Jedi warrior.

In a very basic way, the relationship reflects the essential human experience that children have learning from parents, grandparents and other elders who mentor and assist them as they grow. This happens as same-sex relationships — the old man teaching the young man (father-son) or the old woman counseling the young woman (mother-daughter) — as well as cross-gender relationships. Both situations involve natural tensions, particularly the oedipal rivalry of the father-son relationship. But, ultimately, the dynamics of this wise elder-pupil relationship connect positively on some level. Who but the saddest of individuals hasn't struggled at some point in their young lives, only to realize in the process that they have learned something valuable from someone older and wiser?

Mythic Highlights to Note

• **The roots of universal appeal:** This figure represents the mentor in all of us — the need to nurture and tutor others.

- **Wisdom through experience:** The base of power of this mythic figure is experience. It is the bedrock upon which its credibility is built.
- **Role as an initiator:** The Wise Old Man often helps novices as they are initiated into new situations and experiences. This has a direct link to the role of endorsers in advertising.
- **Heritage in selling:** Heritage, particularly in the form of collected wisdom, can be used as a valued asset for building a brand.
- **A vital relationship:** The Wise Old Man and the young Hero often have an intertwined relationship. This is a source of effective drama.

“**I**n thy face I see,

The map of honour, truth and loyalty.”

William Shakespeare[1]

Mythic Profile
The
Loyalist

15

An Introduction to the Loyalist

We all need friends and confidants. The Loyalist is the friend next door and the shoulder to cry on. This friendship, however, is not without tests and trials. But similarly to the Ultimate Strength, the Loyalist proves his or her character through these tests. The defining trait of reliability guarantees the Loyalist a valued place in the commercial world, sidling up to consumers as "buddy brands". In entertainment, too, this mythic figure is a mainstay. This mythic profile will show why trust and loyalty are effective commercial motivators in the Image Economy as well as exemplary personal traits.

•   **The universal messages associated with this figure:** The Loyalist represents the universal messages of trust, loyalty and reassurance.

•   **Timeless dynamics in summary:** While the testing of the Hero is fundamentally the story of an individual gaining knowledge and self-awareness, the Loyalist archetype connects with people as social beings. Situations involving the Loyalist reflect the universal experience of fitting into society. They also reflect the more intimate experience of forming deep and meaningful personal bonds with others.

But building and maintaining friendships can occasionally be challenging as well as rewarding. While some friendships begin almost instantly, there are plenty of situations where friends must grow on each other. These types of friendships start with a gulf between two individuals. Most people can relate to the experience of realizing that someone they might not have originally considered to be a close friend has somehow grown in their heart and become an important part of their life.

What eventually bring Loyalists together are the trials and tribulations that cement the friendship. The two realize the extent of the bond that has been created only after it has been truly put to the test. There is often a challenge that two friends must overcome together, such as a common foe they must battle, which prompts this realization. In the testing process, there are usually opportunities for one of them to abandon the other. However, the Loyalist doesn't leave the other behind. Instead, by choosing not to abandon the situation and his friend, the Loyalist proves his preparedness to stand shoulder to shoulder with a buddy. The trial of friendship is the anvil on which true trust and loyalty is forged.

The figure of the Loyalist serves as a reminder that we all must look beyond our selfish needs and sometimes make sacrifices for friendship. Friendship, though, is reciprocal. So the lesson of the Loyalist is not simply that you must make sacrifices but also that others will make sacrifices for you, too. Just as people extend loyalty and reliability to friends, they receive assurance and support from others as well. The Loyalist archetype has extremely strong appeal because of the give and take of human relationships.

The Mythic Figure in Advertising and Marketing

• **Reassurance and reliance messages:** This last point is particularly important in modern mythology. Brands must rely on people's willingness to rely on them — a relationship that brands actively propagate amongst consumers. If people weren't willing to be trusting of products, then brands would find it virtually impossible to form enduring bonds with consumers.

Advertising creates the link with consumers by placing products amongst natural Loyalist situations. This is exemplified by one of the most successful advertising scenarios of all time — two friends in a kitchen. This approach, which has become a fairly standard tool of household products over the past few decades, focuses on the kitchen or household situation involving friends and neighbors. This situation is effective because it leverages some strong, subliminal signals. First, you know that there's familiarity and trust between the two because they're in an informal home situation together. The kitchen is the territory of best friends and familiar figures — not distant, formal relations. Second, in this situation, one friend usually gives the other some sort of personal advice about the product. This implies that the product is good enough that friends would be willing to recommend it to each other.

The purpose of portraying products involved in these types of Loyalist situations is the reassurance the association with friendship confers onto products. As we've seen in many of the other mythic profiles, a key function of advertising is to give consumers comfort and familiarity with brands and to reassure consumers that they're making smart, reliable choices. This trust is essential. After all, food manufacturers are asking consumers to ingest their products; cosmetics producers are encouraging consumers to apply products to their face; and automobile manufacturers are encouraging consumers to entrust their lives to the cars. There simply has to be some degree of familiarity and trust for consumers to use products.

It really should be no surprise that utilizing the Loyalist archetype provides such an effective method of selling. After all, when it comes to a recommendation, who are you going to trust most — your friends or the checkout girl at the local supermarket? Peer endorsement is a very credible way of providing reassurance through what is effectively a personal guarantee. Friends are not likely to disappear tomorrow, so their endorsement has an enduring quality to it. The power of peer endorsement is becoming more popular today in the Image Economy through so-called viral concepts. In viral marketing, particularly on the Internet, marketers encourage consumers to pass things on to their friends. And those friends often read about or try things because they trust the person from whom it has come.

A further point about reassurance messaging is that, in some cases, consumers are spending hundreds or even thousands of dollars on a product or a service. Consumers have a natural concern about parting with their hard-earned cash. But it runs deeper than that. Choosing the wrong brand reflects badly on the user. If they choose unwisely, they feel let down by the product. After all, they've bought into more than just the functionality of the product — they've often bought into the brand dream as well. So showing products in relation to Loyalists sends a subtle, yet incredibly important, message of reassurance. Therefore, another facet of the way the Loyalist archetype supports the process of commercial connection is the emotional reliability this figure connotes. Consumers rely upon products in functional terms every day. But, as just stated, consumers have a lot of emotional "skin in the game" as well. Whether they recognize it or not, consumers invest themselves emotionally in their selection of brands and entertainment — they don't make solely rational choices. So the Loyalist archetype is particularly helpful in engendering emotional empathy between brands and consumers in order to build a bond of trust.

•   **Brands as buddies:** Marketers often build this trust by positioning the product itself as a "buddy". This can happen across a number of categories: your sports car can be your buddy (think of all those great times you two had with the top down); your chocolate bar can be your buddy (which gives you a lift when you need it); and your can of soda can be one too. Coca-Cola has long capitalized on being a buddy that provides familiarity and an enjoyable break. This, of course, is no accident; like most other things in modern mythology, it's the result of seeds that have been purposefully planted. A classic Coca-Cola TV spot from the 1970s using the U.S. football legend "Mean" Joe Greene exemplifies how this works.[2] On the surface, the commercial follows a simple story: Joe Greene hobbles off the field after a tough game. A young fan — a boy of 12 — offers him words of encouragement and his Coke. "Mean" Joe downs the Coke, then turns to the child and returns the favor by tossing him his game jersey.

This simple story has a couple of meaningful elements that contribute to the mythology and ultimate effectiveness of the communication. First, there's the obvious juxtaposition of the two — the giant of a man and the boy. It dredges up the age-old image of the elephant befriending the mouse. The gulf between the two is further highlighted by the fact that one is a wounded warrior (he's named "Mean" Joe for a reason, after all) and the other is an innocent child. From appearances, there aren't many people less likely to find a common bond than these two. But in the middle is the product that acts as the intermediary. Their mutual enjoyment of Coke provides the glue, triggering the bond of friendship. Thus, the little boy doesn't hesitate to make an offering of his Coke to the imposing player, and "Mean" Joe recognizes the kindness and courage and reciprocates with his jersey. Their trade symbolizes the instant bond they have struck, catalyzed by their mutual buddy, Coke.

The notion of a product as a "friend" is a very powerful way in which modern mythology creates product affinity and loyalty. The ultimate goal of companies is to have their products find a way into consumers' lives to the point that they are seen as a mainstay and an invaluable part of their routines. Products can become permanent, familiar and trusted fixtures. M&M's chocolates serves as another example of a buddy brand. For many consumers, M&M's has become a friendly comfort — something they can turn to when they want a treat. The colorful M&M's characters, featured consistently in their advertising for many years, provide not only a mnemonic trigger for the brand but also characters to whom consumers become attached. When brands are successful at creating this type of emotional bond, it virtually ensures that a competitive price promotion will pale in comparison to the durable trust and friendship that the product has created.

But this bond also requires advertisers' respect and careful treatment. Even Coke, one of the world's most venerable and best-managed brands, is subject to the invisible forces of archetypes. If it occasionally loses its way, consumers and even its own bottlers can react very quickly.[3] This was the case with a set of edgy commercials that the company produced in the United States a couple of years ago. In one commercial, a wheelchair-bound grandmother flies off the handle at a family reunion when she finds out that there's no Coke available. Another spot featured two high-school friends at their graduation almost getting into a fight for the same reason.[4] This attempt to be irreverent and surprising in order to appeal to a younger audience failed to maintain the consistency of the archetypes that consumers have come to know and associate with Coke, especially as a "buddy brand". When companies stray too far from the archetypes that provide the subconscious foundation for their brand, it can eventually erode the bonds they have worked so hard to create.

The Mythic Figure in Entertainment and Popular Culture

• **Friends and comrades in entertainment:** While grand battles of good and evil make for great films, so does the less dramatic (but equally compelling) story of true friendship. The story of Loyalists coming together generates the basis for many unforgettable stories. In fact, the world of entertainment thrives on stories of human interaction and interconnection.

In various forms of entertainment, the Loyalist appears as the friend or comrade. One commonly recognized form, which we saw already in the advertising process, is the next-door neighbor. By virtue of proximity, neighbors have a natural context for interaction. Many classic shows from the early days of American and English TV, such as *I Love Lucy*[5], focused on situations around neighbors. The interplay of Ricky and Lucy and their apartment neighbors and friends, the Mertzes, was the basis of the show. Over time, programs became more inventive in the locations they chose to show this interaction. Shows also featured places such as the neighborhood bar in *Cheers*[6] that became the setting for the interaction and hilarity of friendship. What has remained consistent in this entertainment genre over the years is that the Loyalist situation encourages the interaction and bonding of friends.

One of the most popular contemporary examples of the Loyalist in modern mythology is the American TV show *Friends*.[7] The program revolves around a group of friends — three men and three women — who live in New York City. They are peers and contemporaries who have a lot in common. But as happens with any Loyalist, they go through trying times together that test their friendship. What has perhaps helped make this show such an enormous hit is the fact that this testing and re-proving of friendship comes in many interesting combinations that stem from having six people who are friends. Sometimes the strife is amongst roommates, sometimes it's the boys against the girls, and sometime it's amongst just two of them as lovers or friends. These different combinations help to keep things interesting and varied, as well as leading to the humor in the show.

The dynamics of the Loyalist can often extend to a wider group that is brought together by some common cause, situation or location. This can happen to people of all ages, as demonstrated in the movie *Stand by Me*[8], which is a bonding story featuring pubescent boys. The wider group dynamic of the Loyalists often happens in war movies as well, which tend to focus on the dynamics of loyalty and sacrifice for comrades that is generated in extreme situations such as war. *Saving Private Ryan, Band of Brothers*[9] and others are examples of this camaraderie and the bonding process.

• **The odd couples:** Loyalists are not necessarily carbon copies of each other. More often, they are diverse or even opposite characters. However, rather than being opposites who compete — such as the Hero and Anti-Hero — these opposites attract and grow together despite their seemingly vast differences. These odd pairings subliminally communicate to viewers the gulf they must bridge to become friends. Yet they discover that they do have valuable common ground, despite their apparent differences.

A classic example of this pairing of opposites is the movie and TV series *The Odd Couple*.[10] Despite the fact that Felix Unger is fanatically neat and his roommate, Oscar Madison, is a confirmed slob, they are bonded as friends — a truly odd couple. They are just one of a long line of unlikely buddies who manage to span the gap. Buzz Lightyear and Woody in *Toy Story* and Han Solo and Luke Skywalker in *Star Wars* are other well-known examples.

Besides being odd, loyalist pairings are sometimes not on even terms either. One of them shows a weakness or perhaps suffers from being an outcast or a misfit. So the process of the two people coming to terms with each other is complex. It not only involves one partner accepting the other; it sometimes involves the weaker one coming of age in the process. The story of *Thelma & Louise*[11] highlights this point. While Thelma (played by Geena Davis) starts out as unconfident and more malleable than her friend Louise (played by Susan Sarandon), she turns out to be hard as nails. When they suddenly find themselves unfairly on the wrong side of the law, the real proving of their loyalty begins. By facing a common injustice, the two discover even deeper bonds and the true extent of their friendship.

The process of building bonds of friendship underscores a couple of universal life lessons. First, the Loyalist uncovers and appreciates his friend's deeper qualities. In the process of interaction, the Loyalist moves beyond the outward characteristics of the partner and focuses on the internal character strengths that make them endearing. The Loyalist re-learns the old moral not to "judge the book by its cover". The second message, which also connects universally to viewers, is that the process of friendship must allow for growth and real exchange between two friends. Friendship is an organic, two-way process, with people learning from each other and changing as a result. The vines of friendship invariably intertwine as they grow.

- **The Loyalist and the TV talk-show format:** TV talk shows today generate huge audiences and have wide appeal around the world, based in large part upon the dynamics of the Loyalist archetype. If you take a close look at the format and style of most talk shows, you'll realize that it's not far off the "two friends in a kitchen" approach that has been such an effective mainstay of product marketing.

First, there's the setting. Guests sit in large, comfy chairs or couches, with the host sitting next to them, coffee mug at the ready. Fundamentally, this setting is meant to create the atmosphere of both congeniality and relaxation that characterizes the atmosphere around proven friends. They are not on guard; they are there to interact and share confidences.

Second, most talk-show anchors pitch themselves as kind, understanding and interested people — confidants. Hosts such as Oprah and Larry King serve as "friends" to the various personalities who appear on their show. They talk with their guests about often intimate subjects, getting them to spill their guts about the tribulations, secrets and traumas in their lives, just as friends share confidences in each other's living rooms or kitchens. This provides entertainment because audiences feel that they too are like friends who are privy to the confidences about how stars really feel. The various guests become a bit more *real* for the millions of people glued to their TV sets. The wider goal, though, of this type of entertainment is to have the hosts themselves become like friends for viewers. Over time, successful hosts become trusted, regular fixtures in many people's viewing schedules. Like products, entertainers can prosper from the dynamics of the Loyalist.

Mythic Highlights to Note

- **The roots of universal appeal:** This figure represents the friend in all of us — the need to form lasting connections with others and to build confidences.
- **Loyalist combinations:** Loyalists come in a multiplicity of groupings, from pairs up to larger groups.
- **Odd couples:** Loyalists often come in seemingly odd combinations, which serves to emphasize the distance they must overcome to form a bond.

- **Friends as endorsers:** In advertising, situations that portray two friends add to the inherent trust and reassurance that friends lend to the "endorsement" process.
- **Buddy products:** Some products pitch themselves in the role of a friend, which will be relied upon like a buddy.

"The earth is my mother —

and on her bosom I will recline.

Tecumseh[1]

Mythic Profile

The

Mother
of Goodness

16

An Introduction to the Mother of Goodness

The Mother of Goodness creates perhaps the most fundamental archetypal bond of all the mythic figures.[2] She is the warm, nurturing source of life and a symbol of the bounty of Nature. Laden with familiar imagery, the Mother of Goodness is present in many commercial images today. She is the archetypal power behind the common advertising messages of purity, wholesomeness and all-natural ingredients. In this mythic profile, we'll see why the Mother of Goodness is the epitome of caring and an effective antidote to an increasingly mechanical and engineered world.

• **The universal messages associated with this mythic figure:** The Mother of Goodness represents the universal messages of purity, nourishment and motherly warmth.

• **Timeless dynamics in summary:** The Mother of Goodness, like the Creator, brings things into existence. However, while the Creator represents creativity and the intellectual powers of invention, the Mother of Goodness stands for creation through corporeal means by giving birth. So, unlike many of the other mythic figures which have unisex dynamics, the Mother of Goodness is a singularly female archetype.

The bond we have with this archetype is part of our survival instincts. From the first moments of life, babies seek the warmth and nourishment of their mother's bosom. But even adults feel an ongoing connection to the Mother of Goodness, given that nourishment is an essential requirement of everyone's physiological needs. As Maslow pointed out in his famous hierarchy of needs, our basic requirements take priority. The Mother of Goodness, therefore, is guaranteed a primary position in the pecking order of importance — a key point that relates to the sales process, as we will see shortly. However, nourishment is more than just a necessity; it is also a key source of human pleasure. People find comfort and a sense of well-being from receiving sustenance. So the Mother of Goodness is both comforting and vital.

Despite the fact that the Mother of Goodness is a bearer of life, she is not a sexual figure. That distinction goes to the Siren archetype, which we've already covered.[3] The Mother of Goodness is completely pure — the expression of warmth and love without sexual connotations. She is, therefore, devoid of the inherent risks and potential dangers that we saw associated with the Siren. In fact, a defining characteristic of the Mother of Goodness is the fact she can be fully trusted. The Mother of Goodness, as Mother Earth, is completely centered.

At times, the Mother of Goodness figure is expressed in an incarnation as a young maiden, who, like the Mother of Goodness, is pure. The young maiden will blossom one day into a Mother of Goodness, who in turn will bring forth life, allowing the endless cycle of nature to continue. Therefore, when we see the young maiden in modern mythology, she symbolizes the power of the Mother of Goodness to provide rejuvenation and regeneration. She serves as a reminder of the potential for new life and vitality.

The Mythic Figure in Advertising and Marketing

The hallmarks of the Mother of Goodness — purity, nourishment and comforting warmth — create very powerful connections in the modern mythology of selling products. We will consider each of these points, starting with the role of purity in products today.

•   **Purity and trust messaging:** As we've seen, technology and engineering are now an integral part of many of the things people consume in the Image Economy. This extends well beyond mechanical products and includes even basic foodstuffs. Consider, for example, the amount of processing that goes into many of the products on supermarket shelves or the increasing presence of genetically "engineered" crops. As a result, while technology is a very powerful force in modern mythology, there is a growing public backlash amongst some consumers against the over-processing of nature. In some cases, technology is even the focus of consumer suspicion.

In this environment, all-natural products, leveraging subliminal connections with the Mother of Goodness, provide an antidote to consumer concern. Many of the New Age corporations that have emerged in the past couple of decades have successfully tapped the latent consumer desire to get back to basics — to the purity of Mother Nature. They provide unadulterated products, ranging from all-natural sodas to facial soaps made from ingredients grown in the rainforest. The all-natural message of these types of products effectively allays consumer concerns by linking them with purity. This is conveyed in advertising and marketing through language that stresses that products are "100%" and "contain no additives", or by using the word "pure" on the packaging or in the advertising. Words such as "fresh" and "gentle" also bestow upon products some of the innate associations we make with the Mother of Goodness.

Over time, this has fostered another equation that has become ingrained as part of consumers' belief systems; namely, that *purity* equals *trust*. In a mythological sense, this trust is completely logical, since the Mother of Goodness figure — a symbol of both purity and nature — engenders a deep and abiding trust. So when products tout their all-natural ingredients, they are leveraging consumers' mythic connections with this archetype in order to create a parallel trust in their product. The associative equation that kicks in is simple: "Since you trust nature, you can trust us, because our products are all-natural."

As we've observed, a basic premise of modern mythology is that it builds consumer connections through both overt and symbolic means. The Mother of Goodness is rich in symbols that trigger deeper associations. Milk, as the mother's water of life, is one of these symbols. Women's facial and skin-care products often highlight the inclusion of milk as a way to convey purity and the wholesomeness of the product. The color white is another symbol, which conveys purity in many cultures. Consequently, white is used predominantly in packaging for products that wish to communicate the purity of their ingredients. This point applies in particular to facial and skin-care products, which require a great deal of trust given their intended use on consumers' skin.

Just how strong the bonds of trust are becomes abundantly clear when something goes wrong. This, unfortunately, was the case with Snow Brand milk from Japan.[4] Over decades, Snow Brand had effectively built its position as the ultimate brand of trust in the Japanese market. This was not due simply to Snow's position as the largest milk producer in Japan. It was the result of its efforts to build an association between the product and purity, as symbolized by the brand name. Consequently the company had become a dominant Mother of Goodness icon, with its milk engendering nearly the same level of trust as mother's milk.

However, this all went completely and tragically wrong when thousands of people became sick from drinking Snow as a result of toxic-producing bacteria in the product. What followed was consumer outrage and a sense of betrayal because people had come to believe so deeply in the mythology of the brand. In the end, the incident shattered a belief, carefully cultivated over years, that the brand genuinely represented a purity that consumers could trust. This example provides a real-world reminder that the Image Economy is an exacting environment. Brand mishaps can have major consequences that reverberate deeply in the psyche of the consumers. It also shows how the archetypes associated with a brand become part of its invisible equity, which must be guarded with great care.

•　**Nourishment and rejuvenation messaging:** Purity and trust serve as the baseline of belief for many products. However, a variety of goods — particularly food products — must also convey how effective they are at providing wholesomeness and enrichment as well. The Mother of Goodness archetype plays a critical role in this aspect of messaging, too, since these qualities are linked to the archetype.

A number of symbols that represent nature's fecundity are used regularly in modern mythology to imbue products with the promise of providing nourishment. Pristine mountain pastures filled with grazing cows, and tropical jungles with waterfalls are commonplace in ads and packaging. So too are fruit and flowers, which immediately convey the richness of the land. Subconsciously, both flowers and fruit have the added benefit of symbolizing pregnancy, since fruit visibly ripens and grows, and flowers bud and then burst forth in full bloom. Their inclusion in advertising and messaging provides a subliminal reminder to viewers of the potency that leads to nature's bounty.

A wide range of products, such as shampoo and butter, use these symbols to link wholesomeness and effectiveness to their products. Tropicana Orange Juice is a good example.[5] The name, with its derivation from "tropical", conveys more than simply orange juice; it gives the brand rich associations with the nourishment of nature in general, since tropical settings are the ultimate expression of nature's verdant potency. Subtly, this helps convince consumers that the product will be good for them and will "work" at giving them nourishment.

The maiden, the young, virginal incarnation of the Mother of Goodness, is also an effective symbol for communicating nourishment. However, she is most frequently linked to rejuvenation — literally, the ability to make something young again. Products often promise to replenish as well as nourish. Damaged, split hair, for example, can be made shiny again, and health drinks promise to invigorate and fortify their users. The frequent inclusion of young women in this type of advertising, particularly for products such as hair care, reminds us of freshness and restored vitality. It also serves as a symbol of regeneration, subliminally supporting the effectiveness of the products to invigorate consumers.

Again symbols of nature play an important, subconscious role, this time communicating rejuvenation. Water is the most common of these key symbols. Water is an essential — the main component of the human body. This essential role of water in replenishing and revitalizing is underscored through language on packaging and in commercials via product names that contain the word "essence" or those that use the word "essential" on the packaging. This is often coupled with visual mnemonics such as waterfalls, rain showers and raindrops. A walk around any grocery store aisle will provide ample evidence of this.

Given the importance of water to life, it has broad symbolic meaning in most societies. In particular, though, water represents purification, as evidenced by its use in most religions. Consequently, the inclusion of water in advertising and packaging is a common way to communicate that a product is pure as well as effective at revitalizing.

- **Products of care and comfort:** The penultimate goal of many advertisers is to leverage the innate association of motherhood with warmth and love to provide their products with a halo of motherly caring. When brands achieve this, people will actually expect — and seek — comfort from these products. Products can elevate themselves to the position of surrogate nurturers that mirror, on a subliminal level, the trust that people have in their mothers. This doesn't happen automatically because a product is all-natural, since even 100%-natural products can sometimes come across as a bit cold if the right mythology isn't actively built around them. A boiled potato, for example, is all-natural and provides nutrients, but it doesn't necessarily win hearts! Modern mythology must encourage the right psychological linkages to make the magic work and build a lasting bond.

In some cases, the product serves as an aid to consumers as they provide love and warmth to others. Baby powder is a good example of this. Many of the category ads highlight the use of the product as part of the mother's loving routine of cleaning and caring for her infant. The advertising doesn't normally focus on the clinical aspects of the product. Instead, it highlights the emotional bonding of providing this care, with the product positioned as playing a meaningful role — the mother's trustworthy helper — in caring for the child. Through the naming of their products, many baby-product companies — Care brand, and Mother's Care products from the U.K., for example — foster the belief that they are nurturers. Nurturing is essential for babies; so, building the mythology of a product as a surrogate nurturer helps to subliminally cement a product's place in consumers' hierarchy of needs.

Baby products are perhaps obvious candidates for a linkage to caring. But other types of products also play a role as surrogate nurturers. Aunt Jemima pancake mixes provide another example.[6] The advertising icon of Aunt Jemima serves as a mnemonic to remind consumers of nurturing and care. Her broad, warm smile on the package is meant to stick in consumers' heads as they tuck into pancakes made from the mix that bears her name. Consumers then feel like she's part of the care that went into the mix, somehow making the pancakes taste better (more like Mom's). This may seem far-fetched, but recall for a moment the case of the Coke and Pepsi taste tests and the powerful effect that the mind can have over a person's taste buds. Consumers, particularly mothers, often like using surrogate-nurturer products because they amplify the natural feelings that they already have about looking after their family. Indeed, modern mythology conditions moms to feel that they are doing a better job of it when they use products that are symbolic of caring.

The Mythic Figure in Entertainment and Popular Culture

Even in an era of violent programming and gratuitous sex, the purity and caring of the Mother of Goodness archetype still wins hearts. The reason is simple: the entertainment process, similar to the sales process, connects people to the fundamental qualities of this mythic figure. When people sometimes seek an escape from the pressures of modern life, stories of purity and innocence offer a temporary refuge. Thus entertainment focused on the Mother of Goodness can provide a feeling of warmth and comfort, just like some products. And, if we go back to the basic point about mythology, we see that mythic figures provide icons that people emulate and from which they learn. Characters or public figures that embody purity and motherly warmth help guide and influence the public psyche.

- **Icons of motherly care:** Julie Andrews as the nanny, Maria, in the film *The Sound of Music*[7] exemplifies how the Mother of Goodness archetype can be embodied in entertainment. In the film, Maria arrives at the Von Trapp family as a fresh, pure maiden — a young nun who has left the order. Although she is not the biological mother of the Von Trapp children, she transforms into the Mother of Goodness in her interaction with them. She nurtures and cares for them, creating a strong bond of trust and love. In the process, Maria also reinvigorates the entire family. When she temporarily flees their home, the children seek her out because of the connection they have with her. Like all Mothers of Goodness, she has become a vital part of their lives. The pristine mountain settings of the film further add to its general ambiance of wholesomeness. The continuing popularity of the movie demonstrates the strong appeal that the Mother of Goodness can have in entertainment and in powering personalities. The role turned Andrews into a symbol of purity and wholesomeness for an entire generation. These traits, in fact, became a defining part of Julie Andrews's ongoing public image well after she starred in the movie, perhaps because people simply wanted to believe that someone as fresh and wholesome as Maria really existed.

Icons of motherly caring can be found in real life as well as in entertainment. The late Mother Theresa is known to millions of people around the world for her charity work. As the head of the Missionaries of Charity in Calcutta, Mother Theresa was much more than a religious symbol. She came to represent human caring and charity in general. Over the decades, Mother Theresa served the destitute and ill and acted as a mother to thousands of orphans. She even provided warmth and care for Calcutta's lepers.[8] Consequently, people of many nationalities and religious faiths came to admire her virtues of purity and purpose. In these seemingly cynical times, societies still genuinely need and seek symbols of motherly care.

• **Icons of innocence:** The defining archetypal traits of purity and innocence also provide entertainment value. A good example of this is the fairy-tale figure of Snow White. Starting with her name, everything about Snow White reflects the essence of the Mother of Goodness archetype in the form of a young maiden. Snow White is a great beauty — the "fairest of them all", according to the mirror on the wall. Yet she is non-threatening in a sexual sense, despite the fact that her evil stepmother sees her as a rival and a threat. Instead, Snow White's innocence shines through, which is why the huntsman who is supposed to kill her takes pity on her. When Snow White eventually comes upon the seven dwarves' house, she takes up the symbolic role of their mother, cooking and cleaning and caring for them. The dwarves, by their diminutive size, seem like children in comparison to Snow White, although she is herself a child. The young, innocent maiden blossoms into the caring Mother of Goodness, right in front of young viewers' eyes.

Children and adults alike have long delighted in this tale, both in books and on screen from Walt Disney. *Snow White* "works" as a piece of entertainment because it connects people back to the root dynamics of archetypes. Disney has shown, through other figures of innocence such as Bambi, how successful and lucrative the tapping of archetypes can be for entertaining people.

A final example, this time from Japan, further illustrates how icons of innocence can be resonant symbols in popular culture and effective money-spinners too. Hello Kitty is a world-famous character that can be found on over 15,000 merchandising items.[9] Everything from toasters to schoolbooks now bears the likeness of this innocent, wide-eyed cat. Hello Kitty's appeal originally started amongst young Japanese schoolgirls. However, over the course of 25 years, Hello Kitty's popularity has spread to cover a wide variety of fans, including men. To some viewers, Hello Kitty is nondescript. However, to loyalists, Hello Kitty is a symbol that provides them with a connection to innocence. The doe-eyed character couldn't be less threatening — a small, pink kitten with soft curves and no mouth.

Yet Hello Kitty still connects in a powerful way that has enabled it to generate an estimated US$1 billion a year in sales through licensing. It seems that fans want to have Hello Kitty on virtually every item imaginable. In explaining Hello Kitty's success, its creator claims that it works on a "heart-to-heart" basis — a clear recognition of the deeper communicative and motivational power of archetypes.[10] The Siren sells effectively because of sex, but clearly the Mother of Goodness, in a very different way, sells too.

Mythic Highlights to Note

- **The roots of eternal and universal appeal:** This figure represents the purity in all of us — the need to hold certain things sacred and undefiled.
- **A strong set of symbols:** The Mother of Goodness has a particularly strong association with a number of symbols, particularly the color white, water and fruit symbolism. These stand for purity and nature's rich bounty, which relate back to their ability to effectively provide nourishment.
- **Products as surrogate nurturers:** Products which build a bond of caring can be seen as surrogate nurturers — products that either help people care for others or make consumers feel cared for by consuming them.
- **The young maiden:** The Mother of Goodness can also be expressed through the young maiden figure that symbolizes rejuvenation.

"A joke's a very serious thing."

Charles Churchill[1]

Mythic Profile

The
Little
Trickster

17

An Introduction to the Little Trickster

On the one hand innocent, on the other hand a terror, the Little Trickster figure[2] angers and frustrates while he amuses and charms. This well-celebrated figure of the Trickster is a delightful entertainer as Bugs Bunny, Dennis the Menace, Pee-Wee Hermann and Bart Simpson. But this figure is more than a delight. Like the best of court jesters, he is able to make stinging barbs and occasional astute comments before retiring from harm's way. As we'll see in this profile, in addition to tickling consumers' funny bones, the Little Trickster can have a serious impact on the sales process.

• **The universal messages associated with this figure:** The Little Trickster represents the universal messages of humor, non-conformity and the element of surprise.

• **Timeless dynamics in summary:** The Little Trickster relishes the opportunity to sabotage the normalcy of the day. In fact, that's his job description. The Little Trickster lives to trick, fool and surprise people with jokes. He also finds himself unwittingly embroiled in surprising situations or predicaments, frequently of his own creation. In the process of disrupting the typical course of events, he exposes a couple of things about his basic nature.

First, the Little Trickster is the joker in the deck; no one knows when he'll appear or what he might do next. Will he suddenly make a wisecrack? Is he hiding something? Will he accidentally break something? Most importantly, is he lying? The most predictable and consistent thing about the Little Trickster is actually his unpredictability.

Second, a key reason he's unpredictable is that he's also uncontrollable. The Little Trickster doesn't toe anybody's line, including his own. Instead, he often succumbs to the temptation to play pranks and can be amazed at his own lack of self-control. It is, however, his nature.

Next, the Little Trickster has an uncanny eye for the absurd. As with the other mythic figures, there's a bit of "Everyman" in the Little Trickster. He reminds most people of their own foolishness and folly as well as expressing some of the things they wish they could get away with. His antics can prompt other people to act absurdly too. In the process, he exposes the ridiculous and the sublime in life. Also, through naïveté or irreverence, he frequently causes people embarrassment. So the Little Trickster acts as a pressure valve, giving people a chance to take a break from the weighty issues of life to stop and have a good laugh. The Little Trickster brings equilibrium to situations through levity.

There is, however, a more serious purpose to the Little Trickster than just fun and jokes. This mythic character fundamentally represents a challenge to conformity and the order of things and therefore can be a critical witness to events. In his own way, the Little Trickster keeps people honest by pointing out hypocrisy and stupidity, although he can also be a liar. The Little Trickster is particularly effective at mocking, since he has the veil of innocence, from behind which he can shoot his barbs at society. He is not evil, but he can definitely be a piercing critic with his comments. So despite the antics surrounding the Little Trickster, this mythic figure is an effective foil for occasionally delivering serious messages that reach deep into people's hearts.

The Mythic Figure in Advertising and Marketing

• **Humor in the sales pitch:** These archetypal traits — in particular, humor — frequently enable the Little Trickster to soften the sales pitch and close the sale. The most obvious reason why humor is an effective sales tool in advertising and marketing is that it can improve the likability of the product. Products are not inherently warm or friendly. An aluminum can full of soda or a new car off the assembly line doesn't warm your heart; it takes the magic of modern mythology to entice people to feel some sort of positive emotions towards products. Using humor elicits an immediate reaction from consumers and builds a lasting, positive association in their minds by attaching delight to products. Little Trickster figures in advertising then serve as mnemonics that repeatedly trigger pleasurable memories connected to the product. Therefore, it's hard not to smile when you think of funny things you've seen and to have a feeling of goodwill towards the products that make you smile.

In some cases, humor is attached to products whose primary benefit is pleasure. Chocolates and other types of food treats are good examples. With these types of products, humor is intended to build a positive association between the product and the happiness derived from consuming it. M&M's chocolates achieve this by using characters that correspond to the various colors of M&M's found in the pack. This is a particularly clever strategy because the Little Tricksters in this case — the characters — are actually the product incarnate. So if you like the M&M's advertising, it more directly equates with liking the actual product. Jell-O brand pudding, for example, ran a famous campaign for years that featured the comedian Bill Cosby interacting with small kids — Little Tricksters — who said funny things about liking pudding.[3] This created a sense of fun and pleasure around consuming the product — another effective way to create consumer bonds.

• **Humor as covert selling:** Even products that involve complex technology or have very serious purposes, such as air-courier services or automobiles, can effectively leverage the archetypal power of the Little Trickster. One way they do this is to use the spontaneity that's a key trait of the Little Trickster to create a *surprise attack* effect with consumers. This old war tactic is effective since humor disarms consumers, causing them to drop their normal defenses of cynicism and doubt. By taking the hard edges off the sales process, humorous advertising can get consumers on the advertisers' side. This makes the Little Trickster archetype a great covert weapon in the war for a slice of consumers' attention.

FedEx is a good example of this point. When it pioneered the overnight-delivery category in the United States, FedEx used a variety of hilarious spots, one of the most memorable of which featured a man speed-talking his way through the day.[4] This humorous approach might have seemed illogical for a product that was trying to get people to both know and trust it. FedEx had plenty of other, serious, communication routes it could have taken, particularly given the opportunity to highlight the sophisticated hardware and logistics that go into running a fleet of planes. But a humorous approach enabled the company to create great recall and awareness — vital prerequisites for a product trying to stake out territory in consumers' minds. Humor, as perhaps the least-expected route for FedEx to take, made an indelible mark in many consumers' psyches. At the same time, the comic foil still allowed it to communicate important messages about its product, such as the fact you can rely on FedEx to get your parcel to its destination overnight.

The figure of Joe Isuzu for Isuzu Motors in the U.S. is another good example of using humor as a cover for a serious sales message.[5] Joe, who acted as the pitchman in a series of commercials for the company, was the quintessential Little Trickster — naughty, unpredictable and a complete liar. In fact, every commercial featured Joe with a goofy, boyish grin lying about the vehicles while subtitles told the real facts. This approach to selling cars was both amusing and brilliantly effective. The use of Joe, who so obviously lies, actually disarms consumers who have become guarded against sleazy car salesmen and the hard-sell advertising approach that is typical in the category. But by using the foil of Joe Isuzu, the company was then able to slip in relevant information about its cars. This was a particularly smart alternative to messages of leadership (via the Power-broker) or technological superiority (via the Change Master) and enabled it to break through in a crowded advertising category. As Joe and others prove, the Little Trickster can make an effective modern mythology using humor and spontaneity.

But a word of caution is required here. The use of the Trickster archetype doesn't guarantee success. Humor, like sex, is too often used gratuitously in the Image Economy. In such cases, the advertising might amuse consumers temporarily, but it usually falls completely flat when it comes to motivating them. For humor to work effectively, it must be linked to something that makes a meaningful point about the product or casts the product in a new light that enhances its relevance and appeal to consumers. A good chuckle, unsupported by any link to the product-user dynamic, can quickly evaporate without a trace from consumers' minds.

The Mythic Figure in Entertainment and Popular Culture

• **Great figures of entertainment:** Since the Little Trickster figure puts us all in touch with the inherent absurdity of things that surround us, he or she is the root of comedy. In entertainment, the Little Trickster's naughtiness and unpredictability amuses and frequently delights audiences. Consequently, expressions of this mythic figure are amongst the most beloved in entertainment: Dennis the Menace, the Lil' Rascals, Bart Simpson, McCaulay Culkin in *Home Alone*[6], to name but a few. All of these Little Tricksters offer a mix of innocence and mischief that causes others, particularly adults, to feel embarrassed and vexed. Sometimes, the Little Trickster is purposely paired with an adult. The asymmetry of child and adult is innately fascinating and funny since it is such a seemingly uneven battle. However, the Little Trickster can often prevail. Luckily, the Tricksters' innocence and youth neutralizes otherwise hostile feelings that adults might have towards them because of the predicaments they are put in.

It's important to note that the Little Trickster needn't actually be little or young. Paul Reubens' comedy persona of Pee-Wee Hermann, of *Pee-Wee's Playhouse* and *Pee-Wee's Big Adventure* fame, is a good example of this.[7] Pee-Wee is a man-child who acts and thinks like any bratty kid. His bow tie and trademark white shoes add to his juvenile, innocent appearance. Yet Pee-Wee's sometime caustic barbs show his colors as a Little Trickster. Of course, true to Trickster form, Pee-Wee laughs after delivering a comment and runs off with a goofy grin on his face.

Other adult stars, such as Jerry Lewis, and Rowan Atkinson as Mr. Bean[8], have built their comedy fame on fundamentally childish characters that could equally be called Little Tricksters. Even Lucille Ball had traces of the archetypal Trickster figure. Despite the fact that she was a middle-aged woman at the height of her comic career, she embodied the spirit of innocence, spontaneity and child-like glee that this archetype evokes.

- **Cartoon humor:** The cartoon medium is particularly well suited to Little Tricksters since an animated format allows them to exaggerate their tricks and pranks. Cartoon characters can change costumes instantly, hold live grenades that don't kill them, and fall off the edge of cliffs, only to dust themselves off and head back for more. As a result, cartoons are fast paced and focused on action that amplifies their character traits.

Also in keeping with the key dynamics of the Little Trickster, cartoon tricks often turn back on those who initiate them. Tom usually gets caught in the trap he's set to catch Jerry, while the rocket that Wile E. Coyote shoots at the Roadrunner invariably boomerangs back on him.[9] This boomerang effect is perhaps one of the most common elements in cartoons because it reflects the randomness of the Little Trickster and trickery in general; once a trick is set in motion, it is out of everyone's control. The wild card of humor can be played on anyone, even the Little Trickster.

Consequently, Little Tricksters are the mainstay of cartoons. Tom and Jerry, Tweety, the Roadrunner, Goofy and Bugs Bunny all embody this archetype.[10] Bugs Bunny, though, is perhaps the epitome of the Little Trickster. He is sassy, clever and a source of complete surprise, whether he's hoodwinking Elmer Fudd or giving someone an unexpected smooch on the lips. This rascally rabbit constantly outwits the others in unforeseen ways, mocking them in the process. He is lovable, funny and (most importantly) completely irreverent. Bugs respects no one and nothing is too sacred to be spared from his parody. The same could be said of Bart Simpson[11] — the modern Dennis the Menace[12], complete with attitude and a flair for mischief. When Bart isn't getting himself into or out of trouble, he is sure to tweak society's nose by telling people to "eat my shorts". Both Bart and Bugs are true to form as Little Tricksters.

The cartoon business is wonderfully entertaining for kids and adults alike. But let's not forget that cartoons are also serious business, generating billions of dollars of revenue each year through licensing and other deals, reflecting the appeal and drawing power of the archetype. The Little Trickster is a big money-spinner in the Image Economy.

Mythic Highlights to Note

•   **The roots of universal appeal:** This figure represents the non-conformist in all of us — the need to maintain spontaneity and irony.

•   **Elements of surprise:** The element of surprise can be a very effective way to enhance the memorability of products in the sales process.

•   **A little trickery never hurts:** Although the Little Trickster figure often fibs, cheats and purposely misleads, there is also a core of honesty to what the Little Trickster says. Jokes and dishonesty can sometimes be an effective foil for getting across serious sales messages.

•   **Challenging the status quo:** Humor can be particularly effective by allowing products to challenge the expected, normal order of the day.

•   **Increased likability:** One of the rudimentary reasons that humor is used in marketing is to make products seem more approachable and likable.

" It is a riddle wrapped in a mystery

inside an enigma. **"**

Sir Winston Churchill[1]

Mythic Profile
The
Enigma

An Introduction to the Enigma

In a world of increasing media scrutiny, you might expect the Enigma to be an endangered species. Yet even the persistent paparazzi can't destroy the innate appeal of the unknown or this elusive figure's place in the Image Economy. The Enigma captures the public's imagination in many entertaining forms such as Zorro, X-Men and Batman[2] as well as the various aliens in shows such as *Star Trek* or *The X-Files*.[3] In the advertising and brand world, the Enigma is at work as the closely guarded secret ingredient or secret recipe and an advertising approach called FUD (fear, uncertainty and doubt). As we'll examine in this final mythic profile, the uncertainty of the Enigma is one of the strongest motivational forces in the Image Economy.

*   **The universal messages associated with this figure:** The Enigma represents the universal messages of mystery, suspense and uncertainty.
*   **Timeless dynamics in summary:** Uncertainty is something we all face on a daily basis, ranging from the small unknowns of whether we'll get a flat tire or spill our coffee, up to the great riddles of our existence on a small planet in an infinite universe. This uncertainty can be the source of a great deal of anxiety and can cause real fear. But equally, it can be a rich source of enduring consumer fascination.

Like the Siren, the mythic figure of the Enigma creates an intense, innate attraction. This stems from the deeply rooted psychological response people have to mystery. The story of Pandora's box and her compulsion to lift the lid — despite dire warnings about the consequences — serves as a symbol of mankind's insatiable curiosity.[4] We are all compelled to try to lift the lid on the unknown. Occasionally, mankind's attempts to understand the inexplicable yield positive results, such as the discoveries of science. But, more often, mankind's best efforts to unlock the mysteries of life are futile.

Still, people continue to seek answers to the unknown. We are an incorrigible lot. Until mysteries are solved, they often continue to generate fascination. Ancient riddles and bygone events are still a great source of interest. Tourists still wonder, for example, about how the great pyramids at Giza or the temples of Machu-Picchu in Peru came into being with such great precision. And UFOs reportedly sighted in the 1950s are still the topic of discussion in some circles today. Always slightly beyond reach, the Enigma keeps things ever so tantalizing by giving flashes and clues, only to recede again into mystery. For this reason, the Enigma tends to have a long shelf life and holds people's attention for a very long time.

The Mythic Figure in Advertising and Marketing

• **Selling products using fear, uncertainty and doubt:** On one level, using mystery and uncertainty to sell products and build brands might seem odd. After all, we've examined numerous ways in which advertisers attempt to build consumers' confidence in them by demonstrating, highlighting and elaborating on specific product benefits. Mystery and uncertainty would seem to run counter to this effort. But we must not overlook the fact that anxiety and concern are strong and effective motivating forces. Fear is a key component of one of our most rudimentary instincts, which is the instinct for survival. Since the days when the first caveman sought shelter from a summer lightning storm, the motivating seeds of fear, uncertainty and doubt — FUD — have been prompting our actions. Communicators invariably seek the most effective routes to connect with consumers. So while some advertisers use grinning actors in front of cars and toaster ovens, others take advantage of the human survival instinct and the motivating power of FUD to generate results.

FUD is a common element in a variety of marketing and advertising tactics in the Image Economy. First, it is frequently used to build the need for certain types of products. Why would consumers bother to buy life insurance or a new set of tires unless a sufficient fear had been instilled in them of grave consequences if they don't? FUD is the proverbial stick that marketers use to beat consumers into action. In addition to prompting consideration of existing products, fear and uncertainty can be used to build new categories. Some advertising alerts consumers to dangers that they never knew existed. Scientific discoveries — such as uncovering the dangers of polyunsaturated fats — play a prominent role in creating a fear which, in turn, drives demand for new products that address these problems.

This leads to the other side of the FUD equation, which is the carrot — the consumer payoff. Marketers don't wish to terrorize the public. Rather, their goal is to motivate potential consumers. To achieve this, they often use the transformational message of modern mythology tied into FUD. The resulting advertising shows consumers a problem in order to then sell them a solution as well. This approach not only reminds consumers of the possible threat they face — shoving the worry under their noses to cause the concern — it also then portrays the product as providing a logical solution that will put them in a position of control against uncertainty. The implication is that consumers can master uncertainty, foresee the unforeseeable and protect themselves as best they can against possible calamity and injury — if they just have the product or service being advertised. The messages are quite familiar to us: "If you want to avoid a possible car crash, buy this car with new anti-lock breaks that will save you" or "Use this insecticide to prevent bugs from quietly eating away at your house". In this manner, FUD often makes enticing subliminal promises to give consumers control over uncertainty.

Another reason why FUD serves as an effective advertising approach is that it connects back to the workings of human memory. In addition to short-term and long-term memory, we tend to have "flash-point" memories, which are defining recollections that stick in our brains. These are often associated with shocks to the system, rather than pleasant stimuli. People tend to remember getting punched in the teeth more readily than a nice kiss. So FUD is used as part of a scare-tactic approach which creates a flash-point memory in association with a given topic or product. Public service announcements are particularly famous for their use of gruesome, scary images to convince consumers to use seat belts or to quit smoking. Fear, like sex, motivates consumers with great immediacy.

•　　**Removing doubt to build the brand:** Many advertisers don't go as far as scaring the bejesus out of you to motivate you. Uncertainty and doubt can be used in subtler forms to prompt the desired consumer response. Hints of the Enigma, blended into the message, can be effective as well. Visa, the credit card company, has a long-standing advertising campaign in the U.S. that serves as an apt example of this point. Its advertising highlights shops and other places that do accept Visa and don't take American Express. While part of the message is focused on the ubiquity of Visa card acceptance, underscored with the promise "It's everywhere you want to be", the underlying dynamic of the advertising also directs consumers towards the concern that they'd be out of luck in that establishment if they had an American Express card instead.[5] The implicit message here is that Visa is an antidote to the concern some consumers might have about a retailer not accepting their credit card. By creating some doubt about the acceptance of other cards, Visa can better highlight the relative certainty its product offers.

The example of Visa highlights another key point about FUD. While uncertainty and doubt can be used to recruit new consumers for a product through the process of giving them a worry, it can also be used to persuade consumers to stick with a current product rather than switch to a different one. The Visa campaign not only makes the case that people should select Visa because it will be accepted in more places; it also reminds the many millions of existing users all over the world not to be wooed by competitive credit cards that could leave them in a lurch.

In general, brand names provide consumers with some protection against uncertainty because they are known, trusted entities. They give consumers a degree of assurance that they won't get burned, if they just stick with them. But new products and brands have usually not accrued consumer confidence. Therefore, a specific tactic that enables some products to get around this problem is the use of a money-back guarantee. This approach spares consumers from taking a leap of faith with a product, since the company promises to fully assure consumers of their happiness. In a more basic way, product sampling also helps consumers get over the hurdle of uncertainty about a product by giving them a little free taste or free trial before they spend their money on it.

•   **The use of secret ingredients to create interest:** Another basic way that the Enigma archetype figures in advertising and marketing is the secret ingredient. As noted earlier, mysteries have a certain appeal to people, and some marketers leverage the enticing aspects of the unknown, rather than using fear to drive consumers. This can be done by highlighting a product's secret formula, secret recipe or carefully guarded process of creation — an approach that is particularly popular with food and beverage products. The Colonel's secret recipe for KFC and Coca-Cola's guarded formula are two well-known examples of this approach.[6]

This is ironic, since products that people consume would seem to be the least-likely candidates for using secrecy; you'd think that consumers would demand to know all the details before consuming it. Of course, popular food products, like all products, have to create a certain baseline of credibility and trust. They could never get away with simply telling consumers to drink from an unmarked can. But touches of uncertainty don't always have to create concern; mystery and secrecy can create brand cachet as well. The root message of this communications approach is that the formula or process is so special and important that it's worth keeping a secret. In truth, some of these guarded secrets would probably be of little real consumer interest if they had been made public from the start. However, denying it to public view enhances the mystique and appeal.

But advertisers must tread carefully in their use of the Enigma archetype. Simply creating mystery around a product without a worthwhile link to a message about product superiority or a consumer payoff can cause consumer disappointment. A well-known example of this is Burger King's "Herb" campaign from the U.S. in the mid 1980s. In a series of commercials and related PR, Burger King created a nationwide search for a fictional character named Herb who had never eaten a Burger King product. Massive hype was built around the mystery of this fellow's identity. However, when it was finally revealed that Herb was a "nerd" who wore glasses and pants that were too short, the hype had clearly exceeded the payoff. The campaign continued on, with Herb making personal appearances in Burger King outlets. However, his notoriety quickly fizzled, and the "Herb" campaign became known in the industry as a big disappointment that did little for the company's image and sales.[7]

The Mythic Figure in Entertainment and Popular Culture

Uncertainty, mystery and fear are effective motivators in entertainment as well, building box-office appeal and audience fascination.

• **Mystery and uncertainty in entertainment:** While most personalities seek frequent exposure in the Image Economy, some stars are renowned for purposely distancing themselves from the public. Marlon Brando, J.D. Salinger, Ingrid Bergman and Stanley Kubrick are classic examples of reclusive stars. Rather than resorting to camera-crazed antics that milk the limelight for their own gain, reclusive stars retreat into a vigilantly guarded cocoon far from the public eye. Ironically, this aloofness often adds to their mystique and further fuels public speculation about them. The more they maintain their privacy, in fact, the more consumers wonder what these personalities are really like. As a result, such stars are sometimes the objects of the public's most intense speculation.

Speculation about enigmatic loners generates interest in on-screen Enigmas as well. Zorro, for example, is an intriguing masked Enigma who vanishes without a trace, leaving only his signature "Z". Batman is a brooding loner who makes an appearance to uphold justice and then vanishes from the scene. The X-Men and The Shadow[8] are further examples of cartoon and celluloid Enigmas who maintain their aloofness. Viewers love to watch these entertainment figures, hoping to gain insights about these mysterious individuals. Often, Enigmas lead dual lives (Bruce Wayne/Batman, for example), assuming a different guise or persona for their "other" activities.

Because Enigmas are unknown quantities, a sense of foreboding often surrounds them. Entertainment thrives on this uncertainty in the form of the mystery and suspense genre. The silver screen and TV are jam-packed with situations and characters that embody the Enigma archetype. An example of the loner figure in films is the renegade U.S. Colonel Kurtz from Francis Ford Coppola's *Apocalypse Now*[9]. Audiences are drawn into a surreal journey as Captain Willard, an American intelligence officer, leads a band of men on an odyssey of uncertainty, deep into the jungle to eliminate the enigmatic Kurtz. In some film and TV situations, no specific individual is the object of mystery and suspense; there is just a general sense of ambiguity and uncertainty that creates the suspense. David Lynch's *Twin Peaks*[10] kept viewers enthralled by creating this murky, often chilling tale about the bizarre undercurrents in small-town America. The book business, too, thrives on thrillers that revolve around shadowy figures of mystery. Agatha Christie, Mary Higgins Clarke and others over the years have created a popular segment of the book business based on Enigmas.

• **Mystics and aliens in entertainment:** Since Enigmas reside near the edge of the unknown, they often bridge this and other worlds, frequently serving as intermediaries with unseen forces and worlds beyond. Fortune-tellers and mystics follow in a long line of seers throughout history, from the oracles of Greece to Rasputin, who have been objects of fascination. In the Image Economy, the business of divining the future has gone high-tech. Astrologers such as Jeanne Dixon are regular fixtures in the tabloids and on popular websites. The medium for dispensing mystical advice might have changed but the root power of these figures is the same. And there will probably always be a fascination with mystics and seers since the mystery of what is yet to come is as compelling as unsolved mysteries of the past.

Fortune-tellers are a subset of a broader group of mystical figures that possess a wide range of magical powers. Magicians, such as David Copperfield, Sigfried and Roy, and Penn and Teller, captivate audiences from Las Vegas to Monte Carlo with their powers of magic and illusion. Magic doesn't require $50 tickets, however. Many kids around the world have become enamored of a young Enigma — Harry Potter — making him one of the most lucrative image franchises of recent years.

Outer space is a fertile and popular frontier for the unknown and a common source of Enigmas in entertainment. Audiences love aliens and other space creatures that stretch the boundaries of expectation. These types of Enigmas are truly beyond comprehension since one never knows what types of powers they are likely to possess. This heightened sense of wonder and uncertainty (and sometimes bewilderment) at these creatures makes for tension and suspense that have become a Hollywood staple. In many such stories, humans seek and pursue the unknown. A perfect example of this is Captain Kirk and his Starship Enterprise who "boldly go where no man has gone before". Unlike *Stars Wars*, which has largely familiar characters representing good and evil, *Star Trek* episodes almost always focus on encounters with something new and seemingly indecipherable, and enigmatic. The appeal of the unknown is really the centerpiece of each episode. The same could be said of phenomenally successful shows like *The X-Files* or movies such as *Aliens* and *Close Encounters of the Third Kind*.[11] *The X-Files*, in particular, has built a loyal following of viewers based on the shadowy forces that fill the show.

• **Fear in entertainment:** An even more extreme form of suspense and fear of the unknown can be found in horror films. Films such as *The Legend of Sleepy Hollow*, *The Exorcist* and the cult film *The Blair Witch Project* all focus on the intense fear that can be generated by the unknown.[11] Ghosts and vampires — incarnations of the Enigma — are also common fixtures in horror films. Like other forms of the Enigma, they use the veil of uncertainty to generate fascination and keep viewers glued to the action.

One of the key reasons that suspense and fear are effective entertainers is the strong emotional and physical reactions they trigger in viewers. The human body reacts to suspense and fear with virtually immediate effect: when the emotional alarm-bells ring, the pulse quickens, the adrenaline surges through our bodies and our muscles are tense and ready. This is accompanied by a greater state of mental alertness and preparedness than normal, as we stand ready to deal with danger. Some people love the "rush" of getting scared, particularly in a day and age when the natural environment around them is so tame and sedate. This thrill of fear is what entices some people to ride on roller coasters, jump out of airplanes, and leap off high places with nothing but rubber bands around their ankles. It is also the thing that motivates a lot of us to sit in dark movie theaters watching various incarnations of the Enigma with rapture and intense concentration. Just as the Enigma creates flash-point memories to sell products, entertainment thrives on flash-point experiences.

As the popularity of these various shows demonstrates, the Enigma is often a rich source of material since it fundamentally stretches our imaginations. It also serves as a reminder that the Image Economy is built on more than what we see: it relies on the deeper mythic workings of a variety of archetypal figures that ensure the things we can't see are often as effective as the things we can.

Mythic Highlights to Note

- **The roots of universal appeal:** This figure represents the mystery in all of us — the need to interpret the unanswered questions in our lives.
- **FUD is a powerful motivator:** Fear, uncertainty and doubt can be used as very effective commercial motivators. FUD can both help sell existing products and be the rationale for creating new types or categories of products. However, FUD cannot be used gratuitously; there has to be a rational connection back to how the product provides a solution.
- **Mystery is a source of enduring interest:** The Enigma can hold consumers' attention for a long time. In the form of brands, this can mean some sort of secret surrounding the product, such as a special or secret ingredient. In entertainment, it means concealing certain elements of the character from the audience in order to hold their interest.

Mythic Figures in Combination and in Local Cultures

19

The Source Code in Action

Some key points should be evident from the preceding profiles. First, although consumers are often completely unaware of it, an archetype is subconsciously at work in every instance of commercial persuasion. Archetypes are the invisible connectors that link people to commercial and entertainment images, producing consumer fascination and shaping their beliefs. Second, the daily deluge of images triggers a wide range of automatic and unconscious responses in consumers' psyches. Consumers are motivated in a number of different directions every day. Messages that are humorous, jarring, scary, or warm and fuzzy can all potentially connect with consumers, despite the fact that they motivate consumers with emotionally disparate forces. The "positive" motivation of a surrogate nurturing brand (the Mother of Goodness) or the "negative" motivation of fear (the Enigma) can be equally effective, depending upon how well it is used. No one bond is necessarily stronger than another, and there is not a single or "right" way to break into consumers' minds. Lastly, the common bedrock of archetypes drives the images that appear in both the sales and entertainment processes, allowing for the fluid and constant crossover that underpins the Image Economy. Popular image franchises, such as the *Star Wars* characters, can easily cross the line from entertainment to selling because of the common foundation provided by archetypes.

Archetypes are indeed efficient and flexible. But as we'll examine next, the way archetypes mix, and the manner in which individual consumers experience archetypes, can add layers of complexity to the creation of effective communications.

The Interrelationship of Archetypes

We have covered the mythic figures in individual profiles in order to focus on what distinguishes and delineates each archetype and to demonstrate how each functions in modern mythology. But do not assume that archetypes exist in isolation. While every archetype has its own place at the table of the human psyche, the individual archetypes are part of a pantheon of archetypes that are all simultaneously active in our subconscious and which intermingle and interact constantly.

If we go back to the dozen archetypes that were profiled, we see that they form a compass of sorts, outlined in Figure 1, which points in virtually every direction. This reflects the point that the human psyche comes with a complete range of feelings; the compass must head in every direction to accurately reflect the complexity of the mind. Archetypes that haven't been profiled here could be added, too, further filling out the circle. The fact that people comprehend all these different emotions is a key reason why all of the archetypes can be used to persuade consumers, albeit in different ways.

Figure 1: The Archetype Compass

As you study this compass, you'll see that the archetypes fall into pairs of approximate opposites. As noted in one of the profiles, every force must have a counterweight to help give it definition. What this means in practical terms is that images and messages can work in opposing directions. The Loyalist archetype, for example, produces effective messages based on the dynamics of *certainty*, while the Enigma archetype can create an equally convincing message using the inverse approach of *uncertainty*. Often, opposing forces are present at the same time. In fact, the intertwined destiny of archetypal opposites is the basis of many timeless themes we find in popular entertainment. The cold war of the sexes, the story of good and evil, and the interaction of dog and cat personalities are all fascinating because they are studies in opposing archetypal forces. The example noted earlier of the cola wars demonstrates how this dynamic of opposite images has practical application in driving consumer fascination with brands.

The rich tapestry of human experience, however, is woven from more than black and white threads. Archetypes can be grouped in countless combinations, involving varying numbers of archetypes. Just as the interplay of the gods in classical mythology fascinated and titillated ancient audiences, modern audiences are also riveted by the interaction of archetypes expressed as different commercial and entertainment figures. They love to see whether the Hero will succumb to the Siren, how the Ultimate Strength will deal with the Enigma, and whether the Trickster can outwit the others. The complexity of archetypal relationships is the essence of drama and the reason why there are so many different types of stories and brand images in the Image Economy.

Multiple Archetypes in Brands and Personalities

In some cases, archetypes work closely in combination, rather than in opposition to each other. Indeed, archetypes can have similar or slightly overlapping characteristics. For example, the Hero, the Wise Old Man and the Loyalist all share similar traits of reliability and steadfastness. Archetypes can therefore have associative or tangential power depending upon how they are mixed. This becomes incredibly important when you actually harness the power of archetypes in modern mythology. Once a company defines its core archetypal values, using complementary archetypes allows it to create greater depth to its image.

This last point has very practical application in the Image Economy. A popular concept in the brand and marketing world is the notion of the "brand personality". However, this term is slightly misleading, because it is often construed to mean that brands have a single personality. But brands, like people, often have multiple facets to their character. They are rarely one-dimensional, despite what many brand pundits say about the need for a single-minded positioning. Indeed, the great brands might stand for one word or idea in consumers' conscious minds, but they often *harmonize* multiple archetypes on a subconscious level, which is the reason for their broad appeal and strong consumer connections. A blend of archetypal powers can add new layers of richness to the image.

General Electric provides a good illustration of this harmonization of archetypal power. The company, which was founded by Thomas Edison, has a natural pedigree for inventiveness. But as we saw in the Creator profile, inventors can have an unpredictable edge. However, through GE's long-running "We Bring Good Things to Life" campaign, a stabilizing element has been harmonized into the underlying stratum of the brand. This communicates that GE not only invents things; it creates products that help and nurture people's well-being. Subconsciously, this brings forth the assurance and reliability of the Mother of Goodness archetype, which provides balance to the Creator.

Consumers respond to this subconscious mix of Creator-Mother archetypes, which is crystallized perfectly in the line "We Bring Good Things to Life". This statement can be read with an emphasis that highlights bringing forth new products (the Creator). But it can also be read with an emphasis on bringing good things *to life,* thus improving people's quality of life (the Mother of Goodness). Additionally, the style of GE's advertising reflects the mix of the two archetypes. The communication imparts a feeling of motherly warmth and care while it highlights the inventiveness of the company. Lastly, GE's communications also feature the various products, from light bulbs to sophisticated MRI scanners, that provide a better quality of life for consumers. Subliminally, this generates positive proof that they really do bring "good things to life". So even though GE is a hard-nosed business organization, the average consumer feels that it is both an inventive and caring company.

Coca-Cola is another globally recognized brand that helps illustrate the way in which multiple archetypal forces can work in combination. Coke has very broad-ranging appeal, in large part due to the range of archetypes subconsciously at work in support of the brand. As an original — "The Real Thing" — Coke has strong Creator dynamics. It is an authentic brand. But consumers also turn to Coke as a friend or include Coke amongst friends. Thus the Loyalist archetype is simultaneously at work making it a "buddy brand". On top of that, Coke has elements of the Hero archetype, built through the "product-as-hero" approach, that produce a halo of trust in the brand. Lastly, Coke has a Change Master dynamic as well, transforming the moment into something fun. Thus, Coke enjoys a broad reach of positive and complementary subconscious associations that give it emotional traction with a wide base of consumers.

In certain cases, a brand's underlying archetypal mix might seem odd or perhaps even contradictory. But unusual mixtures can actually lead to greater consumer fascination. Harley-Davidson is a suitable example of this. Like Coke, the Harley brand has important aspects of the Creator archetype because it is an original. Harley-Davidson's long history and pedigree make it equally the "real thing" for many motorcycle enthusiasts. But the Creator archetype is not generally an expected or intuitive mix with the Anti-Hero, which is another underlying element of the brand. Still, this distinctive mix of archetypal values works, ultimately giving Harley-Davidson a unique image and a brand that engenders fierce loyalty amongst its users.

The mixing of multiple archetypes is pertinent to personalities and public figures as well. People who have complex, sometimes contradictory, traits often generate great interest. An example of this is Princess Diana, who was a magnet for public attention, although she often sought refuge from the public stage. Diana represented a truly engrossing combination of archetypes. On the one hand, she was a Powerbroker who moved in exclusive, elite circles. She was clearly a person in the know, who hobnobbed with the world's powerful people. Yet, Diana was also very vulnerable and seemed to care intimately about close friends, the people she met through her charity work and, particularly, her two children. Thus, she had strong Loyalist and Mother of Goodness associations, too. Yet, at the same time, she was beautiful and alluring — a Siren in some people's eyes. It seemed hard to fathom how these disparate elements could all be embodied in one person — a major reason Princess Di generated so much ongoing public fascination. In addition, more than a few people in the public felt empathetically connected with her because she represented a complexity that they also feel as they struggle to deal with the contrary aspects of their own minds.

There are endless examples from entertainment and popular culture that could be cited to illustrate fascinating blends of archetypal powers. What should be sufficiently clear from the preceding examples is that archetypes are effective at connecting in complex combinations, not just individually.

Archetypes and Culture

As any international advertising or marketing person can readily tell you, connecting across cultures with commercial messages is not a simple task. Why is this, given everything you've read so far about the universality of archetypes and their potential to cut across cultures? This question opens up another important topic to keep in mind as you consider the compass of archetypes — namely, the influence of culture and personal experience in the way individuals interpret archetypes.

Archetypes are innate, universal forms. But we experience life on an individual, not a universal, basis. Therefore, the "universal mind"[1] of archetypes must be reconciled with the personal mind. This happens constantly as individuals subconsciously interpret universal forms through the filter of personal experience and culture.[2] The lessons that people learn as they grow up, the stories their parents and teachers tell them, and their social interaction with friends all contribute to shaping their own, personal, filter through which they interpret the world. Other cultural factors, such as whether people live in a matriarchal or a patriarchal society, also have a huge impact on their personal worldview. Even from house to house within the same culture, people's experience of life varies greatly. All of this leaves an indelible mark on an individual's psyche and ultimately shapes how they interpret the universal forms of archetypes.

As a result, individuals and cultures gravitate to different archetypes — a key reason one image doesn't suit everyone. Asian cultures, for example, tend to revere icons of harmony and group acceptance, while American popular culture, particularly the business culture, celebrates the maverick — the iconoclast that boldly challenges the group and single-handedly takes on the world with new ideas. This is not to say that no Asians revere mavericks or that no Americans appreciate group harmony. As we'll examine later, individual personality type can have at least as much influence as culture. But culture does have a substantial influence on which images people connect with. The validity of archetypes as common elements of the mind is not negated by culture. For underneath the ever-changing overlay of individual or societal interpretation is the constant compass of archetypes.

The Global-Local Balance

The big implication of this for communicators is that they must select the archetypes that are most appropriate for a given brand and then manage their image in a way that is culturally relevant and effective at summoning up the subconscious power of those chosen archetypes. This cuts to the core of the "global versus local" debate that's so prevalent in the marketing world. Marketers spend a lot of time and energy trying to decide whether it will be more effective to create a single image across the world or to create purely local images and products that are tailored to different cultures. Unfortunately, both sides of the debate often fail to reflect the deeper dynamics of what's happening with consumers. Every "global" image must still pass through consumers' personal filters of local relevance. And any "local" image must ultimately connect to a universal archetype to be effective. Regardless of which approach a company takes, there must always be the right balance between the two.

Determining how to do this is not easy. It takes considerable effort to understand which archetypes will be most relevant for a brand. It takes discipline to ensure that all of a company's activities continuously reinforce a set of archetypes once they're chosen. And it takes real insight to understand which symbols are resonant and meaningful in a society and which will therefore trigger the deep archetypal bonds that make for powerful images. Communicators must also contend with the fact that there are invisible, shifting boundaries to the effectiveness of symbols. At some indeterminable point, the potency of symbols can fade from currency. When symbols are no longer relevant, they fail to connect. Equally, new symbols are constantly being created. As noted earlier, new symbols are a by-product of the Image Economy. So it takes constant work to ensure that the bedrock archetypes of an image have a relevant, current face on them. Given the complexity and fluid nature of managing archetypes across cultures, communication can never be reduced to a painting-by-numbers exercise. No one-size-fits-all answer can be given, though the best images often do manage to cross the chasm of culture. Rather, companies have to be vigilant and focused if they hope to be successful at managing these intangible motivators.

Section IV
Harnessing Archetypes

Managing the Intangible

20

Managing the Asset in the Image Economy

While archetypes work their magic in the unconscious, advertisers cannot simply turn their fate over to the randomness of the human psyche. Rather, if they hope to be successful in the Image Economy, companies must identify and consistently manage the archetype(s) they choose to associate with their image in order to guide consumer beliefs. The last major issue to be considered then is how you can best manage archetypes in order to improve your chances of winning in the Image Economy. This entails taking a fresh look at some of the assumptions and processes that most companies have in place for managing their image. It also fundamentally requires that companies start thinking of archetypes as core assets.

At first, the notion of managing these hidden motivators might seem a bit daunting and impractical. But communicators *can* take steps to maximize the return on these intangible assets. The various profiles demonstrate that archetypes have a very logical role as the source code of persuasion and fascination. By understanding the unique dynamics of each archetype, and by following some practical steps, you can guide the brand mythology process more effectively and take advantage of the rich substratum of consumers' unconscious.

A Tangible Payoff

The key thing to keep in mind about managing archetypes is that it's not an ethereal, intellectual exercise. It's also not glorified corporate voodoo or astrology. Rather, managing archetypes is a key part of the value-creation process of business. Archetypes are the hidden reason that a simple, black T-shirt with an Armani logo on it can sell for quadruple the price of one without it. Archetypes, working in the subconscious, connect consumers with symbols such as the golden arches, enabling them to become a significant icon that has huge drawing appeal. Archetypes are the invisible power source that generates trillions of dollars of value in the Image Economy. So the effort required to manage them is clearly warranted.

This does not, of course, obviate the other steps required to build a sound business. Successful companies must still create quality products, provide decent customer service, price products competitively, and get a host of other things right if they hope to be successful. An image alone can't save a poorly run company. However, it's equally true that simply moving goods doesn't add up to having a brand, and endlessly discounting prices doesn't create enduring bonds with consumers. So, while archetypes are intangible and pose a unique management challenge, they are nevertheless worthy of a disciplined approach to nurture them as company assets. If guided properly, these intangible assets can produce very tangible results.

Internal Management Best Practices

The starting point is to reconsider, both internally and externally, the processes by which companies develop and disseminate images. Before anything is ever put in front of consumers, there is a large amount of internal work that goes on in companies. So this is where we'll focus our attention first. If sufficient internal steps aren't taken to manage archetypes properly, it is unlikely that a company will ever enjoy great success with consumers. Of course, companies vary greatly in how they go about creating and managing their image. So a prescriptive approach using one, fixed methodology is not practical. But there are best practices that apply to companies of all sizes and types. By following these best practices, you can enhance your chances for success.

• Testing: Identifying and mapping archetypes

Companies commonly test and track a variety of aspects of their business. This usually involves either pre-testing communication before it's deployed or post-tracking the effect of the communication after it has been in the market for some time. A lot of companies do both in order to get a "before and after" view of the effectiveness of their communications material. Some of the most common performance indicators they use are market share, brand awareness, brand recall and brand affinity (how much consumers say they like a brand). Billions of dollars in marketing funds are then spent or redirected, depending upon the results of these types of indicators. The truth, though, is that these measures don't reach deep enough. They fail to get to the deeper roots of whether the communication is really connecting with consumers.

The reason for this failure is that these measures are focused almost exclusively on how consumers respond on a rational, conscious level, rather than unlocking consumers' subconscious responses. Take "intention to buy" scores as an example. Some companies consider this to be a particularly important measure, since it appears to be the most direct way to assess whether a piece of communication will be effective at delivering the desired result — getting consumers to buy a product. The problem is that most consumers can't tell you their real intentions. If put on the spot, some consumers will invariably say they intend to make a purchase, but often fail to do so in reality. Many more, though, simply don't know what they will really do. Emotions — a key influence at the decision point and a main motivator that binds consumers to brands — are a product of the subconscious, not the conscious mind. It is hard, if not impossible, for consumers to accurately predict their emotions or what truly motivates them. Do you know for certain how you'll feel next week? Do you know exactly why your new tennis shoes or watch make you feel good? By scraping only the surface of the issue, companies often get an inaccurate measure of consumer intentions. This is the reason some companies have a nasty surprise when great communications test scores turn into only mediocre results in the actual marketplace.

What companies need to seek are measurements of the subconscious bonds and associations that consumers have with their brands. These measures can augment the more topical indicators and provide valuable insight about the underlying workings of the communication. You might wonder whether testing something as intangible as archetypes is even possible. After all, by its very nature, the subconscious doesn't lend itself to direct articulation. However, if companies are prepared to take an approach that goes beyond a straight, rational method of testing, they can use associative techniques to help uncover consumers' deeper motivations. The Myers-Briggs personality tests provide a good parallel for how this testing can be done. The purpose of the Myers-Briggs testing, a topic we'll explore a bit later, is to help people understand their personality type. This is essentially an exercise in helping individuals identify the most prevalent archetypal drivers that define them. This is achieved by using associative responses that relate back to subconscious elements. A similar approach for brands can yield new insights about the "personality type" of a brand.

The first step then is for a company to seek better insights regarding the subconscious assets that are at work in their brands. For existing brands, this means conducting an audit of the subconscious consumer bonds they have already created. This should enable companies to identify which archetypes and attendant subliminal expectations are currently at work. The testing results can then be used to help map out the hidden territory a brand occupies in consumers' psyches. Because you're dealing with invisible forces, giving archetypes some sort of shape and definition via a mapping exercise can be particularly helpful. This enables people to visualize the situation and understand better the amorphous equity they are managing.

- ### *Identifying core archetypes: Selecting which archetypes will drive the mythic bonds*

Once companies understand the subliminal contours of their brand, they need to make some important choices about which subconscious assets to develop further. New brands must make some fresh choices regarding the archetype(s) around which to build. Both routes require much more than simply selecting archetypes from a list. Ultimately, a company's strategy about its subliminal assets has long-term implications that should make the decision a natural part of the CEO's territory.

Given the intense levels of competition for consumer attention today, it seems almost inconceivable that some companies aren't prepared to give the proper attention to identifying the invisible strings that will help bind consumers to them. Unfortunately, some corporate heads fail to understand the magnitude of the issue, choosing to focus solely on the tangible assets of the company. Regardless of who in the company is charged with the decision, a professional rigor should be applied.

A practical step that helps the decision is to use the testing and mapping to assess the territory relative to the competition. This can expose what subliminal positions the competition already occupies. It can also help a company see which archetypal assets will give them distinction in the pack, leading to a unique, sustainable positioning. The key thing to keep in mind is that, unlike traditional mapping exercises where brands occupy only one spot or zone on a map, companies have the potential to make a variety of subliminal connections with consumers. The examples in the previous chapter demonstrated how strong brands often harmonize multiple subconscious elements. So the decision about which archetype(s) to associate with a brand provides plenty of room for creativity and requires the company to think about how the archetypes will work in combination.

Companies actually have a lot more latitude in this decision than they sometimes realize. An interesting example to illustrate this point is the marketing of milk. Numerous dairy boards around the world are responsible for determining how to advertise what is essentially the same product. Yet they use a diversity of approaches to connect with consumers. In some cases, milk is portrayed as the Hero, with advertising featuring famous people and heroes who drink milk. In other markets, the Mother of Goodness is used instead. Communication in these markets highlights the all-natural and nourishing aspects of the product. In still other markets, the Change Master or the Ultimate Strength archetypes are used. Communication in these countries shows surprising situations of how milk makes kids healthy and strong.

The diversity of approaches shows that there is not one obvious or "right" route that they should take. Unfortunately, because of the tendency towards "category thinking", companies often feel like there isn't much of a choice in the matter. However, this is almost never really the case. At the key decision point, companies have to be brave enough to step outside their traditional comfort zones if they hope to carve out unique, subconscious territory with consumers.

Apple Computer illustrates this point. Prior to the launch of the Macintosh, computers were generally positioned as being something very rational. Companies had not successfully connected their product with users' creative sides via the Creator archetype. Further, most computer-makers had focused on how computers provided functionality, rather than emotionally empowering their users. That was simply how computer marketing was done. However, the launch of the Macintosh in 1984 changed all that. As a result of its "Power to Be Your Best" messaging, Apple captivated a segment of users who gravitated both consciously and subconsciously to the message of creativity (the Creator archetype) and self-transformation (the Change Master) — a big departure from the category norm. Apple was brave enough to break the mold and generate new archetypal connections for its computers. And, as a result, Apple became a distinctive and potent icon.

- **Codifying the commitment: Communicating and living your archetypal values**

Once a company has set a direction, it must clearly articulate and publicize it. Many companies put their values into a corporate mission statement in order to outline the general principles the company will attempt to follow. In addition, companies often have brand statements or brand prints that give definition to each of their brands. Both the mission statement and the brand print provide a useful discipline. However, too few — if any — incorporate archetypes. These intangible assets deserve clear identification as well. They are as logical a part of the mission statement or brand print as the other elements that are usually included. If companies fail to codify their archetypal values, they will probably fail to adequately communicate the intended DNA of their brands. So another practical step that businesses should take is to reassess their brand prints and mission statements to incorporate the archetypal assets they are managing.

The ultimate purpose of codifying beliefs and archetypes is to help a company steer its actions. The mechanics of writing down the words and sticking them up on the wall won't do much good if companies don't follow through. They must use the statements as guides for their decisions so that they genuinely live what they proclaim. This involves aligning the actions they take with both the conscious and subconscious elements they have chosen to stand for. Consumers have an amazing ability to detect when there's discord between the two.

If you doubt this point, think for a moment about how consumers react to companies when they perceive something to be off the mark. Imagine what consumers would think, for example, if they saw Johnson's Baby Powder sponsoring professional wrestling. Consumers would probably feel that it was "wrong" for the brand, even if they couldn't say why. That's because consumers, particularly those that are loyal to a brand, have subconscious expectations and associations with brands. These aren't inherent associations. As we saw in the profiles, they have been engineered over time by what a company has communicated about its values in order to map out territory in consumers' psyches. When subconscious expectations are either not met or somehow violated, consumers can have strong emotional reactions. So constant attention needs to be given to ensuring that a brand or a company stays true to its ethos.

Successful companies today are often those that have firm beliefs. Virgin, Starbucks and The Body Shop have emerged as well-known companies in large part because they have a commitment to a set of ideals. They don't simply trot out these beliefs as a ploy when it's convenient. Rather, they align everything they do around their values. And because these companies both clearly articulate their beliefs and stick to them, consumers have a very clear sense of what they stand for. Only Virgin can be Virgin. Similarly, The Body Shop stands for a clear set of values. This ultimately pays dividends, since these "brands of belief" engender reciprocal consumer belief in them, leading to loyalty. This all emanates from archetypes, the subconscious bedrock of a company's values and image.

- ### *Ongoing management strategy: Integrating the image*

Even when a company has strong beliefs, it usually takes time to cultivate the consumers' side of the equation. So a company must consistently reinforce its image through a variety of activities. As just noted, consumers have amazingly well-tuned antennae that can pick up when there's a breach in the consistency — on either an overt or an underlying level. This is a key reason why companies must be committed to the essence of their brands and then integrate all their activities around that core.

The brand-creation process is highly dynamic, and communicating with consumers is an ongoing process. Often, a variety of activities such as promotions, sponsorships, press coverage and advertising run simultaneously to support a brand. So brand creation is a multi-dimensional exercise, requiring a number of pieces to come together in the process.

The key benefit of all this effort is the cumulative effect of brand associations. Associations build up over time, just like an ancient city is constantly built on top of previous structures. Loyal Pepsi drinkers today may still be reacting to seeds that were planted in their brains many years ago, as well as to what they see today. So activities must extend from a constant core to ensure that the cumulative effect is consistent. This is the essence of integrated communication. If done correctly, each of the different channels and activities adds a unique dimension to the core, just like facets make a diamond more brilliant. As a result, brands can widen their sphere of influence, creating an effective modern mythology.

The cumulative process of brand creation links users to both outward and subliminal triggers of a brand. The goal is to present the brand in a way that is consistent in "look" and "feel". Most companies focus their attention on the outward manifestations — the logo, the corporate colors, the packaging, and their advertising and promotions. You might think, therefore, that consistently presenting the "look" of a brand should be easy. But a lot of practical experience in this area shows how difficult this can be. Even the biggest and brightest companies sometimes make egregious errors in managing the way their brands "look" to the public. Imagine, then, how scattered the "feel" part of it can be at times, too.

This is where a company's mission statement and brand print, inclusive of a definition of archetypes, can again play a practical role in guiding the image-management process. By focusing not just on the surface elements of brands (which should be improved), but also the amorphous assets of archetypes, companies can shepherd their image more consistently. Essentially, the archetypes should be used as a screen to vet their activities and associations. Given the growing complexity of the Image Economy, there are more and more options to choose from. So companies have to be conscious of the subliminal implications of their activities in the areas of sponsorship, in-store promotions, joint promotions and star endorsements. Another common mistake they make, though, is to consider integration to be just a way to gain exposure. So, if there's a chance to slap their name on something that will get them in front of lots of consumers, they're usually interested. However, these activities often don't meet the relevancy test — namely, exposure that is consistent with the subtext of the image.

What companies should look for in making decisions about their integrated activity are the partners or events that are consistent with their brand at an archetypal level. This enables brands to generate positive proof about their archetypes. So, for example, a company that makes cookies and has the Mother of Goodness archetype at its core should seek other companies associated with the Mother of Goodness archetype for co-promotional activity. Associative testing can help you determine who those companies are. The cookie company can also add to its underlying assets by doing things on its own that reinforce the archetype. So, if it conducts a sampling event, it might give away free milk with the cookies or hold the sampling in comfy chairs instead of using a plastic trial booth. It might even go as far as tying its sampling into donations to children's foundations to reinforce the message about its values, and thereby its core archetype. Everything a brand does as part of an integrated effort must communicate something deeper about it.

For large companies with diverse activities, this process of integration is especially challenging and complex, since there are simply more fronts of exposure to consumers where they might get it wrong. So by ensuring that all activities are "on archetype", they can be sure that they are "on brand" as well.

• Long-term commitment: Maintaining consistency over time

Companies are usually committed to a strategy as long as it's succeeding. But they periodically face down-times as well, which puts their resolve to the test. This results in the commonly seen problem of companies abruptly changing their image. It seems easier to scrap the current effort than drill down and understand how to make it better. This is often a reflection of their lack of conviction about their approach in the first place. Some companies change direction in the hope that a new marketing campaign in a completely new direction will instantly boost sales. Others change images like some people change clothes. But an image is not just an external face to the world — it communicates a deeper set of values that connect with consumers. Consumer attachments don't turn on a dime.

The irony is that for brands that have achieved some degree of success, it becomes even more difficult to make substantial changes in direction. Consumers don't conveniently suffer amnesia because companies wish them to. It can therefore cost companies twice as much and take twice as long to change consumers' minds as it took them to persuade them in the first place.

However, this doesn't imply that companies should never change. It's a business reality that one sales upsurge or hit product needs to be followed year after year with further growth. So companies must also be able to respond to challenges and do things that will spark renewed interest in their brands. The key today is to know how to guide change effectively without abandoning core assets that have taken a lot of time and money to cultivate.

The best-known brands stick to a clear, consistent ethos while they change and rejuvenate themselves. They achieve this by distinguishing between messaging tactics and the core bedrock of their brands. This distinction is perhaps one of the most vital things for a communicator to understand. Those who get it right know that there are often dozens of ways to say the same thing. So instead of changing the essence of what they say, they change the way they are saying it. Take, for example, a car brand that has associated itself with the Ultimate Strength archetype. Its existing messaging strategy might involve torture tests to prove how strong the cars are. If sales start to flag, it doesn't necessarily follow that this is the wrong archetype for the brand. It might seek a change in the way it expresses the archetype, such as by using an endorser who is known for his strength or by switching to other types of performance messaging. These messaging tactics keep the brand centered on the same archetype so that there is a deeper element of consistency while there's something new to shout about in the marketplace.

Through testing, some existing brands might determine that they don't currently represent the archetypal values they believe will give them distinction in the long term. They, too, can change by gradually mixing their old archetype in with new ones. So, for example, a car brand that decides the Ultimate Strength doesn't work might consider an approach using the Wise Old Man. The advertising might be a mix of old and new, focusing on how the brand has built durable, reliable cars over many years. Then, after a period of time, it might focus exclusively on the values of the Wise Old Man, focusing on the heritage story of the brand. This type of subterranean migration of values can help companies avoid the all-or-nothing bet of a new image makeover and the resulting disassociation that consumers sometimes feel.

• Managing your expectations: Determining what constitutes success

As an underlying asset that ultimately produces financial returns, archetypes are worth some form of ongoing monitoring and measure. And since effective measurement is predicated on knowing what types of goals are achievable, companies must have a sense of what to expect in the process of managing archetypes.

Thinking of image building in terms of mythology can help you set your expectations. Mythology is founded on symbolic relationships, so brand builders must understand that the images they are creating will work on a symbolic level as well as a rational level. Second, mythology works its way into consumers' psyches in indirect routes. Once a message is released into the public, it's truly out of a company's control.

Too many advertisers begin the communications process with a false set of expectations about what they will be able to achieve. Some have an unrealistic perception of how much factual information consumers can, and actually will, take on board about their products. Consumers are not VCRs that will learn to replay messages exactly. Many advertisers, though, expect the audience to be glued to their sets, committing every detail of their commercial to memory. This is not only unrealistic, it's impossible, since the human memory is far from perfect. Particularly over time, details tend to fade, except for certain defining elements. Instead, general impressions and feelings form. Also, consumers do not put together an advertiser's image exactly as the advertiser has constructed it. They experience brands in bits and pieces at random moments, from which they construct their impressions of brands. If everything a company has put together is consistent and powerful, it eventually adds up to a clear consumer belief. Frankly, it doesn't much matter if consumers don't remember the model number of the new Mercedes, as long as they come away with a strong belief that they want one. If the image succeeds in achieving that, consumers will be sure to find the right model number when it's time to make a purchase.

So while all the details in communication count, many of those details will be forgotten. But that doesn't mean it's wasted effort because the details make the vital contributions to the overall impression that is left with the consumer. This is the essence of the takeaway, because it includes the core belief that has been created. Sales alone are not the right measure to decide whether archetypes are "working". I've seen plenty of companies with good images who suffer sales dips because of poor distribution, stock-taking problems, poor route salesmen and a host of other issues. It's often easier to change the advertising than it is to face the tough task of improving internal organizations. The measures that should be used to track success should relate back to the things that archetypes are, by their very nature, good at doing. Foremost amongst these is the power to create strong beliefs. The quality of the consumer connection is the ultimate test of success.

Improving Consumer Connections 21

Improving the Persuasion Process

Companies can do all the internal planning that they want to. However, the real challenge begins the moment an image is put in front of Mr. and Mrs. Consumer. It's at this point that the intangible assets of archetypes are activated.

As we observed earlier, the process of connecting with consumers is now more challenging than ever. The persuasion process — identifying a target market, creating a message with an "idea" to reach that target, and then building exposure through repetition — often can't be relied upon to get the job done today. Since this traditional route is yielding fewer positive results, companies need to look for better ways to connect with consumers. This means more than just determining how to get an image in front of consumers more often. The goal is to connect in a way that nurtures stronger attachments and belief systems.

Ironically, many of the emerging "brands of belief" mentioned earlier have had success without using big network TV budgets to hammer home their message. Products as diverse as Snapple, Ben & Jerry's, Virgin, Red Bull, Soho Soda, The Body Shop and Starbucks have attracted loyal followings without going the traditional route. Yet they've succeeded in building strong consumer equity. As a result, they've captured the attention of larger, more traditional product companies that have been eager to acquire the magic that their brands lack. This is not to say that advertising on network TV doesn't work. But influence today relies on more than repetition and exposure through traditional media.

A more holistic approach is required to build a modern mythology and nurture the underlying archetypes on which images are founded. So, in addition to challenging old notions of how companies manage archetypes internally, communicators must also be prepared to re-think some of the basic components of the persuasion process. This entails using an understanding of archetypes to address the four failures of the persuasion process that were outlined earlier: the lack of consumer understanding and insight; the lack of relevancy of the message; the lack of creativity in the messaging; and the difficulty of creating effective exposure.

The following provides some key points to consider as you tackle these issues. Included in these recommendations are some of the insights that were highlighted as part of the archetypal profiles. Again, no single formula can apply to all situations. These points should be taken as indicators that should prompt your thoughts and ideas.

Improving Customer Identification and Understanding

- ### Looking beyond demographics

There's an obvious logic to companies identifying those groups of consumers most likely to consume their products. However, companies often focus on the wrong issues as they try to determine who those people are. The classic "target market" definition, built largely on demographic data, is frequently insufficient. Marketers typically augment these demographic groupings with associated attitudinal assumptions as well. To a degree, it's true that demographically driven segments such as Gen-Xers, Yuppies, DINKS, TINKS and the Grey Market have some common attitudes and related lifestyles. But many marketers' assumptions about target markets are questionable or simply lack real insights. I can't tell you the number of times I've seen the same old research findings trotted out to explain the Youth Market. Researchers often provide little more than hackneyed conclusions that young people form groups around popular activities (thank you, Einstein) or rebel against their parents (again, the earth shakes). By grouping consumers as target audiences based largely on age, sex and income, marketers often ignore the most important driver of their consumers — their individual personality type.

The fact that people fall into different "types" has been recognized for millennia. In fact, Hippocrates originally outlined four temperaments to classify different types of people.[1] Much more recently, in addition to identifying archetypes, Jung outlined 16 psychological types.[2] He used four basic scales or dichotomies to determine these 16 types. Building on that, the mother-daughter duo of Katharine Cook Briggs and Isabel Briggs Myers then developed the Myers-Briggs Type Indicator to help people identify into which personality type they fall. This test, which has been conducted amongst millions of people, is the most popular measure of individual personality type.[3]

It's important to stress here that personality types are not straitjackets. We all have a bit of everything in us. Occasionally introverts will break out of their shell and dance on a table. Equally, an extrovert will want a quiet moment with his/her thoughts. So communicators can't expect consumers to fall within strictly defined lines. But although people can occasionally surprise us, they are generally true to their deeper nature. Therefore, personality types do provide marketers with valuable indicators that, more often than not, match people's tendencies.

Even if you disagree totally with the Myers-Briggs type classifications, you probably recognize from everyday experience that there are different types of people out there. Starting in the cradle, people exhibit their temperament and proclivities. So although people might share demographic similarities as part of a target group, they will react to messages from very different psychological starting points. This cuts across cultures, since a person's personality type can be of greater influence to their attitudes than the culture in which they live. From Japan to Jamaica, there's always a segment of the local population that fancies itself a rebel, a peacemaker or a scholar. As a result, personality type is often a better indicator of consumers' probable reactions than demographic-related attitudes. The key for companies is to come up with some form of workable definition of their consumers based upon personality type.

- ### *Personality type: A constant*

A key benefit of identifying personality type is that it provides stable bedrock on which to build long-term customer relationships. Consumers' demographic particulars are in a constant state of flux as they age, marry, have children and, hopefully, earn more money. However, their core personality types don't change. A young man who is outgoing and talkative is likely to one day become an old man who is still outgoing and talkative. Personality type therefore provides a "fixed" point about consumers. Even if people wished to, they probably couldn't change their personality type, since it's an innate part of the individual code of who they are.

For those brands seeking lifetime value from a customer — which is most brands these days — this point has important implications. By focusing more on the constant elements of consumers — their personality types — companies can gain new insights about which consumers are really most likely to connect with their message over the long run. Brands that are successful manage to stay relevant to different generations by attracting the same type of users, irrespective of their generation.

An example that illustrates this point is Pepsi.[4] In the early '60s, Pepsi hit upon a very powerful idea. As it sought to carve out a unique market position vis-à-vis Coke, Pepsi decided to focus on younger users — the Pepsi generation. This approach resulted in initial success. However, over time, this positioning wasn't tenable on a demographic basis. The young users Pepsi had attracted were getting older. In fact, they were part of the great U.S. demographic shift of the aging baby-boomers. Pepsi certainly didn't want them to abandon the brand simply because they were no longer young enough to be considered part of the "Pepsi Generation". But Pepsi understood that, irrespective of age, consumers who are "young at heart" and a bit irreverent would still find Pepsi appealing. So it adjusted the communication over time to focus more on the mindset and less on the demographics of its users. The hook of the positioning was not the demographics but rather the appeal this type of messaging has to certain personality types.

There are, of course, certain limits to this logic. Four-year-old children are not likely consumers of coffee, no matter how much their personality type might make them a prime consumer later in life. However, companies will factor in the natural limits of their products' use when they expand their target group definitions to include personality types.

Improving Message Relevancy: The Critical Connections

• The subconscious connection

This exercise is critical since a better understanding of consumers' personality types can lead to greater relevancy for your messaging. Specifically, this happens by understanding how your users' personality type(s) subconsciously interact with the archetypes that underlie your brand or image. When type meets type, different instantaneous interactions occur, just like different chemicals mix to create inert matter or highly explosive combinations.

Figure 2: The Connection Points

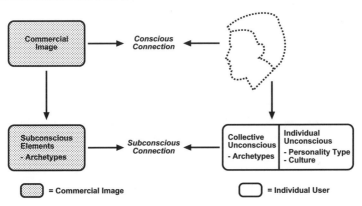

This subconscious intersection of types is the first of two critical connection points of modern mythology. As outlined in Figure 2, when consumers see a commercial image — a TV commercial, a sponsorship, a movie or anything in the Image Economy — they react to it on both a conscious and unconscious level. The unconscious portion of the mind comprises both the collective unconscious, where archetypes reside, and the individual unconscious. As noted earlier, people's personality types, as well as the internalized, subconscious lessons they've learned from their particular culture, shape their subconscious reactions. All of this influences the way that individuals then react to and interpret the underlying archetypes of the image they've seen.[5]

The degree to which an image then resonates with a consumer stems from this subconscious interaction. The mixture determines whether the result is fascination or indifference. It determines how much individual consumers take on that image as "theirs" — a personal symbol which they associate with, are motivated by and, for certain types of products, assume as part of the outward manifestation of who they "are". There's no such thing as a natural Rolex user or Harley rider or Pepsi drinker. But through subconscious association of these brands' archetypes with their users' personality types, certain consumers feel like these brands are a natural selection for them, even if they can't articulate why. When the connection works, it is both powerful and effortless for consumers.

There's also durability to this connection. The right mix can form a bond with a consumer that lasts for years, unless the brand fatefully veers off strategy or does something specific to alienate its consumers. This subconscious matching of company archetypes and user-personality type is one of the reasons that powerful brands often engender long-term loyalty and can appeal to the same consumers over decades. It's also the same reason that certain stars and public personalities attract lifelong fans. Brands, characters and popular personalities become permanent and trusted fixtures in people's lives and emotionally relevant to them because of this sub-conscious connection.

• *Relating to archetypes*

The connection of archetypes and personality types is not a simple issue. What makes one person select a particular brand over another has a number of dimensions to it. But there are some basic principles that you should be aware of as you try to understand how a consumer's personality might mix with the archetypes that support your brand.

First is the principle of self-imaging. Consumers tend to gravitate to those things that reflect who they are, or at least who they think they are and aspire to be. They consciously and instinctively find things that are the "right" match for them. For example, people who have a particularly strong attachment to the Creator archetype as a defining part of their personality are likely to form a strong bond with brands that reflect the Creator. It's natural for people to seek things which they feel are like them. In some cases, they choose things that constitute their inner dreams, even if they don't appear to be a suitable match to others around them.

However, there's more than a one-to-one correlation of archetypes and user types. Consumers don't need to outwardly "see themselves in the advertising" for it to work. A great example of this is a famous commercial for Hamlet cigars. In the commercial, a balding man with a very bad comb-over sits down in a photo booth to take his picture. Through a series of mishaps, he moves at just the moment the picture goes off — three times in a row. Now, this gentleman is not someone who most people would wish to look like. And most people don't want to seem like a bumbling fool, either. Yet the communication works for certain consumers because the underlying archetype of the Trickster connects with their particular personality type. They appreciate and connect with the humor. Additionally, the product itself is positioned as a Hero, rescuing the user from his misfortunes. So while the man in the commercial is decidedly not a Hero, the archetype is effectively blended into the brand. The result is that users who have the personality type that connects with this mix of the Hero and Trickster archetypes form a positive attachment to the brand.

Sometimes the fact that people lack something might cause them to gravitate to an archetype. A consumer who is not strong and powerful — and knows it at heart — might be attracted to the Rolex brand as a way to feel strong and powerful. So the art of utilizing archetypal power is complex and requires communicators to understand both archetypes and personality types for the connection to work effectively. If this all seems like too much effort, remember that the activation of archetypes to generate consumer connections is the engine behind the trillions of dollars in the Image Economy. It's worth your effort.

• *The rational and emotional connection*

While modern mythology creates subconscious connections, consumers also make conscious connections based on rational benefits. They are not manipulated zombies. Consumers must be convinced that they'll buy toasters that toast well, cars that drive smoothly and detergents that clean. The second critical connection to understand, then, is the fusion of rational and emotional elements in the consumer's conscious decision process.[6]

When consumers stand in the supermarket and make a decision, they are not aware of the forces working upon them. In general, except in cases of severe psychological malfunctioning, the human mind works as one unit.[7] So people aren't cognizant of the constant interaction of the conscious and subconscious portions of their minds. They can't pinpoint how something they learned a long time ago is influencing their "rational" decision of the moment. What consumers are aware of is what they think and feel at the time. This provides a critical connection to what's happening above and below the surface of consciousness, since feelings are the products of the subconscious that bubble up into our conscious realm.

Every day, people make decisions that are based on a mix of how they feel and what they think. They go through a constant process of weighing between the two. Perhaps they like one brand more than the other, but rationally they can't justify why it's better; so they "decide" based on product features. In some cases, they toss the rational support to the wind and simply pick the thing they like the most. This is the reality of the Image Economy.

The vital point is to recognize is that there's actually a great fusion of the two elements. Functional benefits tie to emotional payoffs such as feelings of confidence, stature and recognition. For example, revolutionary new disc breaks can mean that the car a person is driving is the most technologically advanced car — which produces an emotional benefit for people who want to own the "latest thing". Or, it could be positioned as a reason why the car is the safest for your family and children, which produces a different type of emotional payoff. If done properly, emotional and rational messages fuse and support each other in the creation of consumer beliefs. The Image Economy produces rational dreams — desires which people must justify in some rational form when they pull out their wallet, and functional products which must create some sort of emotional appeal to be picked out of the complexity of product offerings.

So when communicators are looking to determine how archetypes will help further their cause, they must look at the way these subconscious elements gain conscious expression tied to rational benefits. This is the essence of making a modern mythology that is commercially effective.

Improving Creative Messaging

The purpose of creativity in the material you use to communicate your brand or image — in advertising and in everything you do — is to capture consumers' attention and trigger the deeper associations that will foster beliefs and attachments. This is no easy task. It takes real skill to generate a story or creative "idea" with the potential to touch and motivate millions.

Successful creative work achieves this by the way it uses archetypes as the source code of communication. It's important to recall that archetypes provide the primary, subconscious units which people use to measure and assess the world. So even though you're not aware of it, archetypes in your psyche are constantly helping you form expectations. If, for example, I say that someone is strong, you might envision a person lifting a rock or some weights or even a small car. But you probably wouldn't imagine them lifting a house. It's simply beyond the rational and instinctive measurements that you would apply to size up the situation. So when communication features images beyond the bounds of innate expectation, it jars the psyche.

The nature of the human mind is to try to make sense of things. Particularly when confronted with something new or unexpected, the mind's normal reaction is to try to process what's happening. It's a basic part of our survival instincts. So, an image that takes consumers' minds outside the normal zone of expectation and comfort literally demands their attention on both a conscious and subconscious level.

The best communication preys on this natural human reaction by using images that force consumer attention. People then can't simply cruise on autopilot; they must give it extra focus — at least for an extra split second — in an attempt to process the image they're seeing, hearing or reading. The result can be an asymmetric impact, which gives one image a disproportionately large amount of attention over the others.

The goal of most image makers is to create an indelible mark in consumers' minds through asymmetric impact. Indeed, great movies, books and photos make this type of imprint. Brands, too, stick out in the mind because of exceptional advertising. An example of this is the "1984" spot which Apple Computer used to launch its Macintosh computers in the

U.S. The commercial featured a sledgehammer-wielding woman who charges into an enormous hall filled with subjugated drones seated in rows. Before a group of pursuing storm troopers can subdue her, she hurls the hammer into a giant screen, obliterating the image of Big Brother barking out instructions to his subjects. The symbol-laden commercial was not the light-hearted fare one expects from advertising. But despite being shown only once nationally on the Super Bowl (and a few additional times in local spot markets), the commercial put the computer on consumers' mental maps. And it did so in a way that created an effective "us and them" distinction between Apple and its competitors.

Few commercials create the impact of "1984", which is considered to be one of the best commercials of all time. Most communication requires some degree of repetition in order to be successful. However, in today's Image Economy, communicators simply can't be guaranteed of the frequency of exposure that they'd like. So every time you create communication the goal should be to maximize its impact by amplifying the effect of archetypes. The following are three of the most effective ways this can be done by moving consumers' mental goalposts.

- ***Amplifying the archetype through exaggeration***

The first of the approaches is to amplify the underlying archetype through exaggeration. As a result, viewers feel that the person or object shown has a heightened amount of that archetype, thus turbo-charging its impact. This can happen in varying degrees. Showing a man balancing on one hand, for example, demonstrates strength that is feasible but beyond the norm. Showing a man lifting a house, however, is beyond the norm and infeasible. Both routes can be effective, depending upon your purpose.

Particularly in entertainment, extreme exaggeration is the source of great amusement and entertainment value. The fact that the cyborg in *Terminator 2* morphs into a new form every time he is shot, punched or blown up adds to the sense of excitement and tension in the story.[9] He is not only the Ultimate Strength, he is the epitome of strength. His apparent invincibility leaves consumers wondering how Arnold can possibly overcome him.

In the sales process, exaggeration can be used to highlight key product benefits and trigger the subconscious association of archetypes. An example of this is a car-battery commercial from the U.S. In the commercial, a car is left on a frozen lake in winter with its headlights on for several months — a clear exaggeration of normal circumstances. At the end of the commercial, a person trudges back across the lake, dusts the accumulated snow off the car and then starts the engine. This type of approach really makes the point for the product by amplifying the underlying archetype of strength. Few people doubt the strength of the battery in that car. But exaggeration must be executed carefully since, by law, a product must be capable of doing what it's shown to do. In certain situations, excessive exaggeration might come across as simply a hoax. This would actually hurt the communicator's case, rather than help it. To get around this dilemma, many advertisers turn to the next of the approaches, which is amplification of the archetype through surprising parallels.

- ### Amplifying the archetype through surprising parallels

In cases where the product isn't directly exaggerated for effect, advertisers might exaggerate things around the product instead. An example is the Tag Heuer print advertisement that shows a swimmer (wearing a Tag Heuer) racing in his lane, with shark fins jutting through the water in the lanes next to him. This is a surprising image, which creates an effective parallel with the watch. Through transference, the watch seems exceptional too.

Surprising parallels can also work in the way products are demonstrated or tested. For example, the scene of a person tossing a suitcase around to demonstrate its strength is not particularly surprising. Even if they were to pick it up and throw it around a room, it's still pretty much within consumers' realm of comprehension — they can easily "measure" it in their minds. But how would you measure a gorilla doing the same thing? It would probably make you think a bit harder about how hard a gorilla can throw the case and how strong the case would have to be to withstand it. Well, this is exactly what American Tourister did in a highly memorable commercial.[10] This type of surprising parallel captures consumers' mental attention and amplifies the strength of the underlying archetype by forcing people to re-calibrate their mental measurements.

- ### *Amplifying the archetype through contradiction*

A last strategy to cover is the use of contradiction to create an indelible impression in consumers' psyches. Sometimes, an archetype can best be amplified by doing something that is not in keeping with the archetype. This technique can also range from the subtle to the extreme, with images that can be funny, jarring or even disturbing.

An ad for Hummer off-road vehicles illustrates this point. The visual shows an up-close shot of the front of the Hummer, which looks primed to roll over some tough terrain. However, the copy in the ad takes an unexpected turn. It reads:

> *"You are invincible.*
> *You are all-powerful.*
> *You are unstoppable.*
> *You are on your way to*
> *the Grocery Store."*

While the visual builds upon the standard iconography in the off-road category, the copy mocks it. Of course, until the last line of copy, it is true-to-form in describing the Ultimate Strength: "invincible, all-powerful and unstoppable". But the final sentence runs completely contrary to the macho image of the vehicle. This reversal of expectations sticks out and makes consumers take notice.

The key thing is that even when this contrary approach is taken, the fact that consumers recognize the underlying dynamic of the archetype that's reversed is the reason that it's effective. The Hummer ad leverages the underlying recognition of the Ultimate Strength, even as it mocks the typical category approach of the Ultimate Strength.

A second example of this contradictory approach comes from the movies. Viewers have become so used to the Wise Old Man that they almost expect old men to have gained some wisdom and to have a kind demeanor. This is often far from the truth and can lead to both amusing and touching situations. Jack Lemmon and Walter Matthau as the eponymous *Grumpy Old Men*[11] are the antithesis of the kindly, Wise Old Men. Instead of being serene sages, these two old men bicker and fight with each other constantly, like young boys. It couldn't be more antithetical to the expected archetype. *Shrek*[12] is another film reference that shows how effective it can be when archetypes don't act their part. This is often the essence of humor and an effective way to create notice.

A word of caution is again required here. One of the age-old lessons painfully re-learned during the dot-com era is that capturing consumers' attention doesn't necessarily translate into persuasion and durable beliefs. The use of archetypes in creative ideas should create both cut-through *and* a worthwhile subconscious connection with consumers. Many of the dot-com companies mistakenly thought that simply getting "eyeballs" was enough.[13] In a frenzied dash to build awareness, some resorted to communication antics that were better suited to the big top than network TV, including shooting gerbils out of cannons.[14] Jarring consumers' psyches might create temporary notice or notoriety, but it must ultimately create more than a sense of surprise. It must also foster an underlying psychological attachment to a relevent archetype or set of archetypes that the advertiser has chosen to associate with its products

Improving Exposure

The fourth and final point to consider is the way to generate better exposure. For companies to win in the Image Economy, this means thinking beyond traditional media alone to drive home the message. The goal is to widen the sphere of influence by exposing an image in multiple ways that reinforce its underlying archetypes.

The ultimate purpose of integrated marketing is to build layers of exposure, all based on a consistent core. These layers add new dimensions of conscious and subconscious impact to the image. This stems from the fact that specific qualities are inherent in each communication channel. As the result of the medium used, people feel different types of connections, even when the message is exactly the same. For example, telling your spouse you love them in a postcard has a different impact from that of telling them in person or via a long-distance call. This is the essence of what Marshall McLuhan meant when he said "the medium is the message".[15]

Image makers today should consider every available avenue for generating exposure and then determine the optimal mix of all the available routes. The following are six of the most prevalent types of exposure that, when executed in combination, will build greater presence and influence for your image.

- ### *Frequency exposure*

The first type of exposure is the most familiar, since we've already covered it in detail. The job of traditional media — TV, magazines, radio and outdoor — is to build frequency in order to create conditioning through repetition. In some cases, this is done through mass media that reach a huge audience. In other cases, it's achieved through niche or specialized media that reach a more focused audience. Mass exposure, such as advertising on the World Cup, can generate "stature exposure" too, since being seen on the World Cup or the Olympics communicates subliminally that the advertiser has size and resources. Frequency exposure through traditional media is still a central part of the modern mythology process, but this alone generally isn't enough.

- ### *Advocacy exposure*

There is often more credibility in what others say about you than what you say about yourself. This basic principle applies to the Image Economy. Marketing-savvy consumers know that advertisers toot their own horns. So more companies are seeking advocates who will speak on their behalf and add a layer of perceived impartiality and authority on top of what they say about themselves. This is one of the reasons that PR and the notion of "spin" has grown tremendously in the past few decades.

"Advocacy exposure" is now a critical part of creating influence. If a consumer sees something by a third party — in the press, on TV, at a symposium or wherever they come across it — which echoes what they've seen in paid media, it adds positive reinforcement to the image and builds consumer confidence. The key is to ensure that the message coming through in advocacy exposure is consistent with everything else a consumer sees.

- ### *Viral exposure*

The process of selling and entertaining fits into a complex sociological web that extends well beyond the limited target market defined by most brands. We humans are a social species. So, when advertisers seek greater reach for their images, they must take into account the way people interrelate. This is where "viral exposure" comes in.

Viral messaging is part of our human nature. People recommend movies to each other, share views and pass along funny things they see. They make suggestions and ask advice. So, by creating material that encourages consumers to pass it on, image makers can tap into these natural tendencies. An important point to note is that viral marketing is effective for reasons beyond the exponential effect of word of mouth. When a person passes something on, they naturally and subconsciously apply some sort of screen to the people they think will be the most receptive to the message. Through instinct and experience, they identify those people most likely to respond positively. To put it in viral terms, people naturally identify others who are susceptible hosts for the virus. In modern mythology terms, this means that consumers instinctively know which personality types will find relevancy in the material.

- **_Affinity-group exposure_**

Effective modern mythology connects with both the "me" and the "we" of the unconscious. Archetypes help give expression to people's individuality. Yet as a common source code, they also enable this individuality to be recognized by others. As we've observed, this is particularly important to brands, since badge appeal is predicated on recognition by others.

"Affinity-group exposure" builds upon the group dynamics of images. Affinity groups form around a host of issues and interests. Some are overt affinities that people share when they join the same club, support the same football team or worship the same rock group. However, people share less-obvious and less-defined affinities as well, such as enjoying the same type of humor. Peers form some affinity groups, while other affinity groups cut across all types of demographics and involve a wide array of people. People aggregate in countless combinations, so we all participate in some form of affinity group. What's common to all affinity groups, however, is the formation of a "consensus reality" — a common view about the topic of mutual interest.[16] By agreeing to agree, people generate a joint set of beliefs and behaviors that are both accepted and sometimes expected within the group. Group reinforcement perpetuates these common beliefs. Just watch a group of adolescent kids interact and you'll get a good insight into the strength of consensus realities at work.

Image makers can tap into group dynamics by determining which types of affinity groups are most relevant to their particular message and underlying archetypes. Through sponsorships, grass-roots activities or a host of other tactics, images can become a part of the affinity-group dynamic.

- ### *Contextual exposure*

The next form of image exposure relates to the way images fit into people's daily lives. Consumers are commonly exposed to images at times completely disconnected from the actual use of the product being advertised. For example, people regularly see advertisements for food when they're not hungry and cold-medicine when they're not sick. Since effective images are retained in the subconscious, this exposure is not necessarily wasted. The best images lie dormant in the unconscious until the need for a product causes the conscious mind to dredge them up. But communicators also benefit from creating "contextual exposure" when their images are seen at the specific place or time that is most relevant to consumers.

Examples are all around us today. Drug companies place material and advertising in hospitals and doctors' reception rooms; beverage companies put up signage at points where people are thirsty; and cash-register areas are cluttered with impulse products meant to prompt consumer's attention when they've got their wallets out. These points of presence are intended to generate purchases. But they also deliver on a more subtle level as well, since contextual exposure gives brands ambient presence that affects consumers subliminally. By being in the right place at the right time, brands pluck the invisible chords of attachment, further reinforcing the subconscious bond of the archetypes.

- ### *Experiential exposure*

The most positive proof of anything is your own experience. This is where the rubber meets the road. So in addition to the five types of image exposure just mentioned, companies need to generate "experiential exposure" as well.

Companies obviously gain their most important exposure when consumers purchase and use their products. It's at this stage that products must truly prove themselves. But before that happens, brands find other ways for consumers to "experience" some of the promise of the brand. Sampling, test drives and on-line demonstrations all enable consumers to see how a product performs. But the way a company provides this type of experiential exposure can communicate a lot about the underlying archetypes too. If a luxury-car company provides test drives with white-gloved chauffeurs, for example, it also makes an important statement about the brand, which resonates on a subconscious level. Pepsi's long-running series of head-to-head taste tests with Coke, called the "Pepsi Challenge", provides another example of how experiential exposure makes subconscious connections.[17] The Challenge not only gave people a chance to try the product, it also communicated volumes about the challenging, assertive nature of the brand.

The End Goal: Enduring Beliefs

In summation, it's not hard to create images that will temporarily surprise or shock the public. But that doesn't mean those images will sell. Modern mythology is not about quick hits — it's about forming long-lasting, effective images. All the effort that goes into improving consumer understanding, generating greater relevancy, creating better-crafted images and increasing exposure, should aim to get consumers to watch and believe and then take action. Enduring beliefs are the desired result of effective modern mythology. And unless you're running a state monopoly, this is vital to your ongoing success, since consumers are not obliged to stay interested. Given the robustness of the Image Economy, they have more than a few alternatives for their attention and fascination.

Luckily, the keys to human connection lie within all of us every day. Although people are blind to the influences of the subconscious, it plays an important and influential role in our daily decisions. The unconscious mind is not a wastebin of old material. It contains the seeds of future action.[18] The ultimate drivers of persuasion and the necessary ingredients for success in the Image Economy — archetypes— are innate forms. So you don't have to look far. Through conscious effort and care, you can tap the universal source code of communication and guide archetypes with powerful effect.

Archetypes are the invisible glue that you can use to create better connections with consumers.

The depth of our psyches contains enormous power. That power can do a lot of good, bringing about joy, fascination and amusement. But it can also do damage, if influenced in the wrong direction. So along with power comes the responsibility of how you choose to wield it. The decision about how you choose to harness the source code of archetypes to influence consumers' minds is yours. Now it's up to you. The power to create and connect with others is truly in your hands.

Endnotes

Introduction: A World of Connections

1. Michael Lemonick, "Love for Strangers", *Time*, August 16, 1999, p.53.

2. Jennifer J. Tickle, James D. Sargent, Madeline A. Dalton, Michael L. Beach and Toff F. Heatherton, "Favourite movie stars, their tobacco use in contemporary movies, and its association with adolescent smoking", *Tobacco Control Journal* 2001: 10:16–22 (http://tc.bmjjournals.com/cgi/content/full/10/1/16).

3. Restrictions on tobacco and alcohol advertising vary by country. Regulations can generally be found through the local chapter of the International Advertising Association or the appropriate local health authorities.

4. Joshua Quittner, "Are Video Games Really So Bad?", *Time*, May 10, 1999, pp.41–44.

5. *The Terminator* (1984), Orion Pictures — Metro-Goldwyn-Mayer Studio Inc., and *Forrest Gump* (1994), Paramount Pictures.

Chapter 1: The Image Economy

1. From Roy Johnson's "The Jordan Effect", *Fortune*, June 22, 1998.

2. *Ibid.*

3. *Ibid.*

4. Roger O. Crockett, David Leonhardt, Richard A. Melcher, Mark Hyman, Ronald Grover, Linda Himelstein and Richard Siklos, "Yikes! Mike Takes a Hike", *Business Week*, January 25, 1999, pp.42–44.

5. *Ibid.*

6. Sports Illustrated Tiger Woods Scrapbook, *CNNSI.com*. (http://sportsillustrated.cnn.com/golf/pga/features/tiger/timeline2).

7. "Tiger could be the first $1 billion athlete", *MSNBC.com*. (http://www.msnbc.com/news/424754.asp).

8. Michele Orecklin, Autumn De Leon, Erik Gunn and Jeanne McDowell, "Pokemon: The Cutest Obsession", *Time*, May 10, 1999, pp.38–39.

9. Louis Uchitelle, "More Doubts on New-Economy Gains", *International Herald Tribune*, October 18, 2001, Finance section.

10. Figures regarding the size of the worldwide advertising industry come from "Experts forecast growth in advertising spending this year (1999)", SHOOT, January 8, 1999, BPI Communications, quoting Robert J. Coen, senior VP/forecasting director of McCann-Erickson.

11. Projection of worldwide corporate sponsorship from "Sporting Chance for MasterCard", *Bank Marketing International*, June 1, 1998, Lafferty Publications, p.10.
12. Video and computer-game sales estimates from Alex Pham, "Video Game Marketing Thriving Despite Economic Slowdown", *The Los Angeles Times*, November 20, 2001.

Chapter 2: The Growth Engine

1. Youssef M. Ibrahim, "Fight to Protect Logos Spreads to the Internet. Companies Step Up Trade-Infringement Battle", *International Herald Tribune*, November 13, 1998, p.15.
2. James L. Heskett, Thomas O. Jones, Gary W. Loveman, W. Earl Sasser, Jr. and Leonard A. Schlessinger, "Putting the Service-Profit Chain to Work", *The Harvard Business Review*, March-April 1994, pp.164–174.
3. *Bartlett's Familiar Quotations*, Emily Morison Beck, editor (Boston and Toronto: Little Brown and Company, 1980), p.908:1.
4. "Power in your hand: A survey of television", *The Economist*, April 13, 2002, p. 13.
5. Jeremy Hansen, "1,250 Channels and Nothing On", *Asiaweek*, March 9, 2001, pp.34–35.
6. Figures regarding Nike's sponsorship of the Brazilian national team from "A Black Box", *CNNSI.com*, October 6, 2000. (http://sportsillustrated.cnn.com/soccer/world/news/2000/10/06/pele_brazil/).
7. Kathleen Morris, "This Phantom is a Menace to Toymakers", *Business Week*, July 19, 1999, p.48.
8. WTO press release, "Growth rate of world merchandise trade expected to double in 2000, according to latest report by WTO Secretariat", November 30, 2000.
9. Nicholas Stern, "The Growth Habit is Catching On", *International Herald Tribune*, May 2, 2001.
10. Christy Liu, "Cola Brands Bank on HK Star Appeal", *MEDIA*, May 25, 2001, p.5.

Chapter 3: Hitting the Image Wall

1. Figures for children's exposure to TV commercials from "Children, Adolescents, and Advertising (RE9504)", American Academy of Pediatrics, Policy Statement, Volume 95, Number 2, February 1995, pp.295–297.
2. Joel Achenbach, "Is the Information Age Making Us Any Wiser?", *International Herald Tribune*, March 16, 1999, p.2.

3. Vanessa O'Connell, "Will Marketers' Woes Dent 2002 World Cup?", *The Asian Wall Street Journal*, April 24, 2001.

4. Stuart Parrott, "The golden game", *Asia-Inc.*, April 2002 edition.

5. According to one report studying Asian consumer recall of official World Cup sponsors, three of the top seven companies mentioned most often as official sponsors were incorrect. Source: "World Cup '98 Sponsorship Report" from the Orchard Group (Singapore), 1998. For more information on the confusion caused by guerilla marketers, see Gordon Fairclough's "Nike Ads Spark Suit by Fortune Brands", *The Asian Wall Street Journal*, July 15, 1999.

6. Emily Nelson, "Too Many Choices Can Cause Frustration Among Consumers", *The Asian Wall Street Journal*, April 24, 2001, Media & Marketing Section, p.N4.

7. *Ibid.*

8. Taiwan beer market share information from the Taiwan Tobacco & Wine Monopoly Bureau.

9. Jay Cocks, "The Fall of the King", *Time*, February 9, 1999, p.56.

10. Michele Orecklin, "The King's Ransom Goes on the Block", *Time*, August 16, 1999, p.54.

11. "Old Coke Coming Back after Outcry by Faithful," *The New York Times*, July 11, 1985, p.D4.

12. Walter Mossberg, "Super Set-Top Boxes Put Viewers in Charge, Change TV Habits", *The Asian Wall Street Journal*, February 23, 2001, p.1.

13. Erla Zwingle, "Global Culture", *National Geographic*, August 1999, Vol. 196, No. 2, pp.2–30.

Chapter 4: The Persuasion Process

1. Estimate of up to 4,000% difference in the effectiveness of some commercials comes from Millward Brown's "Advanced Tracking Programme", which uses mathematical modeling of inputs (GRPs behind the campaign) to the output (awareness that the brand has advertised recently) to estimate a statistic called "Awareness Index", which represents the ads' efficiency in generating advertising memories for every 100 GRPs spent behind it.

2. David Ansen, "The Phantom Movie", *Newsweek*, May 17, 1999, pp. 42–44.

3. Virtually all traditional media are sold based on the ability of those media to deliver a certain number of "impressions" (in the case of print, outdoor, etc.) or "rating points" (in the case of TV) to a specific, demographically defined audience. In the case of TV, these are called TARPs or GRPs.

4. The effects of repetition in building memory can be found in *Oxford Guide to the Mind*, edited by Geoffrey Underwood (Oxford: Oxford University Press, 2001), pp.32–33.

5. Ivan Pavlov's experiments focused on what is generally termed as "classical conditioning" or "Pavlovian conditioning". A related yet distinct form of conditioning, called "operant conditioning", is also at work in the positive reinforcement found in many marketing techniques. For more on classical and operant conditioning, see Arthur S. Reber and Emily Reber, *The Penguin Dictionary of Psychology* (London: Penguin Books, Third Edition, 2001), pp.122 and 485.

6. Six Sigma is a popular process that many businesses are following today that focuses on measuring any defects in a process in order to figure out systematically how to eliminate them, resulting in creating near-perfect products.

7. Carole Bula, "Field Trip to Your Medicine Cabinet", *Time*, July 23, 2001, p.47.

Chapter 5: Archetypes: The Source Code

1. Rick Weiss, "Mother of All Plants is Traced to a Single Green 'Eve'", *International Herald Tribune*, August 6, 1999, p.1.

2. For a general overview of Jung's concept of archetypes, see C.G. Jung, *The Archetypes and the Collective Unconscious* (Princeton: Bollingen Series XX, Princeton University Press,1959), "Archetypes of the Collective Unconscious", pp.3–41.

3. For a general overview of the concept of the collective unconscious, see Jung, *op. cit.*, pp.42–53.

4. The distinction between Jung's and Freud's view of the unconscious is noted in Jung, *op. cit.*, p.3.

5. Jung, *op. cit.*, p.4.

6. History of the term "archetypes" noted in E.A. Bennett, *What Jung Really Said* (London: Abacus, A Division of Little, Brown and Company, U.K., 1966), p.58.

7. Jung acknowledged the initial strangeness of the concept of the collective unconscious when he said, "The hypothesis of a collective unconscious belongs to the class of ideas that people at first find strange but soon come to possess and use as familiar conceptions", *op.cit*, p.3.

8. Jung notes the role of the unconscious as the producer of human motivations when he says, "The unconscious produces dreams, visions, fantasies, emotions, grotesque ideas, and so forth." *op. cit*, p.283.

9. Laurent Belsie, "The Short, Simple Human Gene Map", *Christian Science Monitor*, February 13, 2001.

10. For concise comments on the universality of archetypes see Bennett, *op. cit.*, pp.55–56.

11. Jung, *op. cit.*, p.5.

12. Joseph Campbell, *The Hero with a Thousand Faces* (Princeton: Bollingen Series XVII, Princeton University Press,1949), p.4.

13. Campbell further comments on the universal connection of archetypes and mythology in *The Hero with a Thousand Faces*, pp.18–19.

14. Bruno Bettelheim acknowledges the formative guidance provided by fairy tales and myth in his comment, "Therefore, even more than at the times fairy tales were invented, it is important to provide the modern child with images of heroes who have to go out into the world all by themselves and who, although originally ignorant of the ultimate things, find secure places in the world by following their right way with deep inner confidences." Bruno Bettelheim, *The Uses of Enchantment: The Meaning and Importance of Fairy Tales* (New York: Vintage Books, A Division of Random House, 1975), p.10.

15. Bennett comments on the personal nature of the collective unconscious in *What Jung Really Said*, p.59.

16. Jung comments on the primary nature of the "mother" archetype in *The Archetypes and the Collective Unconscious*, p.92.

17. Belsie, *op. cit.*

18. Bennett comments on the role of archetypes in the human "operating system" in quoting Jung in *What Jung Really Said*, p.99.

19. For comments on the instant recognition and usefulness of archetypes, see Bennett, *op. cit.*, "Archetype and Instinct", pp. 54–60.

20. For comments on the motivational power of archetypes, see Jung, *op. cit.*, p.8.

21. Campbell comments on the internal journey of discovery of the hero cycle in *The Hero with a Thousand Faces*, p.28.

22. Jung, *op. cit.*, p.5.

23. Campbell, too, touches on the eternal nature of archetypes and mythology in his comment, "Why is mythology everywhere the same, beneath its varieties of costume?" *op. cit.*, p.4.

Chapter 6: Making Modern Mythology

1. Jung, *op. cit.*, p.5.

2. Jung did not refer to the conscious expression of archetypes as "mythic figures", which is the term I have used as a shorthand for describing them. However, he does address the personification of archetypes in *The Archetypes and the Collective Unconscious*, p.285.

3. Campbell addresses the transformative nature of mythology in *The Hero with a Thousand Faces*, pp.28–29.

4. Jung noted the critical function of symbols in stating, "In this case, knowledge of the symbols is indispensable, for it is in them that the union of conscious and unconscious contents is consummated." Jung, *op. cit.*, p.289. Additionally, Campbell

noted the central role of symbols in stating, "It has always been the prime function of mythology and rite to supply the symbols that carry the human spirit forward, in counteraction to those other constant human fantasies that tend to tie it back". Campbell, *op. cit.*, p.11.

5. The DeBeer's "A diamond is forever" advertising campaign is credited as starting in 1948 and was created by advertising agency N.W. Ayer & Sons. This campaign ranked No.6 on the *Advertising Age* listing of "Top 100 Advertising Campaigns of the Century" (http://www.adage.com/century/campaigns.html).

6. *Mr. Clean*, Procter & Gamble; *Tony the Tiger*, Frosted Flakes, Kellogg's; *Ronald McDonald*, McDonald's; *Charlie the Tuna*, StarKist Tuna; *Felix the Cat*, Friskies Nestlé; and *The Colonel*, KFC, Tricon Restaurants International.

7. The toilet paper reference is to a long-running campaign that appeared in the U.S. for Charmin Toilet Paper, a product of Procter & Gamble. This advertising campaign, starring a figure named Mr. Whipple, ranked No.51 on the *Advertising Age* listing of "Top 100 Advertising Campaigns of the Century".

8. Both Bruno Bettelheim and Joseph Campbell focus on the lessons of myth and fairy tales as primary theses. In particular, see *The Hero With a Thousand Faces*, opening chapter "Myth and Dream", and Bettelheim's *Uses of Enchantment*, "Introduction", pp.5–6. Bettelheim provides more specific comments regarding the resolution of stories in a happy ending and moral in "Fantasy, Recovery, Escape, and Consolation" in *Uses of Enchantment*, pp.143–150.

Chapter 7: Mythic Profile: The Ultimate Strength

1. *Bartlett's Familiar Quotations*, p.388:12.

2. *Ibid*, p.710:1.

3. Frederic Golden, "Who Got There First? George Mallory's frozen corpse turns up 75 years after his last climb — a fresh clue in Everest's greatest mystery", *Time Asia*, May 17, 1999, Vol. 153 No. 19, pp.39–40.

4. For details of Hercules' 12 labors, see *Bulfinch's Mythology* (New York: Avenel Books by Crown Publishers, 1979), pp.144–149.

5. For the story of the clash of Hector and Achilles, see *Bulfinch's Mythology*, pp.221–227.

6. Timex's "Takes a licking and keeps on ticking" campaign originated in the 1950s and continued on through the 1960s. This campaign ranked No.40 on the *Advertising Age* listing of "Top 100 Advertising Campaigns of the Century". (http://www.adage.com/century/campaigns.html).

7. My interpretation of mountain symbolism was influenced by Joseph Campbell, *The Mythic Image* (Princeton: Princeton University Press, 1974), "The World Mountain", pp.76–103.

8. Marlboro's appeal to women is mentioned in a U.S. Centers for Disease Control and Prevention *MMWR Weekly* report "Cigarette Brand Use among Adult Smokers — United States, 1986", September 28, 1990/39 (38); pp.665, 671–673. For further details, see http://www.cdc.gov/epo/mmwr/preview/mmwrhtml/00001783.html.

9. *Mortal Kombat*, Midway Game Inc., and *Doom*, idSoftware.

10. *Survivor*, MMI, CBS Worldwide Inc.

11. *Bartlett's Familiar Quotations*, p.915:10.

12. Reference to Joe Frazier's comments can be found in "The Greatest: Muhammad Ali", George Plimpton, *Time*, June 14, 1999, pp.38–41.

Chapter 8: Mythic Profile: The Siren

1. *Bartlett's Familiar Quotations*, p.459:23.

2. For this mythic figure I have taken the name of the sea-nymphs from the story of Ulysses. For details of the Sirens, see *Bulfinch's Mythology*, pp.242–243.

3. Adam and Eve from *The Holy Bible*, Genesis: Chapters 2 and 3.

4. Michael McCarthy, "Burger King follows urge to jilt Turner", *USA Today* Ad Track, September 25, 2000 (http://www.usatoday.com/money/index/ad318.html).

5. There are a number of versions of Rapunzel which have appeared in books and movies. My reference comes from the story as it appears in *Household Stories from the Collection of the Brothers Grimm*, Translated by Lucy Crane (New York: Dover Publications, Inc.,1963), pp.73–75.

6. My analysis of the Rapunzel tale having sexual dynamics was influenced by Bettelheim's analysis of the fairy tale. See *Uses of Enchantment*, pp.16–17.

7. *Body Heat (1981)*, Columbia-EMI-Warner Bros.

8. *Basic Instinct (1992)*, TriStar Pictures.

9. For the story of Daedalus and Icarus, see *Bulfinch's Mythology*, pp.156–157.

10. The Lorelei serves as a Germanic version of the Siren. The reference comes from Heinrich Heine's poem "Die Lorelei".

11. Movie titles featuring blondes include *Legally Blonde* (2001), Metro-Goldwyn-Mayer; *Blondes Have More Guns* (1995), Filmagic Pictures; and *Gentleman Prefer Blondes* (1953), 20th Century Fox.

12. During a press interview, Marilyn Monroe reportedly responded to the question why she didn't have a tan by answering, "Because I want to feel blond all over". (http://www.geocities.com/mjbleo/mm.html).

Chapter 9: Mythic Profile: The Hero

1. *Bartlett's Familiar Quotations*, p.346:7.
2. For Campbell's comments on the Hero's road of trials, see *The Hero with a Thousand Faces*, pp.97–108.
3. For Campbell's comments on the inner growth of the Hero, see *The Hero with a Thousand Faces*, p.17.
4. For Campbell's comments on the universality of the Hero cycle, see *The Hero with a Thousand Faces*, p.38.
5. Charles Haddad, "Sunbeam's Sole Ray of Hope", *Business Week*, February 26, 2001, p.76A2.
6. John Wayne movies noted are: *The Alamo* (1960), United Artists; *True Grit* (1969), Paramount Pictures; and *The Sands of Iwo Jima* (1949), Republic Pictures.
7. *Top Gun* (1989), Paramount Pictures.
8. *Star Wars* (1977), Lucasarts Entertainment.
9. *Toy Story* (1995), Walt Disney.
10. *Erin Brockovich* (2000), DreamWorks SKG.
11. *Rocky* (1976), Metro-Goldwyn-Mayer Studio Inc.
12. *Gladiator* (2000), DreamWorks SKG.
13. Part of Russell Crowe's acceptance speech for Best Actor at the 2001 Academy Awards. His full speech can be found at http://www.geocities.com/Hollywood/Cinema/1501/maximumcrowe/oscars2001.html).
14. *Forrest Gump* (1994), Paramount Pictures.

Chapter 10: Mythic Profile: The Anti-Hero

1. *Bartlett's Familiar Quotations*, p.63:13.
2. Darth Maul is a character of evil which appeared in *Stars Wars: Episode 1: The Phantom Menace* (1999), Lucasfilms Ltd.
3. Dr. Hannibal Lecter is a character who originally appeared in Thomas Harris' novel *Red Dragon* in 1988. However, he is best known from Harris' book *The Silence of the Lambs* which appeared in 1988, followed by the film of the same name in 1991 (Orion Pictures Corporation), with Anthony Hopkins starring in that role. This was followed by Harris' novel *Hannibal* in 1999.
4. Jekyll and Hyde refers to the novel *The Strange Case of Dr. Jekyll and Mr. Hyde* by Robert Louis Stevenson, published originally in 1886.
5. Jerry Springer is the host of a popular program on U.S. TV called *The Jerry Springer Show* (1991–present) produced by Studios USA, Universal City Studios, Inc.

6. Howard Stern is a well-known American radio personality who appears in his own syndicated radio program, has authored books entitled *Private Parts* and *Miss America*, and starred in a film version of *Private Parts* (1997), Northern Lights Entertainment, Paramount Pictures.

7. "Hit 'em Up", Artist: Tupac Shakur, and "Just Don't Give a Fuck", Artist: Eminem on the "Slim Shady LP".

8. Timothy W. Smith, "A New Jail Term Batters Tyson's Boxing Prospects and His Finances", *International Herald Tribune*, February 8, 1999, p.18.

9. *Angel Heart* (1987), TriStar Pictures.

Chapter 11: Mythic Profile: The Creator

1. *Bartlett's Familiar Quotations*, p.643:6.

2. *Back to the Future* (1985), Universal Pictures.

3. *Barney*, Lyons Partnership, L.P.

4. Comments about Walt Disney's stature in the entertainment world can be found in "Giants of the 20th Century: The Entertainers", *Fortune*, October 25, 1999, p.116.

Chapter 12: Mythic Profile: The Change Master

1. *Bartlett's Familiar Quotations*, p.814:5.

2. For this figure I have taken the term popularized by Rosabeth Moss Kanter's book *The Change Masters* (New York: Simon and Schuster, 1983). However, the description of the character that I put forward is not intended to serve as a summation of the concepts put forward in her book.

3. Viagra marketing activities have included endorsements from former U.S. Senator and politician Bob Dole and the sponsorship of Mark Martin's NASCAR racing car.

4. Moore's Law is named after Dr. Gordon E. Moore, Chairman Emeritus of Intel Corporation. His "law" refers to a prediction he made in 1965 that the number of transistors per integrated circuit would double every 18 months. He forecast that this trend would continue through 1975, yet the trend has continued and is thus considered a key indication of the growth of computing power. Further details about Moore's Law can be found at http://www.intel.com/research/silicon/mooreslaw.htm.

5. Steve Dougherty, "Madonna: The mother of reinvention set a new standard of female fame", *People*, March 15–22, 1999, pp.207–208.

6. *The Wizard of Oz* (1939), Metro-Goldwyn-Mayer Studio Inc.

7. Jane Fonda's workout videos include *Step & Stretch Workout, Lean Routine Workout, Favorite Fat Burners, Complete Workout,* and *Step Aerobic & Abdominal Workout.*

Chapter 13: Mythic Profile: The Powerbroker

1. *Bartlett's Familiar Quotations*, p.615:15.
2. Avis's "We try harder" advertising is credited as appearing in 1963 and was created by advertising agency Doyle Dane Bernbach. This campaign ranked No.10 on the *Advertising Age* listing of "Top 100 Advertising Campaigns of the Century".
3. *The Godfather* (1972), Paramount Pictures.
4. *The Sopranos* (1999–present), Home Box Office, a Division of Time Warner Entertainment Company.
5. *The West Wing* (1999–present) is a popular TV program in the U.S. from John Wells Productions in association with Warner Bros. Television.
6. *Indecent Proposal* (1993), Paramount Pictures.
7. *Wall Street* (1987), 20th Century Fox Entertainment.

Chapter 14: Mythic Profile: The Wise Old Man

1. *Bartlett's Familiar Quotations*, p.140:5.
2. Obi-Wan Kenobi is a figure of experience and wisdom that appeared in the original *Star Wars* trilogy.
3. Both Campbell and Jung refer to the Wise Old Man archetype. Campbell outlines his role as an initiator of young novices in *The Hero with a Thousand Faces*, p.9.
4. Karl Malden appeared as detective Mike Stone in the U.S. TV series *Streets of San Francisco* (1972–1977), Quinn Martin Productions, Warner Bros. Television.
5. Chef Boyardee appears on a range of past products from International Home Foods.
6. Jung addresses the Wise Old Man's role at moments of crisis in *The Archetypes and the Collective Unconscious*, p.217.

Chapter 15: Mythic Profile: The Loyalist

1. *Bartlett's Familiar Quotations*, p.185:16.
2. Coca-Cola's "Mean" Joe Greene TV commercial aired originally in 1979 in the United States.
3. Betsy McKay, "Coca-Cola Seeks Marketing Talent", *The Asian Wall Street Journal*, March 7, 2002.
4. Betsy McKay and Suzanne Vranica, "How a Coca-Cola Ad Campaign Fell Flat", *The Asian Wall Street Journal*, March 20, 2001.
5. *I Love Lucy* (1951–1957), Desilu Productions, Inc.
6. *Cheers* (1982–1993), Paramount Television.
7. *Friends* (1994–present), Warner Bros. Television.
8. *Stand by Me* (1986), Columbia Pictures.

9. *Saving Private Ryan* (1998), DreamWorks SKG, and *Band of Brothers* (2001), Home Box Office, a Division of Time Warner Entertainment Company.

10. *The Odd Couple* (1968), Paramount Pictures.

11. *Thelma & Louise* (1991), Metro-Goldwyn-Mayer Studio, Inc.

Chapter 16: Mythic Profile: The Mother of Goodness

1. *Bartlett's Familiar Quotations*, p.419:10.

2. Jung addresses various aspects of the Mother archetype in *The Archetypes and the Collective Unconscious*, pp.92–94.

3. Campbell addresses the non-sexual aspects of the Mother figure in discussing virginal birth in *The Hero with a Thousand Faces*, pp.311–314.

4. "Japan's Snow Brand hit by new tainted milk finding", CNN.com, August 22, 2000, (http://europe.cnn.com/2000/FOOD/news/08/21/japan.bad.milk.reut/).

5. Tropicana produces a range of fruit-juice products. Further information about Tropicana products is available at http://www.tropicana.com.

6. Aunt Jemima is a brand of the Quaker Oats Company. Further information about Aunt Jemima products is available at http://www.auntjemima.com/tradition/index.html.

7. *The Sound of Music* (1965), 20th Century Fox Entertainment.

8. For background regarding Mother Theresa's work, see Meenakshi Ganguly, "The Road to Sainthood", *Time*, May 17, 1999, p.21.

9. Maria Cheng, "Hello, Kitty", *Asiaweek*, March 9, 2001, pp.44–45.

10. David Tracey, "The Small White Cat that Conquered Japan", *International Herald Tribune*, May 29–30, 1999.

Chapter 17: Mythic Profile: The Little Trickster

1. The Oxford Dictionary of Quotations (OUP, 1999), p.213:20.

2. In naming this archetype, I have used the term "Trickster" from Paul Radin's study of American Indian mythology in *The Trickster* (New York: Schocken Books, 1972).

3. Bill Cosby appeared in a series of advertisements for Jell-O in the mid 1970s. This campaign ranked No.92 on the *Advertising Age* listing of "Top 100 Advertising Campaigns of the Century".

4. The FedEx "Fast Talker" TV commercial aired in 1982 and was created by advertising agency Ally & Gargano. This commercial ranked No.11 on the *Advertising Age* listing of "Top 100 Advertising Campaigns of the Century".

5. Joe Isuzu was a fictional character, played by actor David Leisure, who served as the advertising pitchman for American Isuzu Motors in a series of commercials

from 1985–1989. This campaign ranked No.83 on the *Advertising Age* listing of "Top 100 Advertising Campaigns of the Century".

6. *Home Alone* (1990), 20th Century Fox.

7. Paul Reubens starred as Pee-Wee Hermann in *Pee-Wee's Big Adventure* (1985), Warner Bros., and *Pee-Wee's Playhouse* (1986–1990), R.B. Productions and Pee Wee Productions.

8. Rowan Atkinson stars as the character Mr. Bean, who has appeared in a TV series, *Mr. Bean,* Tiger Aspect (U.K.), as well as in movies.

9. Wile E. Coyote and The Roadrunner are characters from Warner Bros.

10. *Tom and Jerry,* Cartoon Network Inc., an AOL Time Warner Company; *Tweety,* Warner Bros.; *Goofy,* Walt Disney; and *Bugs Bunny,* Warner Bros.

11. Bart Simpson is a character that appears in *The Simpsons* (1989–present), 20th Century Fox Television.

12. Dennis the Menace is a character originally created by Hank Ketcham. The character of Dennis appeared in cartoons, a TV show and in a movie.

Chapter 18: Mythic Profile: The Enigma

1. *Bartlett's Familiar Quotations*, p.743.17.

2. Zorro, X-Men and Batman are figures which have appeared in various forms, including cartoon strips and movies. The respective film credits include: *Zorro* (1998), Columbia TriStar Films; *X-Men* (2000), 20th Century Fox Entertainment; and *Batman* (1989), Warner Bros.

3. *Star Trek* is both a TV and movie series from Paramount Home Entertainment and Paramount Pictures, respectively. *The X-Files* (1993–2002) TV series is a 20th Century Fox Entertainment production.

4. The story of Pandora from Greek mythology refers to Pandora's jar. However, popular interpretations of the story refer to Pandora's box. For the Greek version of the myth, see *Classical Mythology* by Mark P.O. Morford and Robert J. Lenardon (New York: Longman Inc., 1977), pp. 47–49.

5. Details of Visa's "It's Everywhere You Want to Be" campaign are available at Visa's U.S. website (http://usa.visa.com/personal/about_visa/newsroom/visa_brand.html).

6. Details of Colonel Harland Sander's secret recipe are available at KFC's website (http://www.kfc.com/about/secret/html). Coca-Cola's secret formula is mentioned in "Experience the Real Thing", by Jill Rosenfeld, *Fast Company*, Issue 31, January–February 2000, p.184.

7. Brien Murphy, "Flash in the pan Advertising characters face short-lived, and occasionally memorable, moments in the spotlight", *Abilene Reporter-News*, August 10, 2000 (http://www.reporternews.com/2000/features/flash0810.html).

8. *The Shadow* (1914), Kalem Company.

9. *Apocalypse Now* (1979), United Artists.

10. *Twin Peaks* (1992), New Line Cinema.

11. *Aliens* (1986), 20th Century Fox Entertainment, and *Close Encounters of the Third Kind* (1977), Columbia TriStar Pictures.

12. *The Legend of Sleepy Hollow* (1999), Paramount Pictures; *The Exorcist* (1973), Warner Bros.; and *The Blair Witch Project* (1999), Artisan Entertainment.

Chapter 19: Mythic Figures in Combination and in Local Cultures

1. Jung refers to the term "universal mind" in *The Archetypes and the Collective Unconscious*, p.276.

2. Bennett discusses the individual experience of archetypes in *What Jung Really Said*, p.59.

Chapter 21: Improving Consumer Connections

1. Hippocrates, in approximately 450 BC, had outlined the four "temperaments" or "humors" as "Melancholic", "Sanguine", "Choleric" and "Phlegmatic".

2. A concise outline of Jung's 16 psychological types is provided in Bennett's *What Jung Really Said*, Chapter 2, "Psychological Types", pp.20–44.

3. The Myers-Briggs Type Indicator (MBTI) is a registered process created by Isabel Briggs Myers and her mother, Katharine Cook Briggs, in order to put into practical use the psychological types outlined by Jung. The MBTI process enables people, through a series of questions, to identify their personality type.

4. Pepsi had a long-running campaign using the tagline "The Pepsi Generation", which originated in 1964 from advertising agency BBDO. This campaign ranked No.21 on the *Advertising Age* listing of "Top 100 Advertising Campaigns of the Century".

5. My interpretation in Figure 2 reflects Jung's thinking on the personal role of archetypes in conscious expression. Specifically, I refer to Jung's comment "The archetype is essentially an unconscious content that is altered by becoming conscious and by being perceived, and it takes its colour from the individual consciousness in which it happens to appear", *The Archetypes and the Collective Unconscious*, p.5.

6. My assessment of the link of emotional and rational factors in the consumer's decision process takes some influence from Jung's assessment of the interplay of the conscious and unconscious. In particular, see Jung's comments on the role of the unconscious in driving emotions in *The Archetypes and the Collective Unconscious*, p.278.

7. E.A. Bennett describes the constant interchange of the conscious and unconscious portions of the mind in discussing the persona on p.111 of *What Jung Really Said*,

and again on page 100, where he states, "He [Jung] could never think of the mind as partitioned; it was a conscious/unconscious unit".

8. The Apple Computer "1984" TV commercial, created by advertising agency Chiat Day, appeared in 1984 on the U.S. Super Bowl. It was ranked No.1 on *TV Guide's* list of "50 best TV commercials", *Post-Gazette.com Magazine*, June 30, 1999 (http://www.post-gazette.com/tv/19990630commercial4.asp).

9. *Terminator 2* (1991), Tri Star Pictures.

10. The American Tourister "Gorilla" TV commercial aired first in the late 1960s and was created by advertising agency Doyle, Dane Bernbach. This commercial ranked No.94 on the *Advertising Age* listing of "Top 100 Advertising Campaigns of the Century".

11. *Grumpy Old Men* (1993), Warner Bros.

12. *Shrek* (2001), Dreamworks SKG.

13. Jason Sperling, "…and 5 branding campaigns that failed", *Red Herring*, January 2000. (http://www.redherring.com/mag/issue74/mag-and5-74.html).

14. James Poniewozik, "Welcome to the Post-Dot-Com Era", *Time.com*, January 29, 2001 (http://www.time.com/time/sampler/article/0,8599,97137,00.html).

15. The famous quote from Marshall McCluhan comes from the title of his book, *The Medium is the Message* (New York: Random House, Inc. 1967).

16. Mention of "concensus reality" can be found in John Bradshaw, *Bradshaw On: The Family*, (Deerfield Beach, FL: Health Communications, Inc. 1988), p.13.

17. The "Pepsi Challenge" is a comparative taste-test program run by Pepsi-Cola. The program originated in the U.S. but it has been conducted in a number of variations across several international markets.

18. Jung noted the potential of the unconscious mind to drive future actions by stating, "We call the unconscious 'nothing', and yet it is a reality *in potentia*." See *The Archetypes and the Collective Unconscious*, p.279.

References

In addition to the books, periodicals and studies listed in the preceding Endnotes, I would like to acknowledge the following articles and publications that I have referenced as background research for *Building Brands and Believers*.

Barnes, Julian E., "Retailers Hope Harry Potter Sells Toys, Too", *International Herald Tribune*, March 2, 2001, Business/Finance section, p.1.

Barnes, Julian E., "Making, or Breaking, a Megabrand", *International Herald Tribune*, November 23, 2001, Business/Finance section, p.1.

Battaglio, Stephen, "The Late-Night Time Is Still the Right Time", *International Herald Tribune*, September 27, 2001.

Beatty, Sally, "MTV ratings soar off gross humor", *The Asian Wall Street Journal*, April 23, 2001.

Bonk, Thomas, "Woods Travels World Delivering for Sponsors", *International Herald Tribune*, May 20, 2001.

Carter, Bill, "MTV Hopes Its Viewers Now Want Multimedia", *International Herald Tribune*, March 27, 2001, p.19.

Carter, Bill, and Lawrie Mifflin, "Gross-out comedy makes leap to mainstream TV", *International Herald Tribune*, July 21, 1999.

Corliss, Richard, "A Diva Takes a Dive", *Time*, August 5, 2001.

Crampton, Thomas, "Asian Cinema's Rise to Glory", *International Herald Tribune*, May 9, 2001.

Dearlove, Des, "The Life of the Guru", *SilverKris*, October 2001, pp.28–29.

Echikson, William, and David Rocks, "The Name Coke Now Scares People", *Business Week*, July 5, 1999, p.39.

Elliott, Stuart, "With Blockbusters' Prequel, a Galaxy of Tie-Ins", *International Herald Tribune*, May 15–16, 1999, pp.9 and 13.

Emerson, Tony, "Swoosh Wars", *Newsweek*, March 12, 2001, pp.29–31.

Flint, Joe, and Stefan Fatsis, "Tiger's Flop Cuts U.S. Open Ratings", *The Asian Wall Street Journal*, April 20, 2001.

Ghahremani, Yasmin, "Mile-High Mail", *Asiaweek*, March 23, 2001, p.34.

Goodman, Ellen, "Now That Fiji Has TV, Girls Want to 'Go Thin'", *International Herald Tribune*, June 1, 1999, p.9.

Gordon, Devin, "The Dominator", *Newsweek*, June 18, 2001, pp. 44–51.

Gould, Stephen Jay, "Genetic Good News: Complexity and Accidents", *International Herald Tribune*, February 20, 2001, Editorial page.

Halberstam, David, "How He Got Up There", *Time*, January 25, 1999, pp.48–49.

Hansell, Saul, "Web Sites Take Stars to the Fans", *International Herald Tribune*, April 13, 1999.

Kaplan, David A, "The Selling of Star Wars", *Newsweek*, May 17, 1999, pp.45–48.

Khermouch, Gerry, "Consumers in the Mist", *Business Week*, February 26, 2001, pp.77–78.

Khermouch, Gerry, and Jeff Green, "Buzz Marketing", *Business Week*, July 30, 2001.

Khermouch, Gerry, Stanley Holmes and Moon Ihlwan, "The Best Global Brands", *Business Week*, August 6, 2001, cover story.

Kluger, Jeffrey, "When Ads Subtract", *Time*, November 23, 1998, p.64.

Lippman, John, and Betsy McKay, "Warner Bros. Selects Coca-Cola As Marketing Partner for Potter", *The Asian Wall Street Journal*, February 21, 2001.

London, Simon, "Messages that never miss the mark", *Financial Times*, August 7, 2001.

Lord, Richard, "Face-Off Over the Image Issue", *MEDIA*, June 22, 2001, pp.34–35.

Locayo, Richard, and Simon Perry, "Diana", *People*, March 15–22, 1999, pp.134–136.

McDowell, Edwin, "At More Events, Corporations Put Their Names in Front", *International Herald Tribune*, July 17–18, 1999.

McGinn, Daniel, "Self Help U.S.A.", *Newsweek*, January 10, 2000, pp.37–41.

McKay, Betsy, "New Diet Coke Campaign Sexes it Up", *The Asian Wall Street Journal*, March 27, 2001, p.4.

McKay, Betsy, "New Battle Brews in Cola War", *The Asian Wall Street Journal*, April 17, 2001, p.5.

Menkes, Suzy, "Spin Cycle: The Re-Branding of Prince Charles", *International Herald Tribune*, November 13, 1998.

Merida, Kevin, "Unwanted Spotlight Shifts to Caroline", *The International Herald Tribune*, July 20, 1999.

Morris, Kathleen, "$276 Million: Now That's Motivation", *Business Week*, September 13, 1999, p.51.

Nagorski, Andrew, "Hold the French Fries", *Newsweek*, February 26, 2001, reviewing *Fast Food Nation* by Eric Schlosser.

Nelson, Emily, "P&G Plans to Visit People's Homes to Record (Almost) All Their Habits", *The Asian Wall Street Journal*, May 17, 2001.

Olson, Elizabeth, "The Latest in Instant Gratification", *International Herald Tribune*, July 27, 2001.

Pest, Jesse, "Battle for Dominance In the Soap Market Washes Over Nepal", *The Asian Wall Street Journal*, June 28, 2001, p.7.

Piore, Adam, and Stefan Theil, "The Teflon Shield", *Newsweek*, March 12, 2001, pp.26–28.

Redl, Anke, "China showing early signs of advertising fatigue", *MEDIA*, April 27, 2001.

Rosenfeld, Megan, "Fame in America: Munchkins Keep on Truckin'", *International Herald Tribune*, June 26, 2001.

Rudnick, Paul, "The Blond: Marilyn Monroe", *Time*, June 14, 1999, pp. 65–67.

Rule, James B, "An Invasive Trend? It's a Cultural Weed", *The International Herald Tribune*, March 18, 2001, Editorial page.

Schrage, Michael, "Sixteen Tons of Information Overload", *Fortune*, August 2, 1999, p.198.

Scotti, Ciro, "Why His Airness Leaves Such a Vacuum", *Business Week*, February 8, 1999, p.7.

Shapiro, Bill, "Air-ing It Out Again", *Time*, January 21, 2002, pp.42–43.

Shellenbarger, Sue, "Contest Shows Surprising Heroes", *The Asian Wall Street Journal*, June 28, 2001, Work and Family section.

Shenk, David, "How Does Our Memory Work?", *Feed Magazine*, (http://www.msnbc.com/news/278710.asp?cp1=1).

Shepard, Stephen B, "The Oracle Speaks", *Business Week*, February 26, 2001, Information Technology section.

Stein, Joel, "Can We Talk a Little More About Breasts?", *Time*, July 23, 2001, p.56.

Stein, Joel, and Nisid Hajari, "The One and Only Michael Jordan", *Time*, January 25, 1999, pp.40–47.

Tomkins, Richard, "No Logo", *Financial Times*, August 7, 2001.

Underwood, Geoffrey (Editor), *Oxford Guide to the Mind*, Oxford University Press, Oxford, 2001, pp.30–31.

Walker, Sam, "Wheaties Must Dicker With Star Athletes", *The Asian Wall Street Journal*, May 18, 1999, p.6.

Waxman, Sharon, "Fade to Black: Women's Roles in the Movies", *International Herald Tribune*, March 3–4, 2001.

Weiner, Jay, "What do we want from our sports heroes?", *Business Week*, January 25, 1999, p.45.

Weinraub, Bernard, "Hollywood's Gatekeeper to the Stars", *International Herald Tribune*, May 5, 1999.

Wines, Michael, "Sea of Ads Swamp Russia", *The International Herald Tribune*, August 20, 2001, p.1.

Winters Lauro, Patricia, "Old Brand Names Get a New Twist", *International Herald Tribune*, February 11, 2000.

Winters Lauro, Patricia, "Advertising: Perrier Hopes for a Comeback With Its New Ads", *The New York Times on the Web*, June 21, 2001 (http://www.nytimes.com/2001/06/21/business/21ADCO.html).

Zuckerbrod, Nancy, "Study: Cigarette ads have more impact than anti-tobacco efforts", *Canoe.com*, June 6, 2001.

Index

Achilles, 88, 91

Acton, John Emerich, 144

Adam and Eve, 59, 98

Advertised products

    cars, 25, 128–129, 138, 149, 186, 192, 220, 229

    chocolate, 48, 80, 166, 180

    computers, 9, 129, 215–217

    drinks, 26, 11, 82, 177

    food, 22, 24–25, 37, 42, 86, 109, 158

    shampoo, 33–34, 101, 177

    tobacco products, 13, 19, 229

    toys, 20, 48, 113

    watches, 81, 89, 91, 121, 228

    video games, 25

    washing powder, 25, 78, 92, 111

Advertising

    algorithm, 53

    avoidance of, 39–40

    contradiction of, 234–235

    dominant-leadership, 146–148

    humor in, 184–187

    ideas, 125–127

    of all-nature ingredients, 173

    of heritage, 157–158

    of influence, 71

    of invention, 129–130

    of originality, 128–129

    of purity and trust, 174–175

    of reassurance, 164–165

    of rejuvenation, 176–177

    problem/solution, 77–78

    using fear, 192–194

    using secret ingredients, 195–196

Affinity, 167

Agents, 4, 8, 32

Ali, Muhammad, 93–94

Allen, Woody, 113, 132

America, 3, 16, 131, 133, 156

American Express, 13, 156, 194

American Tourister, 233

Anderson, Pamela, 76, 103

Andrews, Julie, 179

Angel Heart, 121

Ann-Margret, 103

Anti-Hero, 117, 123

Apocalypse Now, 196

Apple Computer, 215, 231

Archetypes

    amplification of, 231–235

    as source code, 61

    codifying, 216–217

    definition of, 60

    exaggeration of, 232–233

    expression of, 64–65

    identifying and mapping, 212–214

    individuality of, 65–66

    instant connection of, 229–231

    interrelationship of, 202

maintaining consistency of,
219–221
management of, 217–219
multiple in brands, 203
personifications of, 65–66
persuasive power of, 67–68
relating to, 228-229
selecting, 214, 216
timelessness of, 22, 168–170
universality of, 62–63
Asset, 5, 38, 211
Athletes, 5–6, 28, 32, 77, 109–110
Atkinson, Rowan, 197
Audi, 139
Aunt Jemima, 178
Avis, 150

Ball, Lucille, 187
Barney, 131
Batman, 191
Beatles, The, 4
Best practice, 212–222
Bettelheim, Bruno, 64
Body Shop, The, 217, 223
Bollywood, 29, 132
Brand
    affinity, 20, 66, 213
    building, 31, 94
    definition of, 12
    distinction, 12, 14, 132
    equity, 52-54
    loyalty, 26, 39
    personality, 13, 90, 203
    proliferation, 13, 32–35
    prints, 216
    re-launch, 39, 136-137
    values, 12–14, 136, 147

Brands
    and social interaction, 20–21
    as buddies, 166–167
    as markers, 19–20
    global, 13, 127, 129
    history of, 11–14
    influence of, 34, 36
    of belief, 13–14, 217
    personalities as, 15-16
    power, 19, 91
    under structural challenges,
        36-37
Branson, Richard, 6
Brazil, 4
Bugs Bunny, 5, 17, 188
BusinessWeek, 5
Buzz Lightyear, 113, 169
Byron, George Noel Gordon, Lord,
    96

Cable TV, 8
Campbell, Joseph, 64, 108
Canto-pop, 26
Carey, Mariah, 103
Carrefour, 35
Cartoons, 6, 18, 188, 196
Category killers, 35
Category management, 35
Celebrities
    drawing power of, 3
    familiarity of, 17–18
CEOs
    as celebrities, 15
    as spokesmen, 141
Change Master, 135–143
Charlie the Tuna, 81

Chef Boyardee, 158
China, 5, 21, 25
Churchill, Charles, 182
Churchill, Winston, 190
Cinderella, 136
Clinton, Bill, 38
Clutter
    effects of, 30–61
    reel, 55
CNN, 8, 122, 148
Coca-Cola, 39, 129, 166, 204
Coke, New Coke, 32
Collective unconscious, definition of,
    60
Communication paradox, 43–44
Competition, 14, 24, 33–36, 95, 215
Computers, 9, 129, 215–217
Consultants, 141
Consumer
    assurance, 48, 76, 147, 155,
        196
    code, 55
    cynicism, 30, 32, 187
    loyalty, 51–52, 217
    psyche, 10, 54
Cosby, Bill, 185
Covert selling, 185
Creator, 125–133
Crocodile Dundee, 79
Crowe, Russell, 114
Cruise, Tom, 112
Cupid, 79
Customer Relationship Management
    (CRM), 14
Customization, 14

Daedalus and Icarus, 104
Dalberg-Acton, Lord, 144
Darth Maul, 177
Darth Vader, 74
Data, 8–9
Databases, 8
David, 75, 77–78, 107
Davis, Geena, 169
Demographics, 45–46, 224–225
Dennis the Menace, 183, 187–188
Diamonds, 80
DiMaggio, Joe, 107, 110
Direct marketing, 45
Disney, Walt, 132, 180
Dixon, Jeanne, 197
DNA, 59, 61, 63

E.F. Hutton, 148–149
Earnings, 138
Eckhart, Meister, 151
Economy, 4
Elements, 45, 59, 61–62
Elvis, 4, 38
Eminem, 120
Endorsers
    Hero as, 109-110
    many faces of, 156-157
    Wise Old Man as, 154, 156
Enigma, 191–199
Entertainment, 92–94, 102–104,
        111–115, 139–143, 150–151,
        159–160, 167–170, 179–181,
        187–188, 196–198
Erin Brockovich, 113
Evian, 137
Evil geniuses, 121

Exposure
        advocacy, 236
        affinity-group, 237–238
        contextual, 238
        experiential, 238–239
        frequency of, 236
        viral, 236–237

Fairy tales, 64, 83, 100, 136
Fame as an asset, 17–19
Fear-Uncertainty-Doubt (FUD), 191–
            194, 200
FedEx, 186
Felix the Cat, 81
Focus groups, 55
Fonda, Jane, 18, 141
Ford, Henry, 12, 141
Formula One, 23
Forrest Gump, 113
Fortune, 3
Fox, Michael J., 131
Frazier, Joe, 94
Frequency, 18, 47–50, 233
Friends, 168
Friendships, 163–164
Gecko, Gordon, 151
General Electric, 204
Generics, 36, 129
Genetic, 62–63, 66
Gillette, 13, 138
Gladiator, 114
Global trade, 24–25
Globalization
        of products, 23
        of marketing practices, 26
        of images, 24, 41
        fight against, 41

Grant, Hugh, 38
Greek mythology, 88, 91, 104
Greene, "Mean" Joe, 166
Grimms' fairy tales, 101
Group dynamic, 237–238
Grumpy Old Men, 234
Guerilla marketing, 32

Habituation, 44, 49–50
Hamlet cigars, 229
Harley-Davidson, 39, 122, 205
Harry Potter, 197
Harvard Business Review, 13
Heavy-up, 48
Hector, 88
Hello Kitty, 20, 180–181
Hercules, 64, 88
Hero
        action, 112–113
        as endorsers (see Endorsers),
            109–110
        relationship with Wise Old
            Man, 159–160
        unlikely, 113–114
Hero cycle, 109
Hewlett-Packard, 130
Hollywood, 19, 29, 41, 87, 132, 197
Hong Kong, 4, 26
Human genome project, 62, 66
Hummer, 234
Humor, 110, 168, 183–186,
            188–189
Hypermarket, 33, 35

IBM, 12, 48, 147–148
Icons
    of innocence, 180–181
    of motherly care, 179, 180
Image Economy
    definition of, 7
    impact of, 8–9
Images
    as an asset, 18
    cut through, 55
Indecent Proposal, 150
India, 21
Indiana Jones, 79
Individuality, 65–66, 237
Industrial revolution, 12
In-flight shopping, 22
Infomercials, 4, 140, 156
Information Age, 10
Intangible assets, 13–15, 211–212, 216, 222
Internet, 8, 17, 21, 40, 165
Investor, 37
Isuzu, Joe, 186
Isuzu Motors, 186

Jagger, Mick, 16
Japan, 6, 24, 31–33, 176, 179–180, 225
Jefferson, Thomas, 86
Jekyll and Hyde, 118
Jell-O, 185
Johnson's Baby Powder, 217
Jordan effect, 3, 5
Jordan, Michael, 3–7, 14, 26, 109
Journalists, 18
Jung, Carl Gustav, 60–64, 72

KFC Colonel, 81
King, Larry, 16, 170
Korea, 25

Languages, 41, 65
Lao Tzu, 116
Latin America, 30
Lecter, Hannibal, 117, 121
Lee, Bruce, 4, 75
Lemmon, Jack, 234
Lennon, John, 18
Leno, Jay, 17
Levi's, 158
Lewinsky, Monica, 38
Little Trickster, 183–189
Logo, 12, 14, 23, 79–81, 102, 218
Lopez, Jennifer, 76, 103
Lorelei, 104
Loren, Sophia, 103
Loyalist, 163–171
Lucas, George, 23, 26
Luke Skywalker, 112, 160, 169

M&M's, 167, 185
Madison Avenue, 42, 87
Madonna, 16, 103, 135, 139
Malden, Karl, 156
Mallory, George, 87-88
Malone, John, 8, 149
Mandela, Nelson, 115
Manson, Marilyn, 119
Marketing, 87–92, 98–102, 109–111, 121–122, 127–130, 136–139, 154–159, 164–167, 174–179, 184–189, 192–196

Marlboro, 13, 91
Maslow's hierarchy of needs, 174
Mass marketing, 14, 45
Matthau, Walter, 234
McDonald's, 4, 16, 24, 80
McLuhan, Marshall, 235
Media
    competition, 21–23
    growth of, 8, 21
    MTV, 13, 15
    new, 8, 22
    options, 21–23
    television, 21, 37
Memory
    long-term, 81
    short-term, 81
Merchandising, 5–7, 23
Mercedes-Benz, 138
Michael, George, 38
Michelangelo, 126
Mickey Mouse, 18, 132
Mnemonics, 80–81
Modern mythology
    definition of, 71
    key components of, 73, 164
Mona Lisa, 98
Money-back guarantee, 194
Monroe, Marilyn, 73, 103-104
Montblanc, 20
Moore's Law, 138
Moral lessons, 83–84
Morell, Thomas, 106
Moses, 90
Mother of Goodness, 173–181
Mother Theresa, 180
MTV, 13, 15
Multimedia, 23, 91

Multinational companies, 25, 79
Murdoch, Rupert, 8, 145, 149
Myers-Briggs, 214, 225
Mythic figures
    rituals, 81–82
    stories, 76–78, 82–84
    symbols, 78–80, 149
Mythologies, 63–65

NBA, 3, 5
Nehru, Jawaharlal, 134
New Economy, 7, 13
New media (see Media), 7, 17, 42
Nike, 4-5, 23, 32, 79
Nokia, 32

Obi-Wan Kenobi, 72, 153, 160
Old Witch, 101
Olympics, 31, 112
Oracle, 147–148

Pandora's Box, 192
Pavlov, Ivan, 50–51
Peer endorsement, 165
Pee-Wee's Great Adventure, 187
Pele, 4
People, 6, 139
Pepsi, 6, 12, 93, 127, 178, 226
PepsiCo, 23, 34
Persuasion process, 44–55, 223–224
Planet Hollywood, 19
Pokemon, 6-7, 26
Politicians, 38
Pollack, Jackson, 126

Popeye, 88, 90
Positive reinforcement, 50, 78, 122, 236
Powerbroker, 81, 145–152
Price competition, 35, 37
Prince, The Artist Formerly Known as, 138
Princess Diana, 205
Procter & Gamble, 13
Product(s)
    as Change Masters, 136–139
    as Hero, 110
    as Powerbrokers, 149
    distinction of, 34
    global, 24–26
    new, 33, 127–128
    of care, 178–179
    placements, 6, 32
    proliferation of, 32–33
    re-launch, 137
Promotions, 36–37
Psychographics, 45–46
Psychological types, 225
Public Relations (PR), 7

Rapunzel, 101
Rasputin, 197
Repetition, effects of, 50–51
Retailers, 35–36
Reubens, Paul, 187
Reverse engineering, 34
Rituals, 74, 81–82, 84
Roadrunner, 188
Roberts, Julia, 113
Rocky, 114, 159
Rolex, 81, 91, 121, 228

Ronald McDonald, 81
Roosevelt, Franklin, 15
Rover, 90
Ruth, Babe, 4

Sales, 5, 8, 13, 35, 53, 99, 154, 181, 196, 219
Samson, 87–88, 91
Sarandon, Susan, 169
Satellites, 8, 21
SC Johnson, 13
Schwarzenegger, Arnold, 19, 24
Seduction, 98, 115, 145, 150
Self-help industry, 135, 140–142
Sex, 98–105
Shakespeare, William, 162
Shakur, Tupac, 120
Shrek, 234
Simpson, Bart, 183, 187-188
Simpson, O.J., 36
Siren, 97, 105
Six Sigma, 53, 138
Smoking, effects of, 103, 149, 194
Snow Brand, 176
Snow White, 180
Sony, 48
Source code, 59–69
Spears, Britney, 103
Spielberg, Steven, 125, 132
Sponsorship
    overload, 31
    proliferation of, 7–8
    worldwide value of, 31
Sports, 4–5, 31, 112, 120
Springer, Jerry, 119
Stand by Me, 169

Star Trek, 191, 198
Star Wars: The Phantom Menace, 23-24
Starbucks, 217, 223
Stern, Howard, 119
Stone, Sharon, 103
Subconscious, 10, 58, 62, 74, 227–228
Superman, 90, 135, 139
Supermarkets, 35, 50, 101, 165, 230
Suu Kyi, Aung San, 115
Symbols
    hair as, 100–101
    mnemonic value of, 80–81
    mountains as, 90
    of attraction, 100
    of strength, 90
    water as, 175–176

Tag Heuer, 89, 90, 233
Taiwan, 33
Tangible assets, 13, 214
Target audience, 45–46
Technology, 21, 137–139
Tecumseh, 172
Television, 21, 37
Testing
    blind taste, 14
    clutter reel, 54
    methodologies of, 14
    torture, 89
Thailand, 29
The Iliad, 88
The Odd Couple, 169
The Sound of Music, 179
The Terminator, 75, 87

The West Wing, 150
The Wizard of Oz, 40
The X-Files, 191, 198
Thelma & Louise, 169
Three Little Pigs, 77
Timex, 89–90
Titans, 88, 92
Tony the Tiger, 81
Toy Story, 113, 169
Transformation, 76–78, 139–142
Trojan War, 88, 91
Tropicana, 177
Turner, Kathleen, 99, 103
Turner, Ted, 8
Twin Peaks, 197
Tyson, Mike, 92, 120
Tzu, Lao, 116

Ultimate Strength, 75, 87–95, 220
Unilever, 13

Van Gogh, Vincent, 131
Viagra, 136
Video games, 25
    negative effects of, 93
    worldwide value of, 8
Vietnam, 25
Virgin, 223
Visa, 194
Volvo, 16, 34

Wall Street, 152
Warhol, Andy, 15, 17
Wayne, John, 74, 112

Welch, Jack, 135, 141
Welch, Raquel, 103
Wheaties, 109
Willis, Bruce, 19
Winfrey, Oprah, 16, 19, 110, 141,
        170
Wise Old Man, 110, 153–161
Woods, Tiger, 5–7, 109, 111, 157
World Cup, 4, 31, 112
World Intellectual Property
        Organization, 13
Wrestling
        Sumo, 75, 92
        WWF, 87

Xena: The Warrior Princess, 87
X-Men, 191, 196

Zola, Émile, 124
Zorro, 191, 196